CIVILIZATION AND PROGRESS

CIVILIZATION
AND
PROGRESS

Radoslav A. Tsanoff

McManis Professor of Philosophy
Rice University

The University Press of Kentucky

To

Corrinne S. Tsanoff

ISBN: 0-8131-1255-9

Library of Congress Catalog Card Number: 74-160051

Copyright © 1971 by The University Press of Kentucky

A statewide cooperative scholarly publishing agency serving Berea College, Centre College of Kentucky, Eastern Kentucky University, Kentucky State College, Morehead State University, Murray State University, University of Kentucky, University of Louisville, and Western Kentucky University.

Editorial and Sales Offices: Lexington, Kentucky 40506

Contents

Acknowledgments

QUOTATIONS from other works are acknowledged in the Notes. Where the translator of a cited passage is not indicated, the English version, prose or verse, is mine.

I thank the publisher's reader of this work for his careful examination of my manuscript and for his many suggestions to clear up details in my exposition.

Throughout the entire course of my work I have had the steady help of my wife—now as always during the past half century.

Introduction

DOES THE COURSE of history manifest any significant trend upward and forward? Is historical development an epical rhythm of positive achievement which we can scan; or is it a continual decline; or else is it merely a fortuitous or cyclical rise and fall, or even a random, meaningless succession of events? In fact, are we warranted in speaking at all of historical development and growth? These questions are implicit in the problem of social progress.

This problem has reemerged in a new context of harsh negation. On all sides today we hear grim words. In books and articles and in general discussion the view is expressed that our civilization is on the verge of collapse, that our traditional values are discredited, that our entire social system faces ruin. Many evils now appear in our technical and industrial society, which had been regarded as destined eventually to raise human life to much higher levels. To many, our hopes now appear illusory, our society heading toward disaster.

It should be noted that our age does not disparage technical advance itself. We would not consider declaring a moratorium on scientific research or on technical applications of it. What we deplore is the disparity between technical proficiency and human welfare in our civilization.

In raising the problem of social progress we are probing the principles of critical evaluation of social order and history. We may begin by an explanation of terms. What do we mean by progress? A mere dictionary definition of course will not suffice; all the same, the etymology of the word may be found enlightening. *Progress,* coming from the Latin verb *progredior,* means "going forward." Now, all going is not going forward. Some crustaceans move backward; crabs usually crawl sidewise and can proceed in any direction without really turning. In the crab's philosophy of life the term progress, as moving forward, would be confusing; forward and back, outward and in—all would be one to the crab. And also to many men who see progress mainly as vigorous movement. If the going is ceaseless and energetic, it is judged by some to be progressive, as with the man who "never lets up," or of a community in which "something's doing every minute."

The least reflection should serve to dismiss this identification of progress with mere energetic activity or change, for the most vigorous movement may be most futile or ruinous if it is misdirected. Vigorous and energetic activity and development are, of course, the media through which progress may be achieved. But the decisive factor in progress is the direction of movement: toward what value does activity tend? Progress, individual and social, involves unambiguously personal fulfillment in terms of values that were not but now are, and are yet to be.

The idea of progress emphasizing personal fulfillment may be stated simply as a change for the better in this world. That there is really a "better," is the basic conviction of moral intelligence. It is the great word alike of classical and Christian wisdom, the acknowledgment of a Highest Good or summum bonum, a Pearl of Great Price, the pursuit and possession of which mark the life really worth living. The ABC of morals is this hierarchical outlook on the values of life: that some are to be spurned, and others are to be kept subordinate, while our chief concern is with the highest and supreme values. The dismissal of this selective judgment by thoughtless or skeptical minds is the devil's folly in men's lives.

The second fundamental feature of the idea of human progress is the recognition of its secular aspect. While it transcends the perspectives of mechanical determinism, it is also to be distinguished from the opposite rigid providential determinism of some types of theology. There have always been grave doubts in most of the world's religions that man could achieve progress by his own efforts. The Islamic notion of *kismet* or fate in Muhammadan doctrine, that all of our thoughts and words and deeds have been eternally written in the Book of Allah, rules out any belief in man's own achievement. History could only be the unrolling of Allah's everlasting scroll. Many Christian theologians who do not expound predestination in its extreme form, fatalist or Calvinist or even Augustinian, are yet finally insistent on a providential determination of men's lives and of the whole historical process. In that outlook the idea of progress as man's own active attainment and increasing possession of high values must appear ambiguous, if not impious.

As our historical review will show, the clear idea of progress is a modern expression, emerging since the Renaissance and that "century of genius," the seventeenth. The belief in progress has been called the modern man's secular religion, and some traditional religionists have considered it as ungodly. The important point is to recognize the characteristic perspective in which the idea of progress is manifested significantly: in an outlook on life definitely secular which just as definitely and unambiguously acknowledges personal and spiritual activities and values. In this view of human lives and historical processes we can raise significantly the question of progress; but how is it to be answered?

The first part of our work is a review of the idea of social progress as it has been entertained in the history of thought. The belief in progress was not a vital idea in classical antiquity which in the main did not view history as a progressive achievement. The classical mind generally viewed the course of history either as a continual decline from an original golden age to lower and lower grades of living; or else as a cyclical process of eternal recurrence, in which a round of cosmic processes repeats itself aeon after aeon through measureless time. Some notable classical approaches to a belief in progress, however, are cited as early anticipations of later views.

The second chapter reviews the medieval-Christian tradition which in its orthodox development emphasized both the idea of original sin and a providential determination of human life and destiny not only in men's daily careers but also in its expectations of some coming millennium and in apocalyptic visions of God's final judgment. While the many extravagant expressions of these pious speculations were rejected by more sober religious reflection, the basic conviction of human life under divine Providence resisted any recognition of progress as attainable by man's own endeavors.

The following four chapters, surveying the secular ideas of social-historical progress since the Renaissance, contain a review of alternative affirmations and denials, and some considerable suspense of judgment. Outstanding and generally familiar has been the liberal view of progress derived from the Enlightenment of the eighteenth century. Here human nature is regarded as developing in the process of experience. Under the right conditions of education and social-political order, with governments subject to popular control and sovereignty, men's capacities for improvement would be realized in ongoing progress. The later development of modern Idealism after Kant displayed progress as a universal process of Mind as basic reality ever proceeding to fulfillment and perfection. The ground for this confidence has been the recognition of a growing maturity of critical intelligence so characteristic of the modern temper. The realization of man's "natural desire to know," signalized in the first sentence of Aristotle's *Metaphysics,* has led to almost incredible advance of scientific knowledge and of its technical applications to men's advantage in every field of experience. Some of these theories have traced men's advance in a more thoroughly applied recognition of human rights and personal dignity and worth as the reliable basis of a sound political and social order, the attainment of a true civilization.

But this optimistic liberal outlook has been shocked in our day by the spread of totalitarianism, exploitation and oppression by societies which have indeed been considered enlightened. Thus the confident reliance that spreading enlightenment alone could achieve social progress has been unsettled in our age by two world wars and the brutal destruction of millions by civilized powers. Advancing science and technology, themselves outstanding instruments for progress, have also shown themselves as the producers of unspeakable weapons of war that threaten the utter extinction of civilization, and indeed of all human life. The confidence in the vitality of our civilization has been shaken by the spreading looseness of standards and conduct, creating a state of affairs in which violence may end any prospect of progress or civilization. As a modern reverberation of the theological view of man's unregenerate depravity, the Freudian psychology has been probing chasms of evil in man's subconscious, unsettling any trust in the likely reliability of human betterment.

Resistance, much of it sharply radical, to the traditional idea of progress is not new. During the eighteenth century Rousseau repudiated the cultural theses of the Enlightenment. In his view the course of civilization was a process of corrupting the primitive soundness of human nature. Social progress, if it could be called progress, demanded the reversal of the historical course; it required man's return from the artificialities and injustices of civilization to men's primitive freedom in nature. The revolutionary approach of Marxist "scientific socialism" has advanced the materialistic-economic interpretation of history in its many stages, from ancient slavery to modern capitalism, as corruption and enslavement of men and as leading with dialectical necessity to its own refutation and the total overthrowing of the established order in the proletarian revolution as the only prospect of social-economic progress.

In the biological sciences evolutionary theories have spurred speculation beyond their strictly scientific range. The basic Darwinian thesis of the survival of the fittest in the struggle for existence has been countered by the report of mutual aid as a factor in evolution. In its bearing on ethical interpretation and historical progress, the varying distribution of emphasis between these two evolutionary views has pointed in different directions. Some theories have proceeded from utilitarian ethics of social progress, regarded as advance in philanthropic pursuit of the general happiness and social welfare, and have sought evidence and support in the survey of the evolutionary process. Others, committed to the idea of evolution in the struggle for existence, have regarded moral conduct and more generally social progress as consisting in men's resistance to the ruthlessness of the evolutionary conflict. Still others, more radically, have sought to trace social progress in the very struggle for existence, looking upon competition as the way to advance by eliminating the unfit, thus glorifying conflict and prevailing might as the principles of a heroic ethics. Along a vaster range of cosmic speculation progress has been viewed by some evolutionary metaphysicians as evidence of a creative urge in nature or as an upward emergence from a space-time mechanism to higher levels of existence, to life and then to mind, with a boundless divine prospect. But against any assurance of expanding progressive life and

activity, modern genetics has held that man and all that he is and can become depends upon his genes, his heritage, not alterable by environmental changes and nurture, except by chance mutation.

The modern secular approach to the problem of progress has also influenced some religious views. While readily acknowledging men's own endeavors and attainments, sometimes futile but often successful, many modern minds of religious outlook and spiritual penetration have raised again the old problem, whether men's strivings after perfection can be understood fully in a nonreligious perspective. This sort of critical comment may be expressed in the question: Can man perfect himself by his own efforts alone? More positively, the striving after perfection itself has been viewed as pointing to a spiritual dynamic, the full expression of which requires religious insight.

The review of the idea of social progress in the history of thought discloses in sharp outline alternative appraisals both positive and negative. This does not dismiss but rather accentuates the importance of our basic inquiry: Does the course of history reveal any upward march of humanity in the pursuit and attainment of values, and of the highest values? Conflict and bafflement on this issue is a major aspect of the social crisis in our day.

If we are to preserve balanced judgment we should remember that topics of this sort have always been the province of the special pleader. On the one hand we have placid defense of the course of human affairs; on the other hand, tragic intensity or violent condemnation. The partisan arguments on opposite sides seem to express conflicting temperaments, agreeing only in their tendency to extreme emphasis. But though the extremist may not convince us, we can learn much from him, for his very onesidedness enables him to present very strongly his side of the argument.

Both optimists and pessimists may suffer from another

kind of onesidedness. Starting from too narrow preoccupation with some specific value of human life, which they
regard as all-important and decisive, they may reach their
judgment by trying to ascertain men's achievement in
terms of that specific supreme value. Even a brief report
of the debate about progress readily discloses this one-
sided inspection of human values. Optimists and pessimists might argue whether men's pursuit of happiness
has been successful or futile, but they may not consider
the further question: whether the issue about progress
hangs altogether upon the attainability of happiness, since
other values may be equally important or even more
decisive.

Does the general course of human affairs indicate then
a tendency toward improvement or toward deterioration?
We may judge that our civilization is fundamentally
sound and that it has steadily improved through the centuries, although our generally optimistic appraisal of
human life may be disturbed by signs of lag or corruption
here and there. On the other hand, a pessimist's condemnation of civilization may be intensified by his dour
reflection that things are not only bad, but are getting
worse. Or his dismay may be somewhat tempered by a
grim reflection that life might be worse.

Consider first the optimist's reassuring reply. In the
growing complexity of modern life, surely nothing seems
more obvious than the progressive mastery of the natural
forces and resources available for human use. We are
harnessing nature in more and more various and extensive
ways. We are discovering and utilizing increasing supplies
of food and secure subsistence. We are solving the secrets
of one disease after another and steadily lengthening the
average span of human life. We are perfecting transportation and communication to the point where we have almost wiped out the barriers of space and time. We are
placing within the reach of growing millions the appliances

which make possible a more efficient and comfortable household economy as well as cultural and artistic advantages. Our systems of public education are preparing our young people to outstrip us and move forward to still larger horizons.

But this laudation of modern progress has been scorned by the pessimist. Beneath the garish trumpery is spiritual emptiness and boredom. Granting the great advances of technology, do we find convincing evidence of the attainment of happiness, knowledge, justice, peace? Even in material welfare the luxuries of the few and the comforts of the many are in flagrant contrast to the hardships of multitudes. Our vast industrial expansion has its slimy by-products; it has led to the pollution of our whole environment, air and land and rivers and oceans; it threatens our very survival in the not distant future. While medical science is discovering the cause and cure of one disease after another, the strains and evils of our modern ways of life are breaking down bodies and minds and filling our hospitals and mental institutions faster than our doctors can empty them. From an opposite angle, the very successes of medical science in perfecting sanitary and curative methods, in sharply reducing infant mortality, have released the population flood, and mankind faces ultimate starvation. Our intellectual search leads us to perplexities on deeper and deeper levels. We raise more problems than we can solve and despite our expanding fund of knowledge we find ourselves groping in darkness in our fundamental inquiries. As to justice and peace, it seems a humiliation even to utter these words. Presumptuous statesmen propose to build for ages, but nothing is as forgotten as last year's plans and treaties. In our country the most impressive plans of racial and social reform have been upset and thrown into confusion by lawless riots with their violence, arson, and looting. Throughout the world men are depraved by the devotion which should exalt them.

Patriotism and religion stiffen them into bigotry and inflame them to bloodshed. How can we believe in progressive attainment of the higher values when we see the best motives in us perverted to corruption and ruin?

We cannot dismiss either the optimistic or the pessimistic recitals as merely temperamental reactions, as subjective inferences from personal well-being or woe, or as expressions influenced by periods of relative peace and prosperity or of crisis and chaos. Pessimistic and optimistic accounts of human experience suffer from a confusion which is familiar in the philosophy of history and in the social sciences generally. The available data which might be used as evidence are so vast and complex and so various that by partial selection, one way or the other, a plausible case can be made for either one of two contrary theses. The facts which the optimist cites in his paean of the onward march of humanity are just as genuine as the opposite woeful record which is exposed in the pessimist's damning verdict. Both accounts are in a measure correct, but each may be onesided and neither be a thoroughly true interpretation. We must attempt a broader value perspective if we are to deal more fairly with this great issue.

A basic characteristic of value in the course of the historical process is its bipolarity: that is to say, a moral value must always be expressed in a contending relation to a countervalue. It is never neutrally actual; it has always an impending alternative, challenging and claiming our choice and preference or its resistance to another alternative value. The interplay of contending purposes and directions of our will constitutes the real drama of our lives. Each main value manifests itself in some field of human striving or expression, be it achievement or frustration, positive or negative. Truth is attained and acknowledged through the exposure of error. Justice is pursued and achieved in the correction of injustice and lawlessness.

Likewise with beauty and harmony and honor and friend-
ship and peace.

This means that at any stage in a man's activity and
character, his outlook on life, his emotional attitude, his
will are all engaged across a field of various impending
choices up and down the scale of values, toward eventual
good or evil, or rather toward eventual better and not so
good, worse or not so bad. In this perennial drama of
human life, the good choices and actions are those which
prefer and pursue the upward course that assures the
more nearly perfect fulfillment of personality. But evil
is the misdirecting of the will which leads to stunting
and frustration of character, the perverse choice which
spurns the higher values and indulges lower appetites.

In any individual's life, progress would be the advancing from one right choice of the higher value in one situation to the next similarly right choice in the next situation.
So we may always be facing the rival spur to lower issues
but would steadily reaffirm the better preference and
advance along the higher reaches of conduct toward expanding fulfillment of personality. Now how is this drama
of human experience unfolded on the historical stage in
the course of civilization? Can we say that historical
development itself is a condition and a factor in progress,
and if so, in what sense and to what extent?

The history of civilization manifests the expanding
scope of human activities. It cannot be described fairly
either by an upward curve of progress or by a downward
curve of degradation or by a random line of meaningless
futility. The entire scale of values, for good or ill, for
better or worse, is spread on an increasingly vaster field.
Both fulfillment and frustration of personality become
more extensive and more important. Men's purposes become more far-reaching and their choices more momentous. Men can rise higher to possess a richer treasury of
values, but if they turn the wrong way, their straying and

downfall are more disastrous. In the ongoing course of cultural expansion we can see how much higher and higher men can rise, but also how much lower and lower men might sink.

The historical course of men's advance, from primitive to barbaric to civilized existence, is thus not identical with men's curve of progress. As distinguished from primitive life or from barbaric epochs, our modern civilization is both better and worse; but we should not misunderstand this seemingly evasive appraisal, for in one sense the march of civilization can fairly be called a march of progress. While the historical past does record sublime achievements but also perverse choices, the increasing complexity and expanding range of human powers and activities does provide a field of available high attainments which the earlier historical stages did not afford. Through the ages history has presented to men of the right choice and goodwill an increasingly vaster field of fulfillment and perfection. Civilization is not the assured upward course, but if men do move upward and forward in the achievement of values they can move to much higher levels in the range of civilization. The hazard of the more disastrous failure is always facing civilized man, but in resisting and overcoming this hazard he has the opportunity to achieve values higher than any within the reach of lower societies. In this view one may fairly be an optimist in one's outlook on history, not in a docile spirit of uncritical laudation, but heroically and with a grave sense of responsibility, as clearly aware of the higher prospect as of the mortal perils of our civilization.

We should grasp this point to avoid any ambiguity. While recognizing this aspect of progressiveness in historical development, it is important to insist that our cultural outlook is neither one of pessimistic dismay nor of bland optimism. We aim at clear-sighted and respon-

sible appraisal. The course of history is as the transition
from childhood to adolescence and to maturity. Shall we
praise or shall we bewail this transition which is normal
in everyone's life? The course from infancy to youth and
to advancing age is not be described either as an increasing gain or as a steady loss of values, as either more or
less happy, more or less satisfactory, more or less worth
living. A person's satisfactions are relative to his general
character and development. The joys and sorrows of a
child are both simple. Under normal conditions, with the
proper care, the problem of a child's happiness is soluble
to a degree that it can hardly be in the life of an adult.
But are we to fret about our lost and irretrievable blessedness? Would the pleasures of youth be assured pleasures
to us as adults? In our experience of happiness just as
in the more saintly ways of which the apostle Paul wrote,
as we become men we should outgrow childish ways.

Just as in individual careers so in social-historical
processes and institutions, human abilities sweep out in
both directions, for good or for ill. Men's resources multiply—both their technical and other powers of realizing
their purposes, and their misdirections and perversities
which lead them astray. Achievement and frustration,
creative advance and corruption contend precariously at
each turn of the historical march. The outcome is often
complicated by conditions beyond men's control or reach,
but it depends in large measure upon their choices between alternative interests, purposes, and values. And the
choosing is ever more momentous.

In surveying the historical process to test the idea of
progress, we should be on guard not to identify temporal
sequence with social advance. Progress is not a function
of mere chronology; the earlier is not always the lower,
nor is the latest necessarily the best. That is the confusion
of those for whom the term *modern* is the highest form
of praise. To be sure, we can trace definite human ad-

vancement from primitive to barbarian to civilized societies, and likewise along many lines of activities from
classical antiquity to medieval culture and to modern
civilization. But the historical curve is not altogether
one of a constant upward trend. In the story of humanity
just as in the lives of individuals there are moments or
periods of great achievement and expression, and there
is also decline and backwash. Later years may strive to
regain the lost ground, and long centuries may gain their
inspiration from the lofty ascents of bygone genius to
which they aspire but do not attain. In speaking of
progress we are concerned not so much with the calendar
of humanity as with the ongoing march of civilization in
the realization of values.

This broad view of the meaning and the course of
progress may be illustrated in two fields of experience.
Consider the history of intellectual advance. In science
and in philosophy progress may be measured by the increasing scope of reliably surveyed and tested evidence,
by the adequate and coherent organization of ideas, by
significant interpretation and fruitful theory. In this progress the solutions of critical problems stand out as mile-
stones in the march of reason; but equally important is
the deepening insight that is shown in the recognition of
new and far-reaching problems. The intellectual enterprise is by its very nature endless. Nature has neither top
nor bottom, and human nature is inexhaustible. But in
probing these depths and exploring this boundless range
men can gain in understanding; they can expand the area
of accurate and tested knowledge; they can recognize
more clearly the problems that still elude them. And in
all these directions the history of thought has recorded
real advance.

So likewise in our estimate of the course of civilization
regarding the quest for happiness. The important question here is not whether civilized man is actually happier
than primitive man. Real progress in happiness is in the

development and growing maturity of enjoyment. The problem is this: to what extent are we able to realize the resources of satisfaction which our complex modern life affords, to choose and to experience the riper enjoyments that should be ours in the fruition of civilization. To long for the idyllic joys of bygone days is maudlin and futile. Our real happiness can only be the happiness of our age and of our range.

Our further inquiry in this study must be a testing of the validity or significance of our proposed approach to the problem of historical progress. In successive chapters we shall consider the principal fields of social experience in their historical course so as to test our proposed interpretation of the process of civilization as an expanding range of human capacities that might lead to greater good or to more grievous evil, depending upon an ever more momentous choice between contending purposes and values.

It may not be impertinent here to mention a personal motivation in writing this book. I outlined my broad view of civilization in its relation to progress forty years ago in a chapter on "The Despair of Civilization," in a book entitled *The Nature of Evil*. While my conviction of the essential validity of my basic idea has been confirmed by the turn of events during the past generation, I have felt increasingly bound to reexamine in greater detail the evidence on which my interpretation was intended to rest. And while thus undertaking this inquiry for my own enlightenment I have come to believe that it is timely and likely to be of interest to others who are also seeking their way through the troubled paths of contemporary reflection.

The problem of historical progress faces us squarely today on a worldwide scale. Our crisis arises in the very conditions of modern life that could also become factors in realizing a more perfect civilization. The tragedy of our time is that in its political and economic development modern life has become increasingly global, but we have not attained a global outlook on life and an international morality.

This crisis does not prove that our modern life is hopelessly incapable of progress. Nor can the problem be solved by turning back the pages of historical development, even if that were possible. Our problem and our chances of eventual collapse or progress are as they have been in any society at any time, but the present world crisis has dramatized them most emphatically. The theoretical and technical achievements of modern science have unlocked natural resources and energies available for human use which would enable us to achieve a world community that could be a masterpiece of civilization. We are on the threshold of an age of unparalleled increase in the means of perfecting human welfare in all directions. But the released atomic energies can also be used to destroy, and we find ourselves on the brink of exploding our whole civilization to deadly ashes.

Our belief in historical progress has both an inspiring and a tragic aspect. It should express a clear awareness of the expanding range and complexity of modern life. Before us are marvelous opportunities of unprecedented cultural achievements, but also stunning perils of catastrophic disaster. Our destiny hangs upon our choice between conflicting values. We should confront resolutely our alternatives: what in them is of subsidiary import, to be subordinated and in a threatened fatal conflict to be conceded, and what in them is crucial; where is that crossroad of decision, final and unwavering, and where on that crossroad is the upward and where the downward course? We need that supreme insight and the will to go forward where it directs us. If ever there was an all-human drama enacted before us and within us which sways life itself on the balance, here it is, and we dare not shirk it.

PART ONE

A Historical Review
of the Idea of Social Progress

CHAPTER ONE

Alternatives and Approaches to the Idea of Progress in Classical Antiquity

THE BELIEF IN PROGRESS was not a vital idea for classical minds. The Greeks did not view history as a process of progressive achievement, realization, and expansion of values. Even their greatest historian, Thucydides (c. 460-400), did not contemplate the events of his time in the context of an advancing march out of the past. On his first page he tells us that his inquiries into remote antiquity and into more recent times failed to reveal to him anything "on a great scale, either in war or in other matters." No classical poet sings: "I, the heir of all the ages."

If we follow the example of the chronicler who was content with the bare statement that there are no snakes in Iceland, we shall find that our discussion of the idea of progress in the Christian-medieval period will be just as brief. But then we shall be failing to recognize the distinctive qualities of classical and the medieval Christian ideas of history—radically different views, both unlike our modern outlook. The examination of these differences and contending views should enable us to grasp better the motivation and the range of our modern doctrine of progress.

Before tracing some of the ancient classical approaches to the idea of progress we should examine two Greek

views which also persisted, though not steadily, in Roman
thought: the view of a series of world ages marked by
an increasing degeneration, and the view of the cosmic
process as cyclical, a treadmill of eternal recurrence. The
first of these beliefs pervaded Greek mythology and
characterized the world outlook of some poets and
philosophers. The second was a theory of cosmological
speculation, with significant implications.

It should be stated clearly at the outset that neither
of these ideas commanded general acceptance. Thucydides writes in his account of the rude early beginnings
of the Greek tribes, unsettled in habitation and in customs,
many of them pirates and lawless nomads. While he un-
rolls before us the tragic events of the Peloponnesian war,
Thucydides is not marked by any nostalgia for bygone
primitive glories. Even in its disasters the Athens of his
day could not lose the first memories which he engraved
in his version of Pericles' funeral oration. And he appealed
to the undoubted judgment of the posterity: "I have
written my work . . . as a possession for all time."[1]

The issue between the doctrines of historical degeneration and eternal recurrence was not always drawn sharply.
Both were held by many minds in ambiguous indecision.
And alongside of them there were also some approaches
to the belief in progress.

The view of history as periodic degeneration has been
called the doctrine of cultural primitivism.[2] Traditionally
it was the belief in a bygone Golden Age. Hesiod in the
eighth century gave us an early version of it in his *Works
and Days*. The deathless Olympian gods made first of all
"a golden race of mortal men who . . . lived like gods

[1] Thucydides *History of the Peloponnesian War*, trans. Richard Crawley,
Everyman's Library edition, p. 15.

[2] The doctrine of cultural primitivism has been studied by Professors
Arthur O. Lovejoy and George Boas with thorough analysis and the most
extensive documentation across the entire range of classical literature.

without sorrow of heart, remote and free from toil and grief."[3] The portrayal of their blessed light of existence is in sharp contrast to the series of lower and lower types of humanity which darkened the succeeding ages. Physically and mentally the men of the Silver Age were inferior to their predecessors. And down the scale of baser metals, the Bronze Age and the Iron Age marked the spreading degeneration of human nature.

The golden men lived in justice and ease and joy. Peaceful were their lives and their death was as a gentle sleep. The silver men were slow-witted and insolent, without piety, so that they angered the gods who did away with them. The brazen men were a race of terrible warriors, violent and hard of heart. They crushed and destroyed each other and without any abiding achievement sank into the chill muck of Hades. Hesiod complained: Ours is the age of the men of iron; in toil and grief we grind out our days; wrangling and trickery sully our homelife and our dealings with each other. Neither justice nor reverence are to be found among us, but "envy, foul-mouthed, delighting in evil."[4]

The poet bewailed his lot, that he had been born in the Age of Iron. He interrupted his account of man's deterioration by singing of the great Age of Heroes, between the Brazen and the Iron eras. Some of them were warlike, like the men of bronze and perished in dread battles, but others, nobler and more righteous, still live without grief or want in the Islands of the Blessed. Was Hesiod's heroic episode in the dismal tale of human degeneration a hint of possible future hope of restoration, or was it a note of added dismay? Zeus the farseeing might just as well have allowed us to be born in the heroic mould.

[3] Hesiod *Works and Days* ll. 109 ff., trans. Hugh G. Evelyn-White, Loeb Classical Library.
[4] Ibid., ll. 195 f.

The Golden Age doctrine persisted in the thought of both philosophers and poets, but it was slanted differently in various cosmic outlooks. Plato (427-347) seems to have regarded the myth of the Golden Age, along with some of his own myths, as an imaginative version of a deep truth. The truth would appear to be that individual human well-being and perfection come through divine guidance; but if, or rather when, God's hand is withdrawn, men left to themselves go astray and the whole world reverts toward confusion and evil. This view of the world course, which we may call pendular, has kinships with the doctrine of eternal recurrence. It is also involved in Plato's approach to the abysmal problem of evil. That evil can in any way be attributed to God, Plato rejected emphatically as an impious error. God is the author of good, and of good only. But there is in the constitution of the world a corrupt material strain, and in the very nature of things "there must always remain something which is antagonistic to good." He declared further: "God desired that all things should be good and nothing bad, so far as this was attainable";[5] but left to our own devices we men let our lower impulses prevail. In this Platonic perspective of theodicy the legend of the Golden Age expressed deep significance.

During the Augustan period in Rome the myth of the Golden Age was given an optimistic turn in the prospect of its possible return, as in Virgil's *Fourth Eclogue:* a kind of millennial hope, but hardly ongoing progress. This chant of divine restoration of mankind to a high estate was interpreted by Christian theologians in messianic, providential terms. A closer echo of Hesiod's myth in Roman poetry is found in Ovid's *Metamorphoses.* Ovid glorified especially the primeval perfection of mankind. "Golden was that first age, which, with no one to compel,

[5] Plato *Theaetetus* 176; *Timaeus* 30; trans. Benjamin Jowett (Oxford, 1892).

without a law, of its own will, kept faith and did the right."[6] He also sang in Latin verse the old story of the several ages, but proceeding from the silver and the brazen directly to his age of hard iron, in which "modesty and truth and faith fled the earth, and in their place came tricks and plots and snares, violence and cursed love of gain."[7]

The poetic version of the return of the Golden Age was not only a vision of eventual restoration but also a mediation between the doctrine of cultural degeneration and the cyclic cosmology of eternal recurrence. This second doctrine finds many expressions throughout the entire course of Greek thought, from Heraclitus to Plotinus. The world process goes through the entire scale of possible conditions or events and then returns to retrace its course to the least detail, aeon after aeon.

The basic idea of eternal recurrence was not exclusively or originally Greek. Its various versions may be studied in Babylonian, Brahmanic, Buddhist, and Chinese cosmogonies. It stimulated the Oriental zeal for vastness and infinitude, of which Buddhism provided the most elaborate expressions. The Buddhist *kalpas,* or aeons of world-destruction and world-restoration, were regarded as incalculable cosmic eras: how incalculable, Buddhist speculation taxed its resources to conceive. The monsoon rains of the Bay of Bengal discharge in some four months thirty or forty feet of flood. The Buddhist imagined such a downpour, but of three years' duration: the total sum of raindrops would still come short of the number of years in an *asankhyeya kalpa.* And these cosmic aeons return cyclically, marked by the alternative destruction and restoration of the world. Our folktales begin with the familiar "once upon a time"; but a Buddhist legend is

---

[6] Ovid *Metamorphoses* 1. 89 ff., trans. F. J. Miller, Loeb Classical Library.
[7] Ibid., ll. 127 ff.

more expansive: "Ten quadrillion times a hundred quad-
rillions of *kalpas* ago, there lived a righteous king."[8] A
dim recollection, and hardly a hope, yet Buddhist piety
sought to sustain its serene prospect. Even if in this
kalpa no lotus flower may appear on the primordial deep
(and so no Buddha will come to teach men deliverance
from misery), yet in some incredibly distant future, salvation and enlightenment will again return to wretched
mankind. Even this brief passing mention of Oriental
speculation may enable us to keep in mind the worldwide
spread of the idea of eternal recurrence, as we consider
it more directly in some of its Greek versions.

In Pre-Socratic philosophy the world course of eternal
recurrence was conceived in pendular and in cyclical
terms. Heraclitus viewed nature as a process of endless
change of contending activities, as the opposition of upbuilding and downgrading. All things arising from cosmic
fire are eventually consumed by fire, worlds without end.
Empedocles envisioned a similar counteraction of love
and strife, or attraction and repulsion, throughout the
course of existence. He seems to have entertained also a
cyclical cosmogony and was a believer in the transmigration of souls. These two beliefs found strong support in
the Pythagorean school. Pythagorean influence may be
traced in Plato's advocacy of these doctrines, very definite
in the case of transmigration, only occasional in the case
of eternal recurrence. Aristotle also conceived of the
course of existence in terms of circular motion, for it
alone is continuous and in accord with his view of the
universe as eternal.[9] But while one can cite from Aristotle
passages from which a cyclical doctrine might be surmised, he can hardly be listed with the definite advocates
of eternal recurrence.

[8] Spence Hardy, *The Legends and Theories of the Buddhists*, 2d ed.
(London, 1881), pp. 159 ff.
[9] Compare Aristotle *De generatione et corruptione* 337ª.

In Post-Aristotelian philosophy eternal recurrence was entertained by the Epicurean poet Lucretius (c.94-c.55), found its active expression among the earlier Stoics, and was viewed by Plotinus in a mystical perspective. Lucretius saw in nature a mechanical scrambling and unscrambling of material particles: his world was one of atoms-in-motion-in-space. Thus everything is an impermanent combination or cluster of atoms, and since the number of different combinations, no matter how vast, is yet exhaustible in eternity, there is bound to be recurrence and return not only in general terms but in detail. To a truly cosmic survey, "all things are always the same, *eadem sunt omnia semper*."[10]

The Stoic sages were more explicit and detailed. Reviving the Heraclitean belief in a Cosmic Fire, which they exalted as Directive Reason or as Deity, they conceived of nature as a tension between refining and coarsening processes of material existence. When at long last a world aeon has gone through its whole round of possible conditions and events, it is all consumed in a cosmic conflagration, to start another world cycle recapitulating its predecessors to the least detail. A new Socrates, like so vastly many before him immemorially, again has his trials with his shrewish wife Xanthippe and his trial at court and his final cup of hemlock poison. These doctrines of cosmic conflagration and eternal recurrence were held by the early Stoics, but they were abandoned by Panaetius who introduced Stoicism into Rome, and the Roman Stoics took a linear view of the world process, only occasionally entertaining a cyclical cosmogony.

The doctrines of recurrence and rebirth were revived in the closing period of ancient thought by the Neopythagoreans and Neoplatonists. The greatest thinker of

---

[10] Lucretius *De rerum natura* 3. 945.

that age, Plotinus (205-270), introduced these ideas into his mystical cosmology of divine emanation. Plotinus believed that the spiritual essence of man's soul was not extinguished along with his bodily disintegration. His assurance of personal immortality, like Plato's, was combined with a view of the rebirth and transmigration of souls. In a larger cosmic setting, Plotinus regarded the repeated emanation of the Soul principle as an instance of the cyclical recapitulation of the vast cosmic process of Deity emanating in the three zones of existence—Nous or Rational Spirit, Soul, and Matter. The doctrine of Rational Divine Providence, which the Stoics fused subtly and strangely with their materialistic cosmology, was expressed by Plotinus in unmistakably spiritual terms. The ultimate reality for him was God, emanating radiant perfection throughout the universe at different levels of being.

The legend of the Golden Age and the mythology of world degeneration yielded a dismal view which excluded any real historical advance. The doctrine of eternal recurrence in its various forms viewed the world process either as the cyclical recapitulation of the forms of material existence or as the periodic reenactment of the drama of divine Providence. These ideas may be regarded as dominant in ancient thought.

The view of an upward trend to betterment in the world emerged with the rationalists, but it is interesting to note that cultural advance was recognized and the term *progress* itself was used by the Epicurean materialist Lucretius. Essential to all understanding of Epicureanism is its materialistic cosmology. Like Democritus and Epicurus, Lucretius recognized only atomic particles of matter moving in space, and he explained the nature of everything in terms of the cluster of atoms of which it was compounded, and their motions, contacts, and collisions. No divine guidance was recognized here, no spiritual principles, no dominant purposes and values. All is in a flux; the mechanics of nature is ever changing the composition of things, disintegrating and recombining the masses of atoms throughout existence. Besides this mechanical reassembling of particles, there is always the unaccountable power of each atom to swerve at any moment in any direction. In this world without plan, eternal duration would by the sheer calculation of chances yield eventual recurrence. But how could it afford, let alone assure, genuine and reliable progress?

The thought of Lucretius at this point is versatile rather than consistent. The universal atomic whirl and pulsation are not altogether random and chaotic; as he sees them, under certain conditions certain combinations persist or are transformed in a definite direction. Driven by need or lured by use and advantage, men devised tools, perfected plans and methods which sustained them in what they possessed and opened to them still larger prospects of achievement and even mastery of nature. So gradually in every field of activity, in farming and seafaring, in armament and legislation, in clothing and road building, and in all the arts, men step by step were taught by practice and mental activity to progress, *progredientes,* through time *and by reason.*[11] Surprising in the materialistic outlook of Lucretius is this acknowledgment of directive intelligence.

The recognition of a genuinely progressive course in human affairs by the classical philosophers of more or less rationalistic bent, while it was not dominant, was significant in view of the generally unhistorical outlook of ancient thought to which we have alluded. In Plato's Theory of Ideas the supreme reality is the Idea of Good or the principle of value and prevailing perfection. There

[11] Compare *De rerum natura* 5.1448 ff.

is always evil, and lesser and lower values are always contending with the higher, for there must always be something antagonistic to good and to perfection; but there is also available advance in knowledge and in the arts, and this advance can have no bounds. This view accentuates one aspect of Plato's idealism, and it can be and has been criticized as overemphasis. For all his exaltation of sovereign Reason, Plato's thought is also marked by a deeply tragic conviction of man's finitude in the mastery of values. There is a pessimistic tenor in Plato's social philosophy. His account, in the *Republic,* of the increasing degeneration of society and forms of government might seem like a philosophical pendant to Hesiod's dirge of the stages of men's decline from the primitive Golden Age. In contrast to the aristocratic "pattern laid in Heaven" of his ideal state of dominant Reason, Plato exposed the corrupt strains in human nature that degraded it to lower and lower states, through timocracy to oligarchy and democracy to tyranny.

Aristotle was less dramatic about men; without exaltation, he granted them some reach beyond their immediate grasp. Like Plato he traced the degeneration of the state, but he also pointed out the path of social order and government toward more perfect realization of justice and general welfare. He did not proceed to any rigid conclusion of a final advance or decline, for while in any era some progress in the crafts and arts or knowledge or practice may be traced, the cycle of existence may sweep it all away and like the mythical Pandora's box leave to man only hope.

For more explicit advocacy of human progress, we must turn to the Stoic sages of Rome, most of whom did not maintain firmly the doctrine of eternal recurrence held by their Greek predecessors. Especially noteworthy here are Cicero and Seneca. Cicero (104-43) recognized both progress and the obstacles to it in man's social relations and activities: "Man is the source of both the greatest help and the greatest harm to man."[12] Yet while in so many ways men are hampered and also corrupted by the social conditions in which they have to live, it is in and through society that they can advance in knowledge and in the arts: "Without the association of men, cities could not have been built or peopled. . . . Laws and customs were established, and . . . the equitable distribution of private rights."[13] From small beginnings men proceed to larger gains and advantages, *progressionibus*. Man also should seek to discover and further the development of which he is capable until it is fully attained.[14]

Seneca (4-65) was even more explicit in his belief in the possibility of social progress, yet he combined it with his Stoic austere advocacy of the simple rational life. The plain virtues which he saw in the lives of bygone generations inclined him in retrospect to final resignation. But he also looked to future advance. So he wrote to Lucilius: We should emulate our forebears and advance as they did, going beyond them. Mankind is still in its infancy, and future ages will know clearly much of what now is unknown. We should trust to sound thinking, for "life is the gift of the immortal gods, but living well is the gift of philosophy."[15] Seneca was also nostalgic in his reflections on the Golden Age, in his praise of the long past, in his revulsion at the luxuries and vulgarities of his age. And he viewed with deep concern the possible dissolution of it all, in words recalling the earlier Stoic belief in a cosmic conflagration: "A single day will see the burial of all mankind. . . . All that is famous and all

[12] Cicero *De officiis* 2.5.17, trans. Walter Miller, Loeb Classical Library.

[13] *De officiis* 2.4.15.

[14] Compare Cicero *De finibus* 5. 21, cited by Lovejoy and Boas, *Primitivism and Related Ideas in Antiquity* (Baltimore, Md., 1935), pp. 248 f.

[15] Seneca *Epist. moral.* 90.1, trans. R. M. Gummere, Loeb Classical Library.

that is beautiful, great thrones, great nations—all will
descend into the one abyss, will be overthrown in one
hour."[16]

There is here a characteristic tension between recognition and exaltation of great values, and doubt and dismay
about their final undoing. This tragic outlook may be
noted in the greatest Greek poets. Two examples may
suffice. In the *Prometheus Bound* of Aeschylus (525-456)
the great culture hero recites with justified pride his noble
services to mankind. His eloquent soliloquy reviews every
field of activity in which he had led men, from the savage
burrows in which they groped like beasts into the light
of day to skill and understanding and security and civilized
life. But Aeschylus also portrays the great fire-bringer as
chained to a rock in the Caucasus. Great Zeus had condemned him; his work for man and man's progress are
doomed to ruin.

Akin to the Promethean tragedy is the "Hymn to Man"
in the famous Chorus of the *Antigone,* one of the finest
pages in Sophocles (495-406):

> Wonders are many, and none is more wonderful than
> man; the power that crosses the white sea, driven by the
> stormy south-wind, making a path under surges that
> threaten to engulf him; and Earth, the eldest of the gods,
> the immortal, the unwearied, doth he wear, turning the
> soil with the offspring of horses, as the ploughs go to and
> fro from year to year. And the light-hearted race of birds,
> and the tribe of savage beasts, and the sea-brood of the
> deep, he snares in the meshes of his woven toils, he leads
> captive, man excellent in wit. And he masters by his arts
> the beast whose lair is in the wilds, who roams the hills;
> he tames the horse of shaggy mane; he puts the yoke upon
> his neck, he tames the tireless mountain bull. And speech,
> and wind-swift thought, and all the moods that mould a

[16] Seneca *Quaestiones naturales* 3. 29, cited in F. J. Teggart, *The Idea
of Progress,* ed. G. H. Hildebrand (Berkeley, Calif., 1949), p. 106.

state, hath he taught himself; and how to flee the arrows
of the frost, when 'tis hard lodging under the clear sky,
and the arrows of the rushing rain; yea, he hath resource
for all; without resource he meets nothing that must come:
only against Death shall he call for aid in vain; but from
baffling maladies he hath devised escapes. Cunning beyond fancy's dream is the fertile skill which brings him,
now to evil, now to good. When he honours the laws of
the land, and that justice which he hath sworn by the
gods to uphold, proudly stands his city: no city hath he
who, for his rashness, dwells with sin. Never may he share
my hearth, never think my thoughts, who doth these
things.[17]

"Only against Death shall he call for aid in vain."
This undertone in the "Hymn to Man" seems as dismal
as in the culture paean of Prometheus. And the heroine
of Sophocles is tragic indeed, with her utter commitment
to the ageless laws of heaven and the doom to which her
sublime devotion is bound. Yet the Chorus of Sophocles,
just as the whole tragedy of *Antigone,* does not end on a
note of despair. Is it not Platonic in its unwavering
acknowledgment of the highest values? They have no
easy prevailing power in human lives and societies, but
they alone have right: how, then, could they be ultimately
futile?

[17] Sophocles *Antigone* ll. 332 ff., trans. R. C. Jebb (Cambridge, Eng.,
1963).

CHAPTER TWO

Divine Providence
and Human Progress in
the Christian Tradition

IN HIS *Syllabus of Errors* (1864) Pope Pius IX declared that he could not "reconcile himself with progress, liberalism, and modern civilization."[1] This pontifical pronouncement expressed the traditional ecclesiastical attitude toward corrupt human nature, despite many liberal voices to the contrary. Though evidence might indicate advances in various fields of human activity, church piety has had no faith in secular self-reliance in individual and social achievement. The stricter Christian outlook from the very outset was not historical-progressive but providential. For good or for ill it contemplated not human attainment or failure but rather dependence on divine blessings or judgment, a divinely induced millennium or the crack of doom.

In the language of the theologian the final view of human destinies under divine Providence has been called the doctrine of eschatology, of last things. Itself a verdict on history, this doctrine has its historical origins which connect it not only with Jewish prophetic and apocalyptic ideas but also with nonbiblical speculations in the various ancient civilizations and even in very early societies.

Primitive peoples, faced with lurking danger and stunned by the violent upheavals in nature, saw ultimately the collapse of it all in some final catastrophe. The whole world, they surmised, will at last be wiped out in a deluge; it will shrivel to a crisp in a drouth; it will be burned to ashes; or it will be demolished by earthquakes and cataclysms.

Of more direct interest to us as likely influences on later Jewish and early Christian ideas are the doctrines of the Zoroastrian or Parsee religion. They combined speculations about world-ages with a stern view of final judgment. A basic dualism was taught by Zoroaster (Zarathustra): that the world is the battleground of two creative agencies, the all-perfect God Ahura-Mazda and the evil demon Ahriman. In this world conflict every man is involved on one side or the other, as a thrall of Ahriman or, in good religion, as a co-warrior with God. The cosmic strife covers a span of some twelve thousand years, in four equal aeons. Zarathustra's birth, at the beginning of the last quarter of world history, marks the beginning of true heroic religion among men and forecasts the final age of destiny. During the last thousand years the war of Ahura-Mazda against the evil forces of Ahriman will rage ever more violently. It will finally come to a climax. Stirred to their supreme onslaught by their God-given leader Saoshyant, the hosts of the righteous will rout Ahriman and his wicked cohorts. The whole world will then be melted by fire; it will run through space like a flaming river, consuming all sinners but soothing the righteous. A new world of pure and abiding justice and peace and divine beatitude will then begin.

Zoroastrianism paralleled its visions of final world-destiny with a doctrine of personal immortality and judgment after death. From this life to the next across a vast abyss stretches Khinvat, the Bridge of Destiny. To the righteous man it is as a broad highway that leads him to the threefold Paradise of Good Thoughts, Good Words, Good Deeds; but as the sinner steps upon it, it narrows as

[1] Cited by W. R. Inge, *The Fall of the Idols* (London, 1940), p. 34.

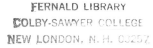

sharp as a razor and hurtles him into the yawning chasm.

These visions of heaven and hell are not dissimilar to those of later Jewish and Christian believers, through which they seem also to have influenced Muhammadan ideas of the hereafter. Islam had its own bridge of divine judgment, Al-Sirat, level and broad to the true believer, but to the infidel a deadly sword's edge.

Recent discovery and interpretations of the Dead Sea Scrolls have impressed upon our minds the relation of early Christian ideas and practices to those of certain other Jewish religious communities with their providential visions of human destiny. The study of the so-called Jewish apocalyptic writings throw light on both the earlier and the later periods of the biblical tradition. Between the Hebrew theocratic hope of a messianic kingdom in Zion and the gospel teaching of the Kingdom of God within us, there is a radical difference but not an absolute gap. The transition may be traced in considerable part through a body of writings, some of them prior to the New Testament, some contemporary with it and with the early patristic literature, the general character of which may be described as being similar to that of our book of Revelation.

The development of the providential eschatology in Judaism and in early Christianity was marked by the gradual universalizing and spiritualizing of the messianic idea: from the prophetic Day of Yahveh to the variety of Jewish and Christian millennial visions and to Saint Augustine's "City of God." The earlier priestly and popular visions were those of a theocratic nationalism. The Day of Yahveh was to be definitely a Day of Israel, the day of restoration of Jerusalem to power and prosperity. The prophets challenged the priestly reliance on ceremonial and ritual; they preached repentance and righteousness as the absolute conditions of salvation from national ruin; else the Day of Yahveh would be a day of disaster. But despite prophets of doom like Amos, Isaiah, or Jeremiah, the Old Testament tradition retained largely this ideal of a national vindication and triumph. There will come an end of tribulation; God will judge his people, destroy their enemies; God's anointed, the Messiah, shall establish his kingdom in Zion. In this messianic kingdom justice and peace will reign in righteous Israel: "the wolf shall dwell with the lamb, . . . and the sucking child shall play on the hole of the asp, . . . for the earth shall be full of the knowledge of the Lord" (Isa. 11:6, 8, 9).

These messianic hopes were shaken but not quite suppressed by the national disasters of the Babylonian exile. "Second Isaiah" inspired the Jews by the rivers of Babylon to renewed comfort and hope through a higher conception of divine Providence. Yahveh is now a universal God of righteousness; he has punished his people for their sins; but he is also a God of mercy, who will lead them back to their homes. Yet even after the return to Jerusalem, post-exilic Israel was wracked by seemingly endless onslaughts of hostile powers. The Syrian king Antiochus Epiphanes built an altar to Zeus inside the temple of Zion and sacrificed a hog upon it in order to crush with his pagan contempt the Jewish spirit of patriotic holiness. In those years of national downfall some of the Hebrews adopted the spreading use of Greek speech and followed Hellenistic ways of thought and life. Others, more resolute in their resistance, spent themselves in the Maccabean uprising and other revolts. Still others retired to lives of hermit devotion in the caves of the southern desert or sought comfort for their spiritual and national anguish in apocalyptic visions of final providential judgment. These last are of especial interest to us, for in their writings we can trace the developing ideals of the kingdom of God on earth and in heaven.

Our best source for the study of these Jewish apocalyptic visions is *The Book of Enoch*, a work of composite

anonymous authorship, some of it written or compiled
during the first two centuries B.C. and some later parts
of it dating from the first Christian century. Extensive
parallel passages in the New Testament indicate that
The Book of Enoch was familiar to the early Christian
writers. Some of the church fathers, among them Barnabas,
cited it as scripture, but as the earlier millennialism was
gradually discredited, especially by Augustine, this work
lost its hold on Christian authority. Saint Jerome called
it explicitly an apocryphal book, but its influence was
not wholly wiped out. Its basic tenor found expression
in sectarian doctrine through long centuries.[2]

Jewish millennialism or chiliasm was concerned with
the belief in an expected thousand-year reign of the Lord
on earth. This figure of 1,000 years was used literally
or interpreted to signify indefinitely long duration. The
apocalyptic seers forecast the future with assurance. The
intolerable oppression and the terrible disasters will get
still worse, and this fateful crisis will itself point to the
final catastrophe and the beginning of the new age. For
the princes of wickedness will not dominate forever; in
its due season divine Providence will prevail. Satan will
then be bound; his foul empire will be destroyed, "shall
melt like wax before the flame," and the advent of the
blessed millennium will signalize the triumph of the
righteous.[3] The expected blessedness of earth was conceived in varying ways. Some of the apocalyptic visions
were earthly: the millennium is to be on earth, and its
joys are to be earthly joys. We read of the expected
material satisfactions: the righteous "shall live till they

[2] Compare R. H. Charles's translation and commentary, *The Book of
Enoch, or I Enoch* (London, 1917); the quotation from Saint Jerome is
on p. xci. Compare also Charles, *A Critical History of the Doctrine of a
Future Life in Israel, in Judaism, and in Christianity* (London, 1913);
J. A. MacCulloch, Article "Eschatology" in Hastings, *Encyclopedia of
Religion and Ethics* (Edinburgh and New York, 1908) and S. J. Case,
The Millennial Hope (Chicago, 1918).

[3] *The Book of Enoch,* trans. R. H. Charles, p. 7.

beget thousands of children."[4] Abundant harvests and fruitfulness beyond compare will reward the tillers of the soil: each vine will bear a thousand measures of olives and "each measure of olives shall yield ten presses of oil."[5] Alongside of these material blessings, justice and righteousness will prevail, "truth and peace will be associated together throughout the days of the world."[6]

The course of apocalyptic speculation is marked by the swaying of emphasis between these two aspects of the expected millennium. Both in Judaism and in Christianity the moral and spiritual interpretation was increasingly accentuated by its most influential advocates, and while in this way the expected millennium was viewed less materially, it also was no longer regarded as a millennium on earth. The earlier visions had been definitely terrestrial. But this sort of apocalypse was radically revised: the vision of the messianic kingdom in Jerusalem was gradually abandoned, and men's hopes of the kingdom of God were translated to the other world and to a life hereafter. So both the millennial hope and the doctrine of immortality were spiritualized. This development of ideals in Jewish apocalyptic writings found not only a parallel but also a more significant expression in the New Testament and in the beliefs of the church fathers, from Justin Martyr and Irenaeus to Augustine.

The interpretation of the millennial hope in the Gospels requires balancing of judgment. There seems to be a certain gradual abatement of the eschatological vigilance, which is more intense in the earliest synoptic Gospel, Mark, than in the other two, and which is still less pronounced in the Fourth Gospel. There is some ambiguity in the words attributed to Jesus: on the one hand, we read declarations of his impending and speedy return

[4] Ibid., p. 25.
[5] Ibid., p. 26.
[6] Loc. cit.

to solemn judgment; on the other hand, we find emphatic negations of the traditional hopes of a messianic restoration of Zion to power and prosperity. "My kingdom is not of this world" (John 18:36). It is not an earthly state of a certain date and location: "Lo here! or lo there!—The Kingdom of God is within you" (Luke 17:21).

This duality of attitude in the Gospels requires some latitude of interpretation. Jesus may have been leading his disciples to his own higher spiritual view; or else, despite the higher ideal of the kingdom of God, traditional versions of it may have been ascribed to him in the oral and the written views of the churches. The opposite ideas are sometimes presented in glaring contrast, as in two successive chapters of the Gospel according to Matthew. When the mother of the two sons of Zebedee asks Jesus to grant that they may sit on his right and on his left hand on the day of his kingdom—as it were, prime minister and chancellor of the exchequer—Jesus replies: "Ye know not what ye ask" (20:20-28). But in the previous chapter he is reported as telling his disciples that they shall sit upon twelve thrones judging the twelve tribes of Israel (19:28). Despite the spiritualized emphasis of the later Jewish apocalyptic writings, the earlier earthly expectation persisted in the popular beliefs. Adolf von Harnack, the leading historian of Christian doctrines, stated explicitly that it is "impossible to reproduce with certainty the eschatological sayings of Jesus."[7] The critical study of these sayings in their bearing on the basic interpretation of the Gospels gripped the searching mind of Albert Schweitzer, whose work *The Quest of the Historical Jesus* is preeminent in its thorough exploration of the entire problem. Jesus' appeal to the higher vision of the kingdom of God is unmistakable, but the lower undertones are not quite silenced. In the developing

---

[7] Adolf von Harnack, *History of Dogma*, trans. Neil Buchanan, 2d ed. (London, 1897), 1: 101.

Christian doctrine of the church fathers there are disagreements. And even though the deeper and more
spiritual insight prevailed eventually, the grosser hopes
were not utterly eclipsed. Across the ages of Catholic
and later of Protestant thought they have been revived
by sectarian visionaries, even to our own day.

Saint Paul's eschatology appears to have proceeded
through two stages similar to those recognized later by
Augustine. In some of his epistles he writes as one ex-
pecting the immediate return of the Lord. He, Paul, will
live to see the solemn day: "The night is far spent, the
day is at hand. . . . Now is our salvation nearer than
when we believed" (Rom. 13:12, 11). But immediately
thereafter he writes to the church of Rome: "Whether
we live or die, we are the Lord's" (14:8). Likewise in
his view of the resurrection Paul revised the current
beliefs so as to emphasize the immortality of the soul, a
spiritual consummation, and yet he did not reject entirely
the belief in the resurrection of the body: "It is sown
a natural body, it is raised a spiritual body. There is a
natural body and there is a spiritual body. . . . Behold,
I shew you a mystery" (I Cor. 15:44, 51).

The preeminent apocalyptic work in the New Testament, the book of Revelation, has been attributed to Saint
John the Divine. In it millennarians have always found
texts with which to defend their hopes of Jesus Christ's
speedy or eventual return to judge the living and the dead.
This book seems to have been written in the days of
persecution that marked the close of the first Christian
century. Even as the Jewish refugees from Seleucid or
Roman tyrants had visions of the reestablishment of Zion,
so the author of this book writes to the seven churches in
Asia as their "brother, and companion in tribulation, and
in the kingdom of patience of Jesus Christ" (Rev. 1:9).
During his lonely exile on Patmos he had a marvelous
revelation and a vision of the Lord's glory. He writes to

the seven churches to admonish them and also to renew
their courage and their devotion in adversity. In their
affliction and oppression he lifts their spirits to see the
supreme dominion and perfection of the Lord, against
whom no powers of evil can finally prevail. God has not
forgotten his children in their sufferings. The Christian
martyrs have not died in vain; their souls cry out to the
Lord for vindication, and on the day of resurrection they
will arise in victory.

The glories of these apocalyptic visions are intensified
by repeated readings despite our familiarity with them.
The author's revelation of God's holy majesty is also a
contemplation of the last days that are at hand. Still more
evil days are in store for the true believers. Satan has
released all his onslaughts to destroy men, but his days
are numbered, and the hour of divine destiny is at hand.
In solemn rhetoric the final doom of the wicked is portrayed—the collapse of the Roman imperial citadel of sin
which is denounced as the Babylon of the West: "Babylon
the great is fallen, is fallen, and is become the habitation
of devils, and the hold of every foul spirit, and the cage
of every unclean and hateful bird" (Rev. 18:2). The
powers of the Lord shall vanquish the far-flung forces of
sin, and Satan himself shall be bound for one thousand
years. In the millennium of the first resurrection the
righteous shall live and reign with Christ. "And when
the thousand years are expired, Satan shall be loosed
out of his prison" (Rev. 20:7). He shall go out to deceive
the nations and shall besiege the saints and their beloved
city. But fire from heaven shall devour the demonic
armies, and "into the lake of fire and brimstone . . . [they]
shall be tormented day and night for ever and ever"
(Rev. 20:10). That will be the day of the second and
last resurrection and of God's final judgment and salvation of his own, in the new heaven and new earth, in
"the holy city, new Jerusalem, coming down from God
out of heaven, prepared as a bride adorned for her hus-

Band" (Rev. 21:2). The last words are those of immediacy and vigilance: "Behold, I come quickly; blessed is he that keepeth the sayings of the prophecy of this book" (Rev. 22:7).

In our study of the patristic millennialism we should keep in mind the intimacy of the church fathers with writings like the books of Enoch and Revelation. The interplay of earthly hopes with spiritual visions is evident in their eschatology as it was in the Jewish apocalyptic writings. One of the earliest church fathers, Justin Martyr, in the second century, wrote with confidence that the Lord's saints shall dwell in Jerusalem for one thousand years and that the millennium will be followed by the eternal resurrection and the Final Judgment. Irenaeus, toward the end of the second century, wrote of the expected millennium in the greatest detail, as the kingdom of God on this earth, with unimaginable earthly blessings. The vindication of the saints was to be in this same world in which they had so long suffered persecution. They were to receive a hundredfold and a thousandfold for all their past tribulations. He quoted Isaiah in saying that the new Jerusalem is to be rebuilt of precious stones of carbuncles and sapphires and jaspers and crystals. His vision of the holy kingdom almost anticipated some of the delights of the Muhammadan paradise. One instance should suffice: "The days will come, in which vines shall grow, each having ten thousand branches, and in each branch ten thousand twigs, and in each twig ten thousand shoots, and in each one of the shoots ten thousand clusters, and on every one of these clusters ten thousand grapes, and every grape when pressed will give five and twenty metretes of wine. And when any one of the saints shall lay hold of a cluster, another shall cry out, 'I am a better cluster, take me; bless the Lord through me.' "[8] Irenaeus insisted on the literal meaning of his expected millennium:

[8] Irenaeus *Against Heresies* 5. 33. 3, in *The Ante-Nicene Fathers* (New York, 1885) 1: 563.

"If any shall endeavour to allegorize [prophecies] of this kind, . . . they . . . shall be confuted."[9]

This sort of millennialism found many advocates. Harnack records the strong support it found in Western Christendom during the third century: "We know of no bishop there who would have opposed chiliasm."[10] Tertullian and Lactantius supported Irenaeus. Tertullian insisted on the resurrection of the dead in the most literal sense. Without any allegory or metaphor, the saints are to be raised to their entire condition, raised in the flesh, with all their organs, and they are to reign with the Lord for one thousand years in the divinely built city of Jerusalem. Have not even heathen attested to a vision forecasting this glorious return of the Lord, how "in Judea there was suspended in the sky a city every morning for forty days"? So the coming of the millennium is not to be doubted, and at its close "there will ensue the destruction of the world and the conflagration of all things at the judgment."[11]

Lactantius also was confident that the prince of the devils shall be bound with chains for one thousand years. He reinforced his biblical assurance with the "inspired predictions" of the Sibyl and quoted Virgil. His millennium was conceived in terms of justice and peace but also of earthly glories and marvelous abundance. Like Isaiah and also like the poets who sang of the reign of Saturnus, he prophesied that "lions and calves shall stand together at the manger," but he also foresaw that "the rocky mountains shall drip with honey; streams of wine shall run down, and rivers flow with milk." At the conclusion of the blessed millennium Satan shall be loosed again and will lash at mankind for the last time. But

---

[9] Op. cit., 5. 35. 1.

[10] Harnack, *History of Dogma*, 2d ed. (1896), 2: 300.

[11] *Tertullian Against Marcion* 3. 25, in *The Ante-Nicene Fathers*, (New York, 1885), 3: 342 f; compare Tertullian *On the Resurrection of the Flesh* 21, 57, 61.

God in his wrath shall utterly destroy him and his wicked followers, and then will come the second resurrection and God's final judgment.[12]

The millennial visions of the earlier church fathers were hopes in despair, the visions of persecuted and martyred devotees who sustained their fortitude with their apocalyptic expectations of final providential triumph. But in fact the Christian movement was advancing from perilous venture to more and more assured possession. Riper intelligence and theological insight also were grasping more firmly the spiritual core of the Christian gospel and the deeper Christian meaning of the kingdom of God. The earlier millennialism yielded gradually to a higher outlook. This development of Christian ideas may be noted in the writings of Origen (c.185-c.254); it finds its fullest expression in Augustine's theology and philosophy of history.

Origen's objections to the notion of a terrestrial millennium, with earthly blessings for the saints, were in harmony with his critical dismissal of some biblical stories which he regarded as mythical and acceptable only as allegory. The literal reading of the stories of creation in the book of Genesis was ruled out for anyone "in his right mind. . . . Who is so foolish as to think that God, like a farmer, planted trees in the garden, in Eden in the East?"[13] And "the Gospels too are full of such things, as when the Devil is said to have taken Jesus to the top of a high mountain." The intelligent interpretation of such stories and beliefs must be allegorical. While Origen reaffirmed his belief in the resurrection of the body, he spiritualized the idea, like Saint Paul. The scriptural accounts of the blessings of the saints and the

12 Lactantius *The Divine Institutes* 7. 24, in *The Ante-Nicene Fathers* (New York, 1886), 7: 219; compare ibid., 7. 26.

13 Origen *De principiis* 2.16, cited by George Boas, *Essays on Primitivism and Related Ideas in the Middle Ages* (Baltimore, Md., 1948), pp. 27 f.

sufferings of the damned are "figuratively indicated."[14]
Likewise he allegorized the eschatology of the earlier
church fathers. Origen was "most bitterly opposed to
chiliasm or premillenarianism and everything that it implied."[15] "Certain persons . . . refusing the labour of
thinking, . . . are of the opinion that the fulfillment of the
promises of the future are to be looked for in bodily
pleasure and luxury."[16] The millennial vision must be
interpreted as an allegory. We must "understand what
we are reading."

Augustine (354-430) was thoroughgoing in his rejection of a terrestrial millennium, and he influenced decisively the main course of subsequent Christian belief.
If we accept the words of Jesus "The Kingdom of God
is within you" and so recognize true religion as the soul's
intimate union with God, then we must dismiss any
external chiliasm as chimerical. The Kingdom of God
is a spiritual kingdom, and it is not to be realized in
some future period of a thousand years in some terrestrial
majesty and abundance. The Kingdom of God is a living
reality right now, in the spirit and the life of the church
of Christ. The blessings of divine worship are spiritual
blessings, and its delights are also spiritual, not saintly
"limitless gourmandizing."[17] Even so "the Devil's binding
has been a fact from the day the Church began to expand."[18] In this manner Augustine reinterpreted the
various apocalyptic passages in the Bible.

This view of the Kingdom of God in human lives involved a philosophy of history, to which Augustine devoted his principal treatise, *The City of God.* "Two

---

[14] *De principiis* 2. 10. 6.

[15] A. C. McGiffert, *A History of Christian Thought* (New York, 1950),
1: 227.

[16] Origen *De principiis* 2.11.2, in *The Ante-Nicene Fathers* (New
York, 1885), 4: 297.

[17] Augustine *City of God*, trans. G. G. Walsh and D. J. Honan (New
York, 1954), p. 265.

[18] Op. cit., p. 272.

cities have been formed of two loves: the earthly by the love of self, even to the contempt of God; the heavenly by the love of God, even to the contempt of self."[19] The earthly city is one of force, oppression and pride and lust; it trusts to victory in wars and in looting prosperity. This city has had many names and habitations, from the Orient to the Roman Empire. Rome never had the life eternal; its heart and soul have ever been corrupt, and Augustine branded it as doomed to destruction and ruin.

The City of God can also be viewed through the course of history, and Augustine traced its spread in the lives of saintly men. Its consummation is being realized in the life of the church, and this Christian life is the life of devout piety, a spiritual state. He declared emphatically: "God and the soul, that is all I desire to know. Nothing more? Nothing whatever."[20] It is in the souls who serve God above all that the earthly city itself finds whatever worth of real justice and peace it may occasionally manifest. And it is through the life of the church that history reveals its upward trend toward Christian perfection, but this progress is not a merely secular enterprise and achievement. Unless it is inspired by pious humility and fructified by divine grace, it is futile and self-defeating. So Augustine, while spiritualizing thoroughly the earlier patristic eschatology, stressed its basic providential note.

This providential perspective of historical appraisal, however, did not rule out completely the acknowledgment of social advance in secular matters, in understanding, and in common welfare. A notable passage near the conclusion of *The City of God* should be kept in mind:

> Has not the genius of man invented and applied countless astonishing arts, partly the result of necessity, partly the result of exuberant invention, so that vigour of mind,

[19] Augustine *City of God* (trans. Marcus Dods) 14. 28.
[20] Augustine *Soliloquies* 1. 7, in *The Basic Writings of St. Augustine*, ed. W. J. Oates (New York, 1948), p. 262.

which is so active in the discovery not merely of superfluous but even of dangerous and destructive things, be-
tokens an inexhaustible wealth in the nature which can
invent, learn, or employ such arts? What wonderful—one
might wish to say stupefying—advances has human industry made in the arts of weaving and building, of
agriculture and navigation? With what endless variety
are designs in pottery, painting, and sculpture produced,
and with what skill executed! What wonderful spectacles
are exhibited in the theatres, which those who have not
seen them cannot credit! How skilful the contrivances for
catching, killing or taming wild beasts![21]

Two statements in the extended passage should not
be overlooked. Augustine cites men's capacities for good
or for ill: "How many kinds of poisons, weapons, engines
of destruction, have been invented, while for the preservation or restoration of health the appliances and remedies
are infinite!" And he adds toward his conclusion: "At
present it is the nature of the human mind which adorns
this mortal life which we are extolling, and not the faith
and the way of truth which lead to immortality." While
he acknowledges in great detail men's secular achievements throughout history, they do not sway his basic
judgment of human life on which all his meditation is
bent, on God and the soul. Those many and various
adornments of our mortal life do not bring the soul any
closer to God; they are not the treasures of life eternal.
It is the gospel verdict: man may gain the whole world,
yet forfeit his own self. Within this devout outlook,
however, Augustine was prepared to recognize realization of human values of whatever source or agency. Knowledge is knowledge, no matter through what mind it
comes to us. The saintly soul may well learn even from
the worldly. Augustine declared clearly: "Let every good

21 Augustine *City of God* (trans. Marcus Dods), 22. 24. Compare John
Baillie, *The Belief in Progress* (New York, 1951), pp. 20 f.

and true Christian understand that truth, wherever he finds it, belongs to his Lord." This fair-mindedness he shared with Saint Ambrose, who had written: "All that is true, whosoever may have said it, is from the Holy Spirit."[22] The divine Spirit may guide some men toward the true church even before they are of the church. But the Kingdom of God is the holy church, and through it is the way to the fuller truth.

If we acknowledge that all true individual good, real and redemptive social well-being, must be finally through the church, can we also maintain that there is spiritual growth in the church itself, a progressive divine revelation, to be realized increasingly through the ages? Or is orthodoxy established providentially on foundations laid once for all, and is the true Christian authoritarianism necessarily retrospective? The Augustinian doctrine does not seem to give an unambiguous answer to this question. Augustine saw no hope of genuine progress through men's secular devices; only through the life in the church with divine grace could man hope to reach personal salvation and really availing social betterment. All this was clear to him. But could he also contemplate a future progress of the Christian truth itself and admit radical new doctrines of self-proclaimed church reformers? He kept resolutely to the reasonable middle road of Christian belief, between extremes which in his judgment led to heresies. Characteristic of his fundamental attitude are the words with which he condemned Pelagius and his teaching that man can be an active contributor to his own salvation, that he has the moral capacity by his own will to choose the good and eschew the evil: "Your doctrines are amazing; they are new; they are false."[23]

The basic position here has ever been the issue between

---

[22] Augustine *Ep.* 166. Compare S. Radhakrishnan, *Recovery of Faith* (New York, 1955), p. 190.

[23] Augustine *Contra Julianum Pelagianum* 3.3.9.

liberalism and strict orthodoxy. Does progressive revelation mean only sound, fuller understanding of the eternal truth once for all revealed by God in Jesus Christ through the apostles; or does it allow the possibility of advance in spiritual insight and vision, progress in revelation itself, basic religious growth? The dominant tradition of the church has emphasized the former alternative and has resisted and rejected the latter. The strict attitude is expressed in the self-declared motive of Scholasticism: Faith seeking to understand—*Fides quaerens intellectum.* Start with the truths of Christian orthodoxy; by analysis and logical inference elicit, deduce, and organize them in the most rational system of doctrines, a *summa theologica;* but in your conclusions repossess and maintain firmly the very first truths with which you started and no other. This is the prayer of Christian consecration of Saint Thomas Aquinas (1225-1274) as he lay on his deathbed: "For love of Thee have I studied and kept vigil, toiled, preached, and taught. Never have I said word against Thee."[24]

Unlike this orthodox procedure of the true Schoolman and doctor of the church, we may note two other streams of religious experience. One of them has been regarded as possibly inspired and deserving the highest tributes of reverence, but also as liable to be spurious and so requiring strict initial caution. This is the mystical strain in religion expressed by persons who have proclaimed their own direct communion with God. The utterances of some of these mystics have been luminous reaffirmations of orthodox truth, and the church has accepted these as eternal truth. But some of these so-called mystical seers have gone astray into sectarian extremes and errors; the church has been doubly resistant to the ardor of their utterances. So there are great mystical saints and there are heretics of mystical aberrations.

[24] Cited in M. C. D'Arcy, *Thomas Aquinas* (London, 1939), p. 48.

The other unorthodox stream of religious experience has been represented by the professed reformers of the church. They have been the radical insurgents against orthodoxy and authoritarianism. Beyond devout advocacy or commentaries or systematic analyses of divine truths, they have sought and proclaimed the new and higher verities of the more mature religion. Not all critical liberalism in religious belief has proceeded to explicit radical conclusions. Within certain limits, not very extensive, the church has admitted critical reinterpretation, as, for instance, the literary-historical or higher criticism of the Bible. But explicit negation of established authority and basic shift of traditional direction have always met with firm resistance as heretical. This theological vigilance against straying from the one true way may express itself in general wariness of undogmatic thinking, scientific or philosophical. The Scholastic piety was on its guard against Abelard's brilliant dialectic and his theological reconstruction of the doctrines of sin and of the atonement. It suspected Roger Bacon's spirit of experimental inquiry. Thus Blaise Pascal (1623-1662), himself a scientist and a philosopher, sought in his pious devotion to repossess the eternal and unchanging truth: "God of Abraham, God of Isaac, God of Jacob, not of the philosophers and the wise."[25]

The opposite, prospective outlook, the conviction that God has revealed himself to men progressively in the past and will manifest his truth in the future still more fully, would seem to expand on a historical scale the familiar words of Saint Paul: "When I was a child, I spake as a child, I understood as a child, I thought as a child; but when I became a man, I put away childish things" (I Cor. 13:11). During the patristic period Montanus declared that the Holy Spirit was revealing to him

[25] *The Thoughts of Blaise Pascal,* trans. C. Kegan Paul (London, 1895), p. 2.

new truths beyond the truths of Jesus Christ in the Gospels. He carried his claim to inordinate extremes, and the church condemned him as an arrogant heretic, but the prospective outlook of Montanism attracted no less a person than Tertullian who spoke of infancy, youth, and maturity of divine revelation, as like the bud, the flower, and the full fruitage of a plant. In a similar vein John Scotus Erigena during the ninth century expounded a doctrine of three stages of spiritual understanding, from the obscure mysteries of the Old Testament law, through the clear light of the Christian gospel, to the perfect illumination of the life eternal in heaven.

In the twelfth century Joachim of Floris taught that history proceeds through three stages corresponding to the three persons of the Trinity. In the first age men live according to the flesh; the second stage is intermediate between the flesh and the spirit; in the third stage men live purely spiritual lives. Corresponding to this triple order of ages are three levels of human lives: the secular, the clerical, and the monastic. Men must prepare themselves for the future age of more perfect piety and fullness of understanding. Here was the urge toward new and deeper insight and more perfect realization of true Christian life, in communities of mystical devotees which spread during the later Middle Ages. They were ready for new gospels of love and illumination. They would reach beyond the traditional doctrines of orthodoxy and interpret for themselves the higher truth of the Holy Spirit. For they regarded themselves as no longer dependent on orthodox dictation; the divine light, they felt convinced, was revealed to every one of them directly.

This conviction was to find fuller expression in the Protestant doctrine of the priesthood of all believers. The condemnation of Joachim's movement by the church aroused his followers and other sectarians to counterresistance. The pope was declared to be antichrist; Saint Francis of Assisi was proclaimed as the leader of the new truly Christian age, and the Second Coming of Christ was forecast for the year 1260. In the teaching of Joachim and his followers a spirit of radical opposition to strict and traditional authority combined with a revival of earlier millenarian expectations. Though these hopes were disappointed, they were never completely abandoned. Various groups even to our time have nourished this sectarian devotion.

These believers were extremists in their advocacy of ideas and expectations which in some degree and form have found expressions throughout the course of Christian history. Even Saint Thomas Aquinas, in his *Treatise on the Last Things,* considered seriously the question whether on the day of resurrection all will rise and be of the same stature, and of the same sex, and more particularly, "whether the hair and nails will rise again in the human body?"[26] Apparently the discussion of such problems still engaged the interest of the thirteenth-century theologians, despite the Gospel verse that "in the resurrection they neither marry nor are given in marriage, but are like angels in heaven" (Matt. 22:30).

There was a millenarian note in some of the movements of revolt against the Roman curia which issued in the Protestant Reformation. The pope was stigmatized as the antichrist; his downfall was forecast and along with it the return of Christ to inaugurate the new age. The Taborites and the Bohemian Brethren, the Anabaptists and their followers in the peasant rebellion of the sixteenth century, who sought to establish a sort of Christian communist utopia, were followed by a succession of English and American sects (Shakers, Irvingites, Plymouth Brethren, Millerites, "Millennial Dawn") who in various tones have issued the same call of Christ's immediate return:

[26] Compare *Summa theologica,* 3 (Supplement), Qq. lxxxi, lxxx:2.

"Behold, the Bridegroom cometh. Go ye out to meet Him!"[27] William Miller set the date of the Advent at 1843, then moved it more precisely to October 1844. Was it Emerson who, when warned that the world would surely end on that day, calmly advised that we should endeavor to get along without the world? The vitality of contemporary Adventism, both at home and in the missionary field, is apparent. The millennial hope in many forms has gained fervor in our days of world crisis.

The Christian-Providential view of social progress should not ignore a fundamental belief of the Protestant reformers, which was expressed with especial thoroughness and conviction in Calvinism. It concerned the relation of the spiritual to the secular, of devout piety to daily practice. It faced the perennial Christian problem of the right way to man's salvation. The Protestant conviction was dual: our salvation is not assured through the traditional "hierarchical redemptive organization of the Church and its priesthood, and to the *opus operandi* of the sacraments,"[28] not through any human intermediation or by any "works" but only and directly through Jesus Christ, by faith. Thus faith, however, is not wholly unrelated to our daily life; it finds expression in all our daily activities.

Against the traditional ecclesiastical idea of a two-level sanctity, lay and clerical, Martin Luther maintained that the farmer at his plow and the housewife in her kitchen could serve the Lord as truly as the priest at the altar. The Protestant outlook was thus in a certain sense secular, but it was not worldly. Its vision of the blessed life was one that pervaded every part of human life to give it religious significance. It undertook to fuse secularism and spirituality. The Protestant reformers' conviction con-

[27] S. J. Case, *The Millennial Hope* (Chicago, 1918), p. 199; compare pp. 188 ff.
[28] Ernst Troeltsch, *Protestantism and Progress.* trans. W. Montgomery (Boston, 1958), p. 61.

cerned their historical outlook: does any human activity whatever have real and final worth unless it is somehow a step toward the one decisive hope, the salvation of man's soul?

The bearing of the basic Protestant principle, rejecting the idea of human progress by man's own efforts, found emphatic expression in Calvinism. Calvin recognized only one supreme authority, the Bible, the word of God. He was guided in his interpretation and in the development of his doctrine by Saint Paul and Saint Augustine, to whom he continually referred. But he went beyond both of them. The fundamental issue concerns the efficacy of man's will: is man in any sense an active contributor to his salvation? Paul's view is remembered mainly by his word to the Philippians: "Work out your own salvation with fear and trembling; for God is at work in you both to will and to work for his pleasure" (2:12, 13). Calvin, with numerous citations, interpreted this Pauline doctrine to support his own conviction that salvation is only through God's grace, that it is neither merited nor earned by men's effort but is due only to God's election of his followers, chosen by his unaccountable will "ages ago" (2 Tim. 1:9). Augustine regarded God's will as active in the election of some to the blessings of salvation. The rest were to suffer justly the dire consequences of their sins.

Augustine held, and Calvin quoted him, that "every good work in us is performed only by grace."[29] The opposite view, held by Pelagius and his followers, that man's free will has the capacity to choose the good and to contribute actively to his salvation, was stigmatized by Augustine as false doctrine. Pelagianism, in strict or in attenuated forms of semi-Pelagianism, has persisted as an alternative interpretation of Christian doctrine. It has

---

[29] Augustine *Ep.* 105, quoted by Calvin, *Institutes of the Christian Religion*, trans. Henry Beveridge (London, 1949), 2. 3. 13.

found its firmest resistance in Calvinism, which maintains that man's righteousness was due nowise to his own human choice but only to God's grace working in him; he held that God's will eternally determined both the election of some and the reprobation of others.

Calvin would have agreed with Milton that man's first disobedience brought death into the world and all our woe; but he viewed it in the eternal perspective of God's omniscience. Left to himself, man is capable only of sin, totally depraved, and as far as his will goes, hopeless. "Man is so enslaved by the yoke of sin that he cannot of his own nature aim at good either in wish or in actual pursuit."[30] Nothing that he does or does not do can contribute in the least to his salvation. That can be attained only by the predestination of God's grace and his "mere generosity." "God of his mere good pleasure preserves whom he will, and moreover . . . pays no reward, since he can owe no one."[31] Furthermore, just as God's grace is deserved or earned by no one but only bestowed, so "the grace offered by the Lord is not merely one which every individual has full liberty of choosing, to receive or reject, but a grace which produces in the heart both choice and will."[32] Both the gift and the acceptance of it are God's work. And even so is the chosen one's abiding humble devotion to righteousness, the gift of perseverance, *donum perseverantiae,* in Augustine's phrase.

The other side of the argument about predestination was pursued by Calvin with the strictest logic. God's eternal election of some to grace and salvation also predestines others to reprobation and to destruction. "Election itself would not stand except as set over against reprobation. . . . Those whom God passes over, he condemns."[33]

30 *Institutes* (trans. Beveridge) 2. 4. 1.
31 *Institutes,* trans. F. L. Battles (London, 1960), 3. 21. 1.
32 *Institutes* (trans. Beveridge) 2. 3. 13.
33 *Institutes* (trans. Battles) 3. 23. 1.

In Calvin's doctrine, God's saving grace and his reprobation proceed to their corresponding fruition in the
daily lives of men. Left to their own wicked devices, the
unregenerate sinners do not and cannot achieve any good.
Their evil ways drive them to their everlasting ruin and
damnation. But while God's grace is never earned by
man's works, it does lead to good work and its fruition.
Calvin not only portrayed these workings of God's grace
in the lives of men of faith; he expected and exacted these
evidences of righteousness in his devout followers, and
first of all in himself. Imperatively he sought spiritual
and also secular expression of Christian righteousness.
This was to be achieved in his Christian theocracy of
Geneva, or rather its "bibliocracy," as it has been called.[34]
It manifested unbending courage and resolution just because the true Calvinist never put his trust in himself but
always in God's will and God's election of him. Thus he
was heroic in his humble piety. The consecrated bearers
of God's charge undertook to refashion human life and
build God's kingdom on earth. How could they turn
back? Calvin assured them of God's irresistible grace.
Their holy work was not only in the life of the spirit but
in the daily secular pursuits and concerns. Mastering his
own weakness and ailments, Calvin overcame great ob-
structions in his reforms in Geneva, in general welfare and
security, in sanitary measures and hospital service, in
public education, in industrial organization and advance.
Beyond Geneva, the influence of Calvinism spread
throughout Western Europe and across the Atlantic. Its
vitality as a socially reforming power marked the history
of French Huguenots, Scotch Presbyterians, and Puritans
in England and America.

The political and economic consequences of Calvinism
have been important. John Knox in Scotland recognized

---

[34] Compare Troeltsch, op. cit., p. 70; Georgia Harkness, *John Calvin:
The Man and His Ethics* (New York, 1931), p. 22.

and declared, despite traditional assumptions of ungodly authority, the divinely justified convictions of a Christian democracy. Calvinists were active in several revolutions or other movements of social-political reconstruction. In the economic field the course of Calvinist influence has been traced in directions disturbing to some minds. Calvin dignified the industry of good men in their daily tasks: with diligent industry, by God's favor and dispensation, men achieved success and even prosperity. If, like Luther's farmer and housewife, the industrialist and the merchant could serve the Lord in their business, would they not see in the growth of their business God's approval of them and then turn more directly to the pursuit of prosperity and economic mastery? Toward this sort of conclusion Max Weber proceeded in his work *The Protestant Ethic and the Spirit of Capitalism.* Weber has not lacked followers, but his thesis has also been subjected to critical revision. The rise of modern capitalism can scarcely be traced to Calvinist sources alone; the names of the Medicis, the Fuggers, and the Welsers mark its tributaries in the Renaissance. Calvin himself would have condemned any strictly secular-economic and selfish emphasis in men's lives. But the ideal of piety as expressed in productive daily industry could not evade the hazard of preoccupation with profits.

The secular-historical applications of Calvinism found more wide-reaching expression in Puritanism, first in early American pioneering and then in the more settled establishment on New World shores. While it has been reckoned that a goodly third of the passengers on the *Mayflower* were a random lot in pursuit of some better chance in life overseas, the leading spirit of the men and women on that ship and on the many that followed it was that of a holy mission. Those voyagers were truly Pilgrims going to a Promised Land in which they were to carry out a divine charge of blessed transformation. A preserved proclamation of a certain Captain Edward Johnson expresses this animating conviction: "Oh yes! Oh yes! Oh yes! All you people of Christ that are here Oppressed, Imprisoned and scurrilously derided, gather yourselves together. . . . Know this is the place where the Lord will create a new Heaven, and a new Earth in new Churches, and a new Commonwealth together."[35]

Calvin's theology had proceeded from his conviction of election by God's grace of men of true faith toward insistence on unremitting industry as the daily fruition of true piety. For Calvin's Puritan followers in a savage land, unremitting labor was a stern condition of survival in which they could be sustained only by their faith and their conviction that they were the Lord's chosen laborers. Grueling daily toil gained both dignity and reassurance when seen as a mission in a holy perspective. Cotton Mather would have underscored Calvin's own admonition: "If the end of selection is holiness of life, it ought to arouse and stimulate us strenuously to aspire to it, instead of serving as a pretext to sloth."[36] The Puritan aspiration to holiness in Massachusetts sought its spiritual but also its daily practical expression: "The God of Heaven had carried a nation into a wilderness upon the designs of a glorious reformation."[37]

Cotton Mather (1663-1728) lived and wrote from the vantage point of many years of productive Puritan labors. He and his father were both graduates of Harvard College, the establishment of which, within twenty years after the Pilgrims' landing on Plymouth Rock, was an outstanding expression of the Puritans' resolute devotion to what was to them a divine charge and also a historic mission. Nonetheless earnest in their holy aspiration,

[35] Compare H. W. Schneider, *The Puritan Mind* (New York, 1930), p. 8.
[36] Calvin *Institutes* 3.23.12, cited by Williston Walker, *John Calvin* (New York, 1909), p. 415.
[37] Cotton Mather, *Magnalia*, 3:1, cited by Schneider, op. cit., p. 31.

they could take a historical view of their New England wilderness that was no longer trackless but plowed and fruitful. Mather was concerned lest men's partial fulfillment of God's purpose for them would make them yield to invading worldliness. The Puritan urged himself to be vigilant in unflagging devotion to his godly duty: he in his New England as Calvin in Geneva said: "Let us not cease so to act that we may make some unceasing progress in the way of the Lord. And let us not despair at the slightness of our success; for even though attainment may not correspond to desire, when today outstrips yesterday the effort is not lost. . . . It is this, indeed, which through the whole course of life we seek and follow."[38]

In some ways the Puritans, in England as well as on American shores, were sterner in holy rigor than Calvin; in other ways, more accommodating to secular considerations. Sabbath observance in Geneva was largely limited to imperative church attendance; but in Massachusetts all work had to end at three on Saturday afternoon, with penalties for walking or playing before Sunday night. In the economic field, however, Richard Baxter, in old England, not only allowed but dignified piously a man's honest pursuit of the better bargain: "If God show you a way in which you may lawfully get more than in another way (without wrong to your soul, or to any other), if you refuse this, and choose the less gainful way, you cross one of the ends of your Calling, and you refuse to be God's Steward."[39] In the expansive range of American economic opportunity, this sort of godly reflection might naturally inspire the quasi-virtuous zeal in building up the business which led to larger and eventually to a vaster prosperity.

In the course of the progressive secular development

[38] Calvin *Institutes* 3. 6. 5; compare *A Calvin Treasury,* ed. Wm. F. Keesecker (New York, 1961), p. 103.
[39] Compare Georgia Harkness, op. cit., pp. 118, 184 f.

of the colonies, the Puritan rigor did not abate so much in its pronounced edicts as in its actual conformity to them. From the outset New England had its unregenerates, and their number increased with the more secure colonization. To rekindle the ardor of its early piety and stir its relaxed conscience, Puritanism needed a Great Awakening, a rededication to the Lord, in which Jonathan Edwards (1703-1758) was a leading spirit. As stern a Calvinist as any Puritan, Edwards rejected any free will or human productive capacity. Yet, while holding inflexibly to divine election to grace and to reprobation, he admonished the unregenerates to repent or face an awesome doom.

This brief statement of the tone of Edwards's sermons, such as "Sinners in the Hands of an Angry God," would not do justice to his philosophical grasp and insight. Beyond the imprecations of his sermons was a systematic probing of the problem of ultimate teleology, the fundamental divine purpose in all creation. "As God delights in his own beauty, He must necessarily delight in the creature's holiness."[40] Man's rise in virtue and godliness must be an advance from pious expediency, from thoughts of heaven and hell, toward pure disinterested love of God. In this spirit one may transcend the worldly outlook; secular considerations, success and progress or tragedy would be seen in their eternal setting, as elements in the perfect divine order. For even our own salvation cannot be our concern, but God's. Our concern must always be to know God and to glorify Him. In his exalted contemplation the sternest of Calvinists may be seen as rising above the range of any secular tasks or achievements or progress.

The rekindled ardor of piety in the Great Awakening faded erelong into cool worldly practicality, but some

---

[40] Jonathan Edwards, *Works*, Hickman's twelfth edition (London, 1879), 1: 101.

deep spiritual convictions of the Puritan conscience proved vital and enduring. In their secular expressions they influenced the historical development of the American way of life. The Puritan's consciousness of his life as a divine mission fused humility of spirit with dignity in resolution. The course of history was seen as the ongoing reenactment of God's plan of salvation and reprobation. And the ways of divine Providence need not be man's ways. The conviction that God is not a respecter of persons might lead to some precarious or even sinister reflections, but it was also an admonition not to spurn the weary and the heavy laden, to whom the gospel was explicitly addressed. The pious concern for the least of these our brethren might—and in the course of Puritan history did—find a secular expression in the democratic principle of the natural and inviolable rights and personal dignity of all men whatever, a principle essential to modern doctrines of political progress. Thus the Puritan "equalitarianism before God suited well the democratic conception of the equal title of all members of society to be its beneficiaries and the sources of its authority."[41]

The historical role of religion in its cultural setting has its own secular aspects, which have significance in the growth of the belief in progress. The providential outlook in its Jewish and Christian expressions, however, does not recognize the possibility of true progress by man's own activity, nor secular historical advance. It sees human life, past and present, as under divine Providence, and it contemplates the full measure of God's judgment in some solemn finality. The unambiguous modern idea of human progress, expressing a far different view of nature and of human nature, has been called the modern man's secular religion.

[41] R. B. Perry, *Puritanism and Democracy* (New York, 1944), p. 194.

CHAPTER THREE

The Upsurge of the Idea of Progress during the Renaissance and the Seventeenth Century

THE RENAISSANCE was marked by a shift in men's thinking: in the authority they recognized and in the direction and range of their prevailing interest. Men increasingly abandoned their submission to ecclesiastical authority. They rather relied on observation and experiment or on critical analysis and inference, both in seeking knowledge and in testing the truth of their ideas. Corresponding to this basic change of method was an equally radical change in outlook. The theological perspective was replaced by an insistently secular study of physical and human nature.

The abandonment of religious authoritarianism left self-reliance as the only alternative for modern thinkers. But critical self-reliant thinking required a standard of validity to replace the earlier dependence on dogma, and this ground was contestable. After their dismissal of divine authority, where were men to find assured truth? One certainty at least the early modern mind possessed firmly: the conviction of a boundless range of knowledge and its applications. In the early stages of the turn from the medieval to modern culture, a philosophical cardinal, Nicholas of Cusa, had expressed this stirring sense of infinite mental prospect: "To be able to know more and more without end is the type of eternal wisdom."[1] Knowledge and the practical application of it are conceivably boundless, but are they within our reach? To what degree are they attainable by our minds? And as it is with knowledge, pure or applied, so it is with the other values on which the worth of human life depends. Right here is the problem of progress in its modern setting.

One strain of Renaissance thinking manifests both a departure from medieval reflection and a kinship to it. The disavowal of the medieval dependence on dogmatic authority and theological commitment signified a resolute pursuit of critical investigation with a secular outlook. But it had not quite outgrown the medieval sense of spiritual indigence. The earlier conviction of sinfulness was replaced by the unnerving doubt of man's spiritual capacities. This skepticism also unsettled the world of values, but its invasion of the realm of knowledge was most disturbing.

Modern naturalism itself posed the skeptical challenge. The medieval Schoolmen meant to proceed from eternal verities of faith to deductive analysis and systematic elaboration. That was the declared Scholastic program, *fides quaerens intellectum,* faith seeking to understand. Firm orthodox commitment allowed no lack of confidence that God-given reason could achieve a system of orthodox truth. Where reason could not ascend to the heights of orthodox certainty, faith would consummate the quest: beyond reason, yes, but not against reason. The secular thinkers of the Renaissance, on the other hand, meant to achieve their own entire statement of knowledge, but found, in their first steps, both their data and their premises questionable. The insistence on an exacting standard led many minds during the Renaissance to indecision and skeptical quandary. Montaigne's motto expressed both their demand and their wavering before it: "*Que sçai-je?*—What do I know?"

---

[1] Compare *Progress and History,* ed. F. S. Marvin (London, 1921), p. 11.

Whether the demand or the wavering was more emphatic depended upon the mental temper. In the case of Montaigne (1533-1592) a genial temperament proceeded from a pervading sense of inconclusiveness to a dismissal of strict logical demands. He found no stability or reliable base, but did observe a most interesting random variety; so he centered his attention on the passing show of himself and others. Montaigne's *Essays* are prose lyrics of the protean nature of man: intellect, feeling, and will, all unstable and undependable, but nevertheless most interesting. He would avoid unwarranted commitment and fanaticism of any sort.

So had Erasmus (1466-1536) before Montaigne been wary of final espousal, wary of the pope's offer of a cardinal's hat and also of Melanchthon's Lutheran overtures. His *Praise of Folly* was a Renaissance recall of Nicholas of Cusa's *docta ignorantia,* instructed ignorance. The Erasmian virtue was tolerance, urbane recognition of our various pursuits of the truth, variously plausible, variously short of finality. But though not conclusive in the attainment of truth, our critical and tolerant search after it is of great worth, for it emancipates us from superstition and bigotry, and it realizes the degree of spiritual attainment that may well be within our reach. In this more positive tone of his thinking Erasmus must be distinguished from Montaigne.

The unstable borderland between creative zeal and indecision thus became characteristic of the Renaissance. The modern issue between confidence and distrust deeply affected many theologians in their view of man's spiritual prospects, progress or frustration, but it was especially marked in some of the leading minds of the transitional period who came to the problem of progress from their reflection on science or philosophy or social and political principles. These men differed in the directions of their emphasis, but they agreed in their keen awareness of the contending issues. The mere mention of two of them should suffice to illustrate this pendular movement of thought.

Giordano Bruno (1548-1600) was the outstanding philosopher of the sixteenth-century Renaissance—adventurous, critical, constructive. He rejected the geocentric astronomy and cosmology of the ecclesiastical Aristotelians; he pursued the new Copernican principles to their ultimate implications. He found the chief worth of man in his supreme devotion to infinite truth, but he also had a tragic conviction that men's minds are not equal to that noble quest. Is not man's life in pursuit of ideal perfection a life of actual ultimate frustration?

In the next century Blaise Pascal (1623-1662) revived but also defied the skepticism of Montaigne. He recognized man's basic ignorance but he refused to accept it. In his earlier reflections he had expressed some of the modern confidence in men's intellectual capacities, in their ability to learn from their own past experience and from the recorded knowledge of their forebears. "Men altogether progress continually." He contemplated the historical succession of men and nations as one man, ongoing and ever learning.[2] These Pascalian ideas are often quoted, but they were not Pascal's last word. He was not a believer in steady progress; he called attention to the narrow range of man's reliable knowledge. He asked after Montaigne: "*What* is it that I know?" and exposed the limits of man's mind. An infant prodigy and a most brilliant scientist of his day, Pascal both praised and questioned his geometrical method. It proves best what it undertakes to prove, but it does not give man the first principles of knowledge nor the final saving truths which his spirit needs: the assurance of God's existence, man's imperative principles of the godly life, man's immortal destiny under divine justice and grace.

"Reason clamors in vain; it cannot fix the worth of

[2] Pascal, *Oeuvres*, ed. L. Brunschvicg and P. Boutroux (Paris, 1908), 2: 139.

things. . . . Justice and truth are . . . so subtle that our instruments are too dull to grasp them exactly."[3] What would be more decisive in our thought or in our life than to be certain of God and his eternal judgment of us? But this certainty is beyond our reach. And what prospects of growth or advance can we regard as reasonable? Pascal drew a zigzag curve on his page as he contemplated the history of mankind. Like the tides of the sea, there is ever a going and a returning, forward and backward. The alleged progress is but a flow and an ebb: no assured conclusive achievement and advance.[4]

What are we to do, then? Pascal's way out of his quandary was through his "wager of faith." Stake your daily life on the possible alternative of God's eternal providence, which alone is of sovereign importance to you. Live and act as if you believed in God; go to mass, take holy water. So he urged himself; but his reason could not be silenced altogether, and his wager moved him to tragic irony: "*Cela vous fera croire, et vous abêtira*— That will make you believe, and will stultify you."[5]

This decisive issue regarding man's spiritual capacities, to know the truth, to pursue and attain virtue, engaged not only scientists and philosophers but also the theologians, who restated their old alternative views of Christian faith in terms of the problem of progress. This theological contrast of beliefs can be studied to good advantage in the controversy between George Hakewill and Bishop Goodman. Goodman's book *The Fall of Man* (1616) had maintained a doctrine of dismal piety, a dire judgment on mankind and on the whole world as tainted to the core and doomed to spreading decay. In the abuse of his reason, in his disobedience and sin, man is like a tumor of corruption, fouling all creation. "Now I have brought man to his grave. . . . I have cast heaven and

[3] Pascal, *Pensées*, ed. Brunschvicg (Paris, 1925), § 82.
[4] Compare *Pensées*, § 355.
[5] Op. cit., § 233.

earth upon him, and together with man entombed the whole world." The entire universe "shall stand in an uproar, the heavens with the elements, the elements with the heavens, and all together confounded."[6] This degeneration can have only one result: inevitable death and dissolution. But though man and his world are incapable of any sound growth and progress, their final decay and ruin will not be the ultimate result. God in his infinite providence will then bring forth his new creation, perfect and uncontaminated by any evil, which will endure for eternity. We may recall the Zoroastrian blessed finale after the utter rout of Ahriman and the ensuing world conflagration.

Against Bishop Goodman's dismal judgment of our human nature and its capacities, George Hakewill in his *Apologie* maintained not only an assurance regarding God's final triumph over evil but also a conviction regarding the upward course of creation. Despite the many lapses and bad turns, the record of history and our own experience justify not dismay but confidence in the future.

Hakewill did not proceed from Goodman's extreme to the opposite. Between a steady advance and inevitable decay, he undertook to prove "that there is both in wits and arts, as in all things besides, a kind of circular progress as well in regard to places as times: . . . they have their birth, their growth, their flourishing, their failing, their fading, and within a while, after their resurrection, and their reflourishing again."[7] This universal resilience of men and things is itself irrefutable evidence of the basic soundness of nature. The reasonable faith in Providence regards the corruptions which beset us as we view the fading and falling leaves of autumn. Winter does come, but after it comes the new life of spring.

Hakewill is wary of undue complacency or Stoic-

---

[6] Cited here from Victor Harris, *All Coherence Gone* (Chicago, 1949), pp. 26, 34.

[7] Hakewill, *Apologie*, 3d ed., two vols. in one (Oxford, 1635) 3.6.2.

Pelagian self-reliance that would ignore man's dependence on God's grace. But he searches the historical record to show that by the grace of God men have risen from low to high and then to still higher ground. Hakewill explores every field of human activity, and everywhere he notes the upbuilding powers of men, in insight, in efficient construction, in artistic creation, in virtuous conduct, in worthy endurance. The later ages are a match for antiquity in strength, in wit, in social order, in resistance to tyranny, in heroic martyrdom.[8]

Even Bishop Goodman's own strictures were turned to good account in the *Apologie*. The bishop held that "nature in all things degenerates, and therefore must be supplied by art. . . . Almonds wanting good husbandry prove bitter, but the bitter will never recover their sweetness."[9] Hakewill might have replied that good husbandry is available in the orchard and likewise good training in the home and school. He observed that we still have good almonds, so the past with its alleged degeneration could hardly be regarded as without some power of maintenance and restoration. Whatever instances of ancient classical greatness Goodman might cite to humble our modern esteem, Hakewill replied that surely our forebears were better than their own ancestors, so the alleged degeneration could not have been universal.[10] His supplementary volume, a tireless controversy in which he challenged the bishop's reasoning point by point, has been called "the greatest pitched battle of the two schools of thought," in which Hakewill "carried the day easily and almost by acclamation."[11]

The long-pitched battle showed the tenacity of the two opposed positions. Hakewill's victory indicated a decisive turn in social outlook not only among the general

[8] Op. cit., 4.2.7, 9, 11.
[9] Compare *Apologie* 5: 98 f.
[10] Compare *Apologie* 5: 178.
[11] E. L. Tuveson, *Millennium and Utopia* (Berkeley, Calif., 1949), p. 72.

public but likewise among a considerable group of theologians. Numerous divines had been opposing the view that the world runs down like a clock, that the dregs and puddle of all ages are sweeping us down.[12] New voices now swelled the confidence in progress. The Cambridge Platonist Henry More (1614-1687) recognized a positive power for progressive goodness in man, a "boniform faculty."[13] Thomas Burnet (1635-1715) revealed man's progress not only in this life but eternally in the hereafter, "a doctrine of cosmic progressivism."[14]

This spread of the belief in progress and the resistance to it, can be traced in the science, the social philosophy, and the general literature of the seventeenth century. Renaissance literature gave brilliant expression of the basic alternatives in Machiavelli (1469-1527) and Rabelais (1490-1553) who agree in their dismissal of the medieval tradition but differ in their estimate of men's character and capacity for progress and in their social and historical outlook. Machiavelli's *Prince* was a negative evaluation of human nature, a divorce of politics from morals, and emphasis on force as the decisive test of statecraft. Two convictions contended for dominance in Machiavelli's thought: his view of men as always driven by the same base desires and lusts, despite high professions, and his exaltation of classical antiquity as the apex of human achievement. These ideas held no hope for historical progress. Men are ever stirred by their passions; the amazing capacity for great achievement which reached fruition in classical antiquity was unprecedented and unapproachable; it was inevitably followed by degeneration. So Machiavelli turned from the strange classical interlude of greatness to portray the usual run of men and nations as

[12] Compare Harris, *All Coherence Gone*, pp. 133, 154.

[13] Compare Henry More, *Enchiridion Ethicum*, trans. Edward Southwell (1690), 1.3; quoted here from the reprint of the Facsimile Society (New York, 1930).

[14] Compare Tuveson, *Millennium and Utopia*, p. 128.

base and ineffectual, mean tools for the strong hand of a despot.

Some modern criticism has revised our generally held ideas of Machiavelli's motivation and of his basic views, but these revisions would not alter radically his meaning as understood by his age. Even more debatable would be any explicit formula of the uproarious book of Gargantua and Pantagruel by François Rabelais. Was it a specific satire in an allegorical version, or an obscure outpouring of derision for everything stodgy and respectable? What interests us here is Rabelais's proposal to modern men to replace their discredited submission to dogmatic authority. What he urged on his age was the rejection of all tradition whatever, of all scruples and inhibitions, the full release of men's energies, desires, curiosities, and fancies, the freest interplay of ideas and passions alike. His was the Book of the Great Unloosing. The motto of his "Abbey of Thélème" was the great word of his confidence in man and of his hopes for men: "Do what you will, *Fay ce que vouldras.*" Give the new age the fullest scope and chance. Men need this free release to try and taste whatever they will; only thus unhampered will they put forth their utmost and realize the new perfections of their nature, the new and deeper truths, the riper experience, the fuller and more intense joy of living, the more humane social order.

Here were two brilliant masters of modern literature who each in his way elated the radicals and scandalized the respectable.

A different sort of thinker and writer was Jean Bodin (1530-1596). His *Republic: Six Books* was perhaps the first systematic work which the modern age could put alongside the *Politics* of Aristotle. Bodin agreed with Aristotle in treating political order as the social expansion of the moral organization of values. The good state is as the good man's life, the normal development and fruition of man's character. Government and laws should express concern for the people's welfare, and they are finally subject to social control. But all reform should be gradual and cautious. Do not lock the gates to further progress, but never remove the lock.

Here was a patient and moderate liberal, but unfortunately he was a diffuse and tedious writer. Even so, Bodin's pedestrian but most respectable exposition persuaded many whom Rabelais had only scandalized; and it was Bodin, not Machiavelli, who expressed the conviction of the new age.

For our best understanding of Bodin's advocacy of the belief in progress we should look especially to a shorter work, the appeal in his *Discourse to the Senate and the People of Toulouse on Education to Be Given to Young People in a Republic.* This is a true manifesto of the Renaissance, a vista of the emerging modern world and the new life available to men, with directions for their advance to master it. Bodin urges men to look across the entire span of human experience: we cannot ever enumerate all the great works of the new age, its discoveries and inventions, its refinements of culture and political wisdom. Never before in history was so much knowledge and practical mastery available to young men through the right humanistic education. More than in any previous age, Bodin declares, we live in "an epoch in which, throughout Europe, the humanities flourish, talents abound, the sciences progress."[15] Likewise in his work, *The Method of History,* Bodin repudiates the belief that mankind has degenerated. The lauded Golden Age of classical legend would be as iron if compared to the modern. Our knowledge and virtue vie with those of antiquity. Nature's treasure is inexhaustible, and our progress in possessing it can have no limits.[16] But we

[15] Compare *Oeuvres philosophiques de Jean Bodin,* ed. Pierre Mesnard (Paris, 1951), vol. 5, pt. 3: 36, 62, 38.
[16] Op. cit., pp. 427, 429.

should not conclude that Bodin was a thorough liberal or that he had full mastery of the modern idea of progress. He retained many traditional superstitions, a crude belief in witchcraft, and a bigoted advocacy of persecution.

The Renaissance proceeded from the humanist revival and exaltation of the ancient classics to its own productive achievements in every field of human endeavor. In this advance ancient authorities were upset by better evidence and more thorough logic, and modern thought was moving to higher and more solid ground. Already in 1543 the works of Copernicus and Vesalius had marked the advance of scientific method in astronomy and anatomy— and Harvey, Kepler, Galileo, and Newton were still to come. Vasco da Gama and Columbus were discovering new worlds, and after them a hundred minds were sailing the boundless seas of thought, charting new routes to those "Americas of the mind" with which Goethe was to inspire a later age.

The new spirit in scientific research and in general social outlook was often cramped by persistent bigotry. In this strife of ideas, Francis Bacon (1561-1626) was less hampered than Bodin but not entirely free in his modern temper. He was critical of specialized research which was already achieving productive results. He did not appreciate the far-reaching importance of the work of Copernicus and Galileo, nor even that of Harvey, his personal physician. For all that, Bacon was dedicated to the promotion of "inductive" science and undertook to formulate the method and principles of its procedure. He boldly dismissed the traditional Aristotlelianism of the theologians and by contrast to the medieval syllogisms called his inductive logic the "Novum Organum." He repudiated dogmatic authoritarianism and the precon- ceptions or "idols of the mind" which had caused science and general knowledge to stagnate for long ages. He urged his contemporaries to turn their minds from an- tiquity to their own age and to its advancing future. We are older than the ancients, he declared; we have had more experience; classical antiquity was but the youth of the world.[17]

Bacon proclaimed a "Great Instauration" of productive thought, the exploration of nature and the possession of its resources for men's use and expanding mastery and happiness. His was a mind of boundless confidence in man's capacity to advance. "By far the greatest obstacle to the progress of science and to the undertaking of new tasks and provinces therein, is found in this—that men despair and think things impossible."[18] Possible, and in fact surely within our reach, are not only specific achievements but also the complete reconstruction of society for the progress of mankind. The Renaissance was an age of utopias, visions, and outlines of the perfect state. Bacon's *New Atlantis* was a scientific-technological utopia, the socialized promotion of scientific research regarded as the main purpose of government, to investigate all fields of nature, to discover and formulate its laws, to utilize them for the betterment of human life and its progress in every direction.

Seventeenth-century thought was moving toward more definite grasp and expression of a theory of progress, and the eighteenth gave systematic philosophical formulations of it. This onward course of thought may be studied in the works of Descartes, recognized as the father of systematic modern philosophy.

Three conditions required for a definite theory of progress have been recognized in the thought and method of Descartes (1596-1650): the unambiguous rejection of any deferential attitude toward classical antiquity as unapproachable, the candidly secular evaluation of knowledge for mundane use and application, and the sure foundation of science on the principle of the uniformity

---

17 Compare *The Advancement of Learning*, in *The Philosophical Works of Francis Bacon*, ed. J. M. Robertson (London, 1905), p. 58.
18 Bacon *Novum Organum* 1. 92.

of nature and its invariable laws.[19] We should note his philosophical self-reliance, which was not always firm, but note even more, the progressive, decisive tenor of his ideas. He may vow to make a pilgrimage to Notre Dame de Loretto in gratitude for his grasp of basic truth, but the truth which he was achieving was secular, a key that would unlock the secrets of mathematics and of physical science alike. When he was asked what authorities he had read in his library for the exposition of his ideas, he pointed to his courtyard where a calf was being dissected: "There is my library . . . now."[20] The original title for his *Discourse on Method* had been "Project of a Universal Science Which Can Raise Our Nature to Its Highest Degree of Perfection."[21] Cartesianism combined reliance on rational analysis with emphasis on the uniform mechanics of nature. The progress of science was assured by this conviction of nature as a mechanical system subject to logical analysis and to research and formulation of invariable laws. Men's sense of their spiritual indigence under divine Providence yielded to men's growing assurance of their progress in the mastery of the laws of nature.

Of the two outstanding features of the Renaissance, the revival of the ancient classics and the rise of physical science, the latter was definitely in the ascendant, but the resistance of the classical humanists was still vigorous. The issue between the ancients and the moderns was contested along the entire front of cultural interests. On both sides, extreme partisans pressed their arguments beyond reasonable limits. Scholastic Aristotelianism still had its solemn protagonists in the universities; but Petrus Ramus (1515-1572) chose for his doctorate in Paris the thesis that "everything which Aristotle taught is false,"

[19] Compare J. B. Bury, *The Idea of Progress* (N.Y., ed. of 1955), p. 66.

[20] Compare E. S. Haldane, *Descartes: His Life and Times* (London, 1905), pp. 53, 280.

[21] Compare É. Gilson, *René Descartes: Discours de la méthode* (Paris, 1930), p. xii.

and Thomas Hobbes (1588-1679) spurned his Oxford learning as "Aristotelity" and dismissed Peter the Lombard and Duns Scotus as "egregious blockheads." On the literary side, Julius Caesar Scaliger (1484-1558) idolized "august Virgil, . . . our divine man," as he called him. Against such classical devotion, Étienne Pasquier (1529-1615), in his *Recherches de la France,* proudly proclaimed Pierre Ronsard as the incomparable poet, greater than any poet of classical Rome.[22] In this debate two leaders of the modern idea of progress exercized great influence: Charles Perrault and Fontenelle.

Perrault (1628-1703), who is remembered by French children for his fairy tales, devoted his old age to a systematic "Parallel of the Ancients and the Moderns." In his championship of the modern cause against the classical tradition, he was wary of going to unreasonable extremes. He did not defy the facts by portraying history as an undeviating advance of human achievement. He recognized that the great age of classical antiquity was followed by long centuries of undistinguished production and then by an eclipse of culture. But this in his judgment only shows that the course of history, as an individual's career, has its ascents and declines. There were the Dark Ages, but there is also the Renaissance, and both have their causes and reasons. What is important to recognize is that, despite periodic retrogressions, the creative mind of man regains lost ground and advances to higher levels.

The seventeenth century need not look up to any previous age, Perrault declared: in one short generation French and English genius had made more discoveries and achieved greater mastery in physical science than the whole of antiquity ever attained. But this progressive note in the retrospective outlook is betrayed by its own enthusiasm; it tends to lapse into a new type of modern-

---

[22] Compare Hubert Gillot, *La querelle des anciens et des modernes en France* (Paris, 1914), pp. 72, 115 f.

classical complacency. Perault saw his century as "arrived in some sort of the highest perfection. . . . Very likely we have not many things for which to envy those who will come after us."[23] The full conception of progress, of a future prospect of boundless advance, was not grasped by Perrault.

Fontenelle's life (1657-1757) spanned the seventeenth and the eighteenth centuries, from the death of Descartes through the youth of Kant and the childhood of Goethe. He is not to be compared with those masters, but in his own way he expressed characteristics of thought which the great names recall to us: a conviction of the consummate productive power of reason, a readiness for thorough critical reconstruction of ideas, a serene view of nature and human nature as infinite in their range and significance. With a fine sense for epigram, he salutes his age in which "authority has ceased to have more weight than reason."[24] No longer rigidly codified, ideas are in active interplay. Locke and Newton contend with Descartes in French minds, and with creative criticism, new conceptions expand men's outlook, infinitely diverse, and stimulating future progress. From London and Paris, scientific societies and academies multiply across Europe.

The development of Fontenelle's thought in itself epitomizes a trend of ideas from the skepticism of Montaigne to the systematic advocacy of progress during the Enlightenment. In his early work, *Dialogues of the Dead*, published in 1683, Fontenelle shows an ironical turn of mind not only in his style but in his outlook on history and on human life in general. The third of his "Dialogues of Ancient Dead with Modern," between Socrates and Montaigne, confronts Socratic irony with the "What do I know?" of Montaigne's *Essays*. The Frenchman tells the Athenian of his modern age, in every way changed

---

[23] Compare F. J. Teggart, *The Idea of Progress: A Collection of Readings*, ed. G. H. Hildebrand (Berkeley, Calif., 1949), p. 194.

[24] Compare Gillot, op. cit., p. 555.

from the ancient, and all for the worse: quite different from the ancient probity and uprightness. Ironical Socrates, on the contrary, had expected that man at long last would have outgrown the vices and follies of his old days. It seems that mankind never learns and never forgets, but keeps to its same stupid and corrupt ways. Externals may alter, but the heart of man and the general order of nature remain constant.

From this view of human life and the course of history Fontenelle turned later in his long career to an expansively forward-looking and progressive view of human affairs. He revived the vision of Pascal's pre-skeptical youth, of the history of mankind as the life of a man ever growing and learning. More positively than Pascal, he insisted that "this man of all ages will never be old"; again and again humanity renews its youth and its productive powers. The true understanding of the ancients is to see each period of history in its right perspective. Fontenelle admired the classical masterpieces. (Like Scaliger, he preferred the Romans to the Greeks.) What he condemned was the servile acceptance of them as final authorities or models of perfection. French genius has surpassed the ancient, but it also is short of finality. We should not raise new idols nor "run after Descartes," as our ancestors ran after Aristotle.[25] We should prize the great past, cherish the greater present, and be alert to the still greater demands and prospects of the future. Here was the conviction of unlimited progress. The systematic theory of it was being formulated in the closing years of Fontenelle's amazing and vigorous longevity, during the eighteenth century.

Fontenelle's confidence in expanding progress was shared by many minds across the Channel. The advance-

---

25 Fontenelle, A *Discourse concerning the Ancients and the Moderns,* trans. Hughes, appended to *Conversations with a Lady on the Plurality of Worlds,* trans. Joseph Glanvill (London, 1719), p. 210; compare pp. 202, 186.

ment of scientific investigation in all fields of nature, in which the Royal Society of London led the vanguard, was championed with documentation and eloquence by Joseph Glanvill (1636-1680) in his *Plus Ultra, or the Progress and Advancement of Knowledge since the Days of Aristotle* (1668). We should remember that Glanvill combined his advocacy of scientific research with some basic skeptical reservations and with superstitious "philosophical considerations" about witchcraft. In *Plus Ultra* he declared confidently that the members of the Royal Society of London, established in 1662, had witnessed more scientific progress in six years than the Aristotelians could match in their eighteen centuries. Glanvill outlined two ways in which knowledge could be advanced: by enlarging, in Bacon's phrase, "the history of things," through detailed information about the various fields of nature, and by improving the communication of ideas. In a succession of chapters he gives a classified inventory of modern scientific advance in chemistry, anatomy, mathematics, astronomy, optics, geography, and other fields, and in the perfecting of scientific instruments. He expounds the efficient institutional organization of the Royal Society, its undogmatic pursuit of truth and its remarkable achievements (in the reporting of which he gives special attention to the "illustrious Mr. Boyle"). He regards it as absurd to make "Comparison between the advantages Aristotle had for Knowledge and those of later ages."[26]

This conviction of endless advance was shared by many; it found expression in the promotion of scientific projects to improve civilization by ameliorating social conditions, from plans for international peace to proposals to abandon the celibacy of the clergy. Many of these projects were confused and ill advised; some were the notions of odd eccentrics; but others failed of success

[26] Joseph Glanvill, *Plus Ultra*, chapt. 15.

only because they were ill timed or premature. The discrediting, deserved or undeserved, of some of these proposals affected the reputation of their advocates whose basic ideas should have earned some of them more enduring recognition.

We have been tracing the upsurge and the spreading impact of the idea of progress in the seventeenth century. This idea clearly involves a more expansive view of the effective range of man's spiritual activity. Although the age was marked by the rise of secular thinking, with radical reconstruction and new and original ideas, the traditional theology with its providential judgment of history was not eclipsed entirely. Its most brilliant advocate, Bishop Bossuet (1627-1704), was a contemporary of John Locke but a spiritual brother of Saint Augustine. Like Augustine's *City of God*, Bossuet's *View of Universal History* interpreted the course of man's existence through the ages as under the direction of divine Providence. Bossuet's charts of history under its epochs and periods are not of major importance to us. In the first part of his work he brings his historical survey to the Age of Charlemagne and then devotes the remaining two thirds to a long review of the progress of religion and a much briefer discussion of the progress of empires. While continually expounding scripture in a somewhat patristic style and eloquence, he is also keenly conscious of the spiritual needs of his age. Modern skeptics and libertines need solemn admonition; they must hear again the verdict of God. Human life is not random, nor is history a mere interplay of blind forces. God reigns over all nations. "Let us talk no more of chance, or of fortune. . . . What is chance, in regard to our uncertain counsels, is a concerted design in a higher counsel."[27] Growth, progress, decline, and fall, all are under God's decree. They that govern find themselves under that higher authority, and

---

[27] Bossuet, *View of Universal History*, trans. J. Elphinston (London, 1778) 2: 280.

they that submit and obey, owe their ultimate loyalty to "the blessed and only Potentate, the King of kings, and Lord of lords."[28]

The involvement of the idea of progress in the new cosmologies and social philosophies of the age may be studied in the impacts made by the theories of Thomas Hobbes and John Locke. No other English thinkers aroused such strong and far-reaching reactions not only in Britain but also in Europe. Locke's influence in France was especially noteworthy, for it turned the direction of eighteenth-century thought and defined important aspects of the French Enlightenment. The coupling of these two names nowise indicates any basic agreement of the two philosophers, but it is interesting to note, despite their radical disagreements, their respective bearing on the problem of progress.

Hobbes (1588-1679) assumed a position of thorough going materialism. Nature, in his view, is mechanical system all the way through, and human nature likewise. Both physiology and psychology should be treated as chapters in physics. The heart is like a spring; the joints are so many wheels; our so-called mind and its ideas are mechanical processes determined by the ways in which the outside world impresses or strikes us—literally. Emotion likewise is simply a kind of bodily motion. From this point of view Hobbes portrayed men in the state of nature as contending with each other for self-preservation, self-satisfaction, and prevailing power and mastery. Every man is to every other man a wolf or a lamb, and human life is a state of actual or threatened universal war. (Our present-day terms are shorter: hot or cold war.) This natural state of human affairs is insecure, with "continual fear, and danger of violent death; and the life of man, solitary, poor, nasty, brutish, and short."[29]

[28] Ibid.
[29] Hobbes, *Leviathan,* in *English Works,* ed. Molesworth (London, 1839), 3: 113.

This portrayal of man in the state of nature was a materialistic pendant alongside of the traditional theological account of man's sinful depravity. Hobbes, however, did not proceed to intone "There is no health in us" and to seek salvation by supernatural means, through divine grace. He did speak of God as the Creator and Final Judge, but only after a fashion, as a respectable gesture. Hobbes's salvation of men from their brutish lot in nature is again through nature. Men's natural desire for security leads them to organize themselves into a society, by each agreeing to subject his will to the will of the absolute Sovereign, Leviathan. In this political theory, the formation of the state is made possible by the mutual negation of all egoistic wills; but this suppression of selfish behavior is itself motivated by the natural self-seeking concern for security.

This warlike account of human character aroused wide criticism. For a long century respectable moralists and social philosophers refuted Hobbism. But Hobbes's *Leviathan,* perverse as it appeared to his critics, provided in its own way an added argument for the belief in progress. Prior to Hobbes, the advocates of progress had been mostly optimists with a positive estimate of man's spiritual capacities. The *Leviathan* took a mechanistic view of men, low and dismal; yet it showed, even in men's insatiate selfishness, their natural motive that must lead them all to form a system of government. Even in the crassest view of men, they are still capable of social progress.

Locke's contribution to the belief in progress is through his theory of the nature of men's minds and the processes of experience and knowledge. His *Essay Concerning Human Understanding* (1690) was the systematic treatise of British empiricism, and it directed in both Britain and France the new outlook on men and societies. This empiricism traced the origin of ideas to the processes of sensation and reflection. All that we are, whatever we perceive, think, feel, or act, is derived and determined by the course of our experience. There are no innate ideas, nor is there any inborn and unalterable character of men and societies. The ongoing course of our experience shapes and modifies everyone; the historical course of events shapes and modifies the order of societies and governments. Political regimes are not set up once for all by divinely ordained principles. Governments must serve the people's needs; they depend upon the people's approval and are subject to reform or abolition at the people's demand.

Here was a philosophical platform for liberal reconstruction. But while it resisted any dogmatic conviction it also disavowed any expectation of certain knowledge or assured prospect in dealing with the factual course of experience. With his characteristic candor Locke avowed that our ideas of substances ("Somewhat I know not what") can yield only degrees of probability, likely surmises, not factual certitude. By careful survey of our data we can record the actual details of our experience and can follow its likely trends, but we cannot ascertain necessary connections or definite prospects.

While Locke's direction of thought provided no platform or program of universal conviction, it did allow a range of probability in foresight sufficient for planning and pursuing reforms. Locke's *Essay* and his writings on education and government became the manuals of French radicals who looked beyond the ancient monarchical regime toward some new order of advance in justice and liberty and social welfare. His works were read overseas in America not only by some of the Founding Fathers but also by thousands of people in the expanding Western land. Locke did not deal directly with the ideas of progress; the term scarcely appears on his pages. But his empiricist accounts of the mind's capacities and of the processes of human life and institutions, as growing in complexity and maturity and as molded by changing circumstances and conditions, laid the grounds of the psychology of the Enlightenment. New and effective approaches were provided to the systematic theories of progress which were to engage eighteenth-century thinkers.

CHAPTER FOUR

Philosophies of Progress
in the Eighteenth Century

THE IDEA OF PROGRESS was a dominant theme of eighteenth-century thought, but in dramatic interplay and reversal. The vitality and perfectibility of social values was affirmed during the first half of that age with a confidence which proceeded in many cases to excessive optimism, both godly and secular. The succeeding period was marked by a wave of social and religious negations and by spreading skepticism. There were voices of discontent and dismay challenging the optimism of the early Enlightenment; on the other hand, the assured and boundless perfectibility of mankind was reaffirmed even in the darkest days of the revolution in France.

The issues of skepticism which embroiled the Renaissance continued to disturb later thinkers. The abysmal problem of evil engrossed and baffled both theologians and metaphysicians. Cosmology and social philosophy reflected contending theories of man and his place in nature. This running summary of tendencies in early modern thought may gain in definiteness by specific references. On the judgment of skepticism and theodicy—the problems of knowledge and evil—the main issues were argued by Bayle, Leibniz, and Shaftesbury. The ideas as well as the lifetimes of these three span the turn of the eighteenth century.

Pierre Bayle (1647-1706) was the master controversialist of the period. In his *Historical and Critical Dictionary* the various heresies of Christian tradition were reexamined, and the claims of orthodoxy were reappraised critically, with conclusions humiliating to faith and reason alike. Assuredly, reliable knowledge depends upon sound evidence and rational demonstration, but these are not available in the all-important matters of religion. Most vulnerable to searching criticism are the orthodox explanations of the nature and origin of evil, committed as they are to recognize the deep-lying corruption of human nature and yet to regard it as nowise reflecting on the infinite perfection of the Creator of man. Despite all our quandaries, however, we must and shall hold fast the verities of faith; only, Bayle urged, let us not delude ourselves that they have any sound rational basis.

The challenge to this skeptical dialectic was met in the *Theodicy* of Leibniz (1646-1716). This treatise appeared only several months after *The Moralists* (1709) of Shaftesbury. Both works were marked by a spirit of cosmic and social optimism which proved widely influential and which even set definite patterns and directions in the literature of the period.

Leibniz was confident that the reliable method of rational demonstration, which he had followed in his systematic philosophy, could solve the problems of religion in sound theology. Rightly analyzed and understood, evil is neither an ineradicable taint in man nor a blot on the Creator's infinite perfection. We need a clearer understanding of the right method required for dealing with our problem. Leibniz here appealed to the principle of the "compossibility" of God's attributes. It is not enough to ask whether our nature is evil because God either could not or would not create it perfect. This dilemma is due to inadequate reflection. We should recognize that the many evils in the world cast no blame on the Creator's infinite goodness nor on his omnipotence, if we also take into account God's omniscience, his infinite insight into the nature of finite beings, which even our own rational analysis can disclose. Any created world is bound to have *some* imperfections characteristic of its finitude. Therein we differ and shall eternally differ from God. But we can be sure that, of all conceivable worlds, God's goodness has chosen, and God's omnipotence has created, the one least imperfect. This is Leibniz's doctrine that ours is "the best of all possible worlds," a comforting thought to pious acquiescence, but with some dismal undertones which resounded later in the century.

Leibniz's application of his theodicy in his social philosophy expressed his forward-looking activism. This world of God's creation, in its very nature not absolutely perfect, is characteristically perfectible. Two ideas seemed to have contended for Leibniz's emphasis. One was the conclusion of his theodicy, that we live in the most perfect world possible. The other idea was the conviction of the inexhaustible resources of our spiritual activity. Finite in actuality, we are yet in a sense also infinite, that is, in our eternal prospect. "We must recognize a certain perpetual and very free progress of the whole universe, such that it is always going forward to greater improvement. . . . No end of progress is ever reached."[1] Our chief merit must be in the fulfillment of our rational capacities. In this characteristic realization of ourselves as centers of intelligent activity, we progressively aspire to membership in the Republic of Minds, God's masterpiece on earth.

The thought of Shaftesbury (1671-1713) was marked by a spirit of generous affability. The usual accounts of evil in human lives, be they sufferings or sins, did not seem to have disturbed him overmuch. His attitude was not quite the serene fortitude of the Stoic but rather the

[1] Leibniz, *The Monadology and Other Philosophical Writings*, trans. Robert Latta (Oxford, 1898), pp. 417, 350, 351.

placid conviction that basically and ultimately all was well. Any degree of pessimism seemed to him to be evidence of one-sided and unbalanced judgment of things, seen in the wrong perspective. When viewed truly in its proper place and role in the universal system, every-thing manifests its characteristic perfection in its con-tribution to the cosmic harmony. Shaftesbury was carried away by this complacent assurance: "When [Nature] seems most ignorant and perverse in her productions, I assert her even then as wise and provident as in her goodliest works. . . . 'Tis good which is predominant; and every corruptible and mortal nature by its mortality and corruption yields only to some better, and all in common to that best and highest nature, which is incorruptible and immortal."[2]

The long-range career of these two optimistic doctrines in the history of ideas seems to have been one of diminish-ing returns. It is commonly recognized that Leibniz's philosophy is of increasing importance in contemporary thought. Even Spengler, in his dirge on the collapse of Western civilization, hailed Leibniz as "without doubt the greatest intellect in Western philosophy."[3] But this superlative tribute must be despite the *Theodicy* and not because of it. Shaftesbury's temporary fame was followed by comparative oblivion, and it can hardly be said that his ideas command today more than historical interest. But for our study of the social outlook of the eighteenth century these two thinkers are very significant, for their influence is reflected in the religious and social thinking of the age, and even more strikingly in its literary ex-pressions on both sides of the Channel.

The most familiar poetry of this placid tenor is, of

2 Shaftesbury, *The Moralists,* in *Characteristics,* ed. J. M. Robertson (London, 1900), 2: 22, 23.

3 Oswald Spengler, *The Decline of the West,* trans. C. F. Atkinson (New York, 1930), 1: 42.

course, Alexander Pope's *Essay on Man*. With his marvelous felicity for epigrams, Pope rhymed the current wisdom of world-laudation:

> All nature is but Art unknown to thee;
> All chance, direction which thou canst not see;
> All discord, harmony not understood;
> All partial evil, universal good:
> And spite of Pride, in erring Reason's spite,
> One truth is clear, Whatever is, is right.[4]

This sort of complacency became epidemic, and in some cases it reached the limits of absurdity. Professed sages in verse and in prose joined in the cosmic rhapsody. So, for instance, Albrecht von Haller: "Perhaps this petty speck of error and of dole/Swells the perfection of the universal Whole." So likewise Senator Brockes, in his eulogy of the goose, divinely designed in its entire anatomy to serve the needs of men:

> Goose-grease doth relieve consumption; goose-gall
> lotion, too, is good;
> Goose is good to eat; for dizzy spells we often use its blood;
> Skin and feathers likewise useful: doth not this bird radiate
> God's omnipotence, God's wisdom, and God's love for
> man's estate?

And the psychologist David Hartley: "All individuals are actually and always infinitely happy."[5]

The definite turn from this general laudation of cosmic and human conditions to the affirmation of their progressive character is also notable in eighteenth-century writers. The superlative declaration of actual and universal perfection might have seemed to imply an optimistic denial of general and ultimate progress. A later poetic comment

[4] Pope, *Essay on Man*, 1: 289 ff.
[5] Compare R. A. Tsanoff, *The Nature of Evil* (New York, 1931, 1971), pp. 132 f., 119.

by Robert Browning comes to mind here: "Best being best now, change were for the worse."[6] Shaftesbury might recognize progress in nature's happy use of partial discords to swell its larger harmonies. But other thinkers, less enthusiastic about actualities, were yet confident of the future advancement of humanity to ever higher levels of knowledge and general welfare.

This trust in progress fired the zeal of men in many directions of radical reform. In France, the vast campaign of the Encyclopedists, with Denis Diderot in the vanguard, expressed, through their resistance to social injustice and their scorn for dogmatic superstitution, their confidence in the power of spreading enlightenment to emancipate men and guide them to ever increasing progress in every direction. With similar confidence Bishop Sprat had written a century earlier in his *History of the Royal Society:* "While the old philosophy could only bestow on us some barren terms and notions, the new shall impart to us the uses of all the creatures and shall enrich us with all the benefits and fruitfulness and plenty."[7]   Adam Ferguson (1723-1816), in tracing the history of civil society, maintained "not only the individual advances from infancy to manhood, but the species itself from rudeness to civilization."[8] With greater authority Edward Gibbon (1737-1794) declared: "Since the first discovery of the arts, war, commerce, and religious zeal have diffused among the savages of the Old and the New World, those inestimable gifts; they have been successively propagated; they can never be lost. We may therefore acquiesce in the pleasing conclusion that every age of the world has increased, and still increases, the real wealth, the happiness, the knowledge, and perhaps the

---

[6] Robert Browning, "The Sun."

[7] Cited here from G. M. Trevelyan, *English Social History* (New York, 1942), p. 258.

[8] Compare E. L. Tuveson, *Millennium and Utopia* (Berkeley, Calif., 1940), pp. 195 f.

virtue, of the human race."[9] But these comforting words come at the end of Gibbon's "General Observations on the Fall of the Roman Empire in the West," to express his confidence that our civilization need not fear another devastation by barbarian invaders.

This boundless optimism and this belief in universal progress were shaken but not swamped by a wave of skepticism and denial of the vitality of social values. The course of historical events before and after the French Revolution and the contrary appraisals of them expressed both spreading pessimism and resistant buoyant faith. While the thinkers of the Enlightenment sought to develop a systematic philosophy of progress, their century likewise expressed a negative evaluation of the historical course of events. Fontenelle had been content, while citing specific advances or backsliding of civilization, to regard its basic processes as more or less invariable and constant. But some of his younger contemporaries in the period of the Enlightenment questioned man's capacities for general progress. Advances in one field are gained at too heavy a cost in others. Knowledge and freedom prove too expensive. At any time we are liable to stray toward frustration and ruin. In that vaunted age of systematic philosophies of progress, L. A. de Caraccioli in 1759 blasted civilization in violent diatribe:

> Already this century has run through more than half of its course, and we have nothing to offer our successors but insipid novels, miserable plays, impious philosophies, and extravagant opinions. How corrosive this generation has been! Since the beginning of the century fifty-eight years have passed, and each of them has been a step downward from the worth of our fathers. Our fathers occupied themselves in self-study while we dissipate, they sought only truth while we love only illusion; they drew their argu-

[9] Gibbon, *The History of the Decline and Fall of the Roman Empire,* ed. J. B. Bury, 4th ed. (London and New York, 1911), 4: 168 ff.

ments from religion, while we persist in establishing systems which contradict that religion; they drew from original sources while our knowledge of the ancient authors derives only from citations; they questioned their souls while we are attentive only to our senses; they permitted themselves recreation only as relaxation from arduous labor while we believe that one should live only to enjoy the most criminal pleasures. In a word, they meditated and we talk, they were profound and we are superficial, they reasoned and we wander aimlessly.[10]

The contending historical valuations may be read in the two outstanding men in French literature and philosophy of the eighteenth century, Voltaire and Rousseau. Voltaire (1694-1778) set out with the advocates of universal harmony. While he was never a friend of the ecclesiastics, he was convinced of a design in nature and relied on it for his belief in God and in the basic soundness and good prospects of mankind. Though he was pleased that Alexander Pope shared his ideas, he did not go the whole length with him or with Shaftesbury. He never glossed over the bigotries, vices, injustices, or sufferings which he noted on all sides. Still, his earlier reactions to those evils was that of Leibnizian lenience. Man is finite and imperfect, but still he has the capacity to advance toward his higher destiny.

Voltaire's personal career, however, as well as the social and political course of events in his time, increasingly darkened his view of life. His initially confident theology was shocked by the Lisbon earthquake in 1755, and the remaining twenty-odd years of his life were marked by skepticism. While he remained "on speaking terms with God," as he put it, he could no longer profess any understanding of a divine design in nature or in human lives. What sort of teleology could find meaning in a Lisbon

[10] L. A. de Caraccioli, *La jouissance de soi-même* (1759), pp. ix-x, cited here from Henry Vyverberg, *Historical Pessimism in the French Enlightment* (Cambridge, Mass., 1958), pp. 79 f.

disaster, or what Providence could justify the thousand foul corruptions and tyrannies of history? His persistent reflections multiplied his perplexities. "Alas!" he exclaimed in his poem on the Lisbon disaster, "I am like a doctor: I do not know."

An incomparable master of raillery, Voltaire turned his own early convictions to ridicule. Leibniz's best of all possible worlds sounded to him like unintended irony. If this world is the best possible, what could the others be like? So he wrote his satire *Candide, or Optimism,* in which his hero, if one could so call his chief character, is on a quest of Eldorado but is driven from disaster to disaster. The providential design in nature and the universal order and harmony were exposed to a cynical parody: "Flies are born to be chewed by spiders, which in turn are eaten by swallows, and swallows by shrikes, and shrikes by eagles, and eagles are born to be killed by men, who in turn live to kill each other and to be consumed by worms, or by devils in a thousand cases to one." The same satirical tone marks the article *"Tout est bien—All is well,"* in his *Philosophical Dictionary,* aimed at Shaftesbury, Bolingbroke, and Pope's "All partial evil, universal good": "An odd general good indeed, composed of gall stones and gout, and all the crimes and sufferings, and death, and damnation."[11]

In this world of unsettled values and precarious outlook, Voltaire saw only one possible ray of hope: in the slow process of enlightenment. In the six volumes of his historical *Essai sur les moeurs* he does not apologize for his tireless chronicles of superstitions and tyrannies and crimes, but neither does he emphasize a final note of despair. Through all historical changes, he points out the abiding reality of certain basic values: "Virtue alone never changes. It is like the light of the sun." Despite all the bigotries and cruelties throughout history, "humane

[11]Voltaire, *Oeuvres,* ed. Moland (Paris, 1877-1885), 17: 584, 585.

philosophy" has also been molding the lives of men. "Finally we should believe that reason and industry will always make new progress." The useful arts will advance, prejudices will be abandoned, and philosophy "will console somewhat for the calamities which it will endure in all ages."[12] We ourselves must do our bit in the work of civilization. "Let us cultivate our garden." This conclusion of his *Candide* was not placid confidence but a somber ironic resolution. "There are always barbarians in the most civilized nations and in the most enlightened times."[13] Around us are the jungles of evil; beyond are the seas of ignorance; our garden plot is small and weedy, and its crop uncertain. Let us keep on cultivating it. Beyond reassuring words like these, what does Voltaire finally have to say about the ongoing preservation and advance of social values? In his *Philosophical Dictionary* he discusses all conceivable topics—articles on Prayers, Prejudices, Pretensions, Priests, Privileges, Prophets, Providence—but there is no article on Progress. Nor is there an entry about Progress in the voluminous index to the ninety-five volumes of his *Works*.

Jean Jacques Rousseau (1712-1778) judged about men's actual condition and of their prospects of improvement in direct opposition to Voltaire. Against Voltaire's growing skepticism, Rousseau refused to doubt the natural soundness of God's creation. The historical process of progressive enlightenment, in which Voltaire saw his single though precarious hope for any human advance, was in Rousseau's view a process of man's corruption. Prior to any program of human progress, and fundamental to any true reform, must be the exposure of the root of evil in men's lives. Rousseau did not glorify primitive man unreservedly. Call the savage a human animal if

---

[12] Voltaire, *Oeuvres complètes* (Paris, 1827), 19: 288; (Paris, 1828), 24: 383, 384.
[13] Op. cit., 24: 385.

you will; still it was a sound and healthy animal, without depravity and without artificial barriers to natural improvement, to growth and perfection. In the state of nature man had freedom to realize his capacities in increasing measure, to perfect his natural intelligence, and to attain mastery in speech and in productive labor and a just and satisfactory common life. But the lure of private property, which promised to a small number of strong men the chance to exploit the labor of the many for their own aggrandisement, led to the establishment of governments, whose chief function has ever been the protection of the exploiting class.

Thus the original natural freedom of man was replaced by a vastly organized system of human enslavement and oppression of the poor masses and by the luxury and corruption of the wealthy classes. Our historical past has been a dismal course of degeneration. Yet even in our civilized system of oppression and corruption, the natural soundness of human beings has not been utterly depraved. Can it ever be restored? Rousseau preached the gospel of return to the primitive bosom of nature, but in his romantic quest he could scarcely expect to retrace completely or to efface the historical past. The more realistic approach to his problem was in the program of reform proposed in his *Social Contract*. How must existing social-political institutions be reconstructed so as to regain for man the most of his lost natural freedom and soundness? Rousseau's philosophy was a project of human emancipation, of bringing men again within reach of their early liberties, their rightful values, and at least some of their native capacities for healthy development. It was a program of radical social regeneration as a prerequisite to any genuine progress.

Rousseau's romantic nostalgia for the original freedom of men accentuated the primitivism which had been a recurring theme in theology, philosophy, and literature,

sometimes dominant, sometimes contending with progressivism. As might be expected, there were extremists
on both sides of this debate. Pope, with his assurance
that "Whatever is, is right," had sung "Lo! the poor
Indian," but the eulogy of the Red Indian or of the Hindu
virtues did become a popular motif in a multitude of
eighteenth-century novels. "Away with your refinements!
enjoy the freedom and simplicity of nature. Be guiltless
—Be an Indian!"[14] Leibniz himself intended nothing sinister or ironical by his doctrine that ours is the best of
possible worlds; but the best English social historian
records the negative undertone in the self-complacency of
the mid-eighteenth-century Englishman to whom "England appeared to be the best country possible in an
imperfect world."[15] Robert Louis Stevenson's later nursery
rhyme comes to mind:

> Little Indian, Sioux or Crow,
> Little frosty Eskimo,
> Little Turk or Japanee,
> O, don't you wish that you were me!

Conversely, universal optimistic commitment might be
annoyed by evidences that the world of men fails to
perform according to the placid expectations. So dour
Dean Swift wrote to Alexander Pope: "I tell you after all,
that I do not hate mankind: it is *vous autres* who hate
them, because you would have them reasonable animals,
and are angry for being disappointed."[16]

Voltaire's blast at optimism in his poem on the Lisbon
earthquake and in his *Candide* did not subdue all the
advocates of historical progress. In England the belief

[14] This passage and others like it may be read in Lois Whitney, *Primitivism and the Idea of Progress in English Popular Literature of the
Eighteenth Century* (Baltimore, Md., 1934), pp. 121, 118 ff.

[15] Trevelyan, *English Social History* (New York, 1942), p. 340.

[16] Compare T. O. Wedell's article, "On the Philosophical Background
of Gulliver's Travels," in *Studies in Philology* (October 1926), 437.

in man's basic soundness and in his unlimited capacity for improvement was reaffirmed with confidence but also challenged skeptically. Richard Price (1723-1791) fought on many battlefronts in his resistance to bigotry and injustice and oppression, without faltering in his conviction of a better future: "Such are the natures of things that this progress must continue. During particular intervals it may be interrupted, but it cannot be destroyed."[17] Likewise Charles Darwin's grandfather contemplated the eternal progress in nature: "It would appear, that all nature exists in a state of perpetual improvement by laws impressed on the atoms of matter by the great CAUSE OF CAUSES; and that the world may still be in its infancy, and continue to improve FOR EVER AND EVER."[18]

The keenest British mind of the age, David Hume (1711-1776), found no basis for such cosmic or historical confidence. In his *Treatise of Human Nature* Hume pursued a method of radical empiricism. He rejected any doctrine of substances, corporeal or mental. We have only the course of our experience, a succession of ideas, and in dealing with any complex idea we should trace it to its initial sources, in immediate sense-impressions. Thus in considering the idea of the causal relation between two events Hume recognized their contiguity in space and their succession in time, and also their constant conjunction in the course of experience. But he explained our notion of their necessary connection as due to our association of ideas which leads us habitually to expect their continued future conjunction.

Where no basis for assured objective certainty of causal relation was available, what empiricist ground for historical confidence could be expected? Hume regarded any cosmic optimism with ironical disdain. The best of all possible worlds indeed! How many worlds have we

[17] Compare Whitney, op. cit., pp. 221 f.
[18] Erasmus Darwin, *Zoonomia* (London, 1801), 2: 318.

compared, to descant so complacently? One world at a
time, he urged, our own, the only world we know, and
that quite imperfectly. In this world we can trace no
steady improvement but rather growth and decay, without any ascertainable pattern of universal or prevailing
trend one way or the other. To proclaim this sorry world
as God's masterpiece would hardly be a tribute to the
Creator. It might be more comforting to our piety to
consider this cosmic togetherness as a rough sketch,
headed for the wastebasket of the Almighty, like others
that might have been botched and bungled. A better
cosmic insight might be forthcoming; an improved trend
in human affairs might be in prospect, but these may be
only our fond surmises. We really do not know. Man's
ways are at bottom as unaccountable as those of the
universe.

We noted the spreading influence of Leibniz's *Theodicy*
in theological and poetic reaffirmation of the teleological
argument for God's design in nature for man's increasing
and perfect good. A whole shelf of theological treatises,
now lost or dust-covered but in their own day notable,
undertook to prove the perfection of divine Providence
from the intelligent order manifested in the various fields
of nature: from the world of fish, of trees, of stones:
ichthyotheology, dendrotheology, petrotheology! These
were prose pendants to Senator Brockes's rhymes in pious
eulogy of the goose and its manifold utility to man: "skin
and feathers likewise useful." But the general ascendancy
of German systematic thought after the middle of the
eighteenth century manifested itself in theories of progress which were important alternatives of Leibniz's theodicy and not merely extravagant inflations of his optimism. We can mention only two men, but they were in
the front rank of German genius during that age: Lessing
and Herder.

Gotthold E. Lessing (1729-1781) was the elder statesman of the German Enlightenment, famous for his historical and cultural criticism as well as for his literary masterpieces. His entire life was dominated by his liberal spirit, tolerant and forward-looking. No words could express better his philosophy of life than his declaration that if God should offer him the choice between the possession of all truth and the endless pursuit of it, he would humbly but unhesitatingly choose the quest.[19] Lessing's brief work *The Education of Mankind* expressed his theological and historical outlook. He regarded the history of the world's religions as man's progressive spiritual education, as God's self-revelation to growing humanity. In his idea that each of the great religious teachers has made a characteristic contribution to the spiritual growth of mankind, Lessing was also advancing a positive view of historical progress. He traced this advance likewise in the moral sphere. Men are admonished to pursue righteousness lest they suffer punishment here and now; then they would beware of wickedness for fear of eternal damnation but as they grow to moral maturity they come to feel loyalty to the moral law itself and they seek virtue for its own sake. And as more and more of this "everlasting gospel" comes to possess the will of men, history will register the higher rise of civilization to justice and peace and moral perfection.

In various writings Lessing surveyed the vast historical span. At one end of it is the savage, prostrate before his idol trumperies; at the other end is enlightened humanity dedicated to spiritual ideals. And this vast progress in the moral and religious sphere is paralleled in other fields of human activity: in science, in the arts, in social and political institutions. This conviction of our expanding energies and capacities is itself a powerful dynamic in

---

[19] Lessing, *Erziehung des Menschengeschlechts*, section 1ff., 32 85, 86, 93f., in *Gesammelte Werke* (München, 1959), 1: 1009-32.

human progress. We do not remain mere spectators of the pageant of civilization; we step in line and join the march.[20]

Lessing's outline of a philosophy of historical progress was developed in the great work of J. G. Herder (1744-1803), *Ideas for the Philosophy of History of Mankind.* We may call this work a historical version of the argument from design. Herder interpreted history as manifesting the progressive self-manifestation of God's purpose for man in nature. This manifestation is implicit in the very structure of nature, but man's historical life has expressed it most fully. The entire process is one of gradual unfoldment. Herder opposed any dichotomy between nature and human nature. He would portray nature as the matrix of spirit. Organic structure was to be revealed as the framework of developing character. Man's erect posture and anatomical organization, his physiological adaptation to a great variety of external conditions, the sense organs which he shares with the animals, and his powers of reflection, of speech, and of cooperation with others—these are all indications of his naturally varied and unfolding social and historical destiny. So we may read the gradually manifested purport of the world process.

From stardust to spirit the gradation is an unbroken rise, and it can have no assignable limit. "The general connectedness of powers and forms is neither retrogressive nor static but progressive."[21] Social institutions and cultures have issued in relation to suitable natural conditions; man's highest expression, religion, has been the full spiritual fruition of nature. This historical arrow of growing perfection has not been single; like rays of light it has spread in all directions, for nature is boundlessly fertile

[20] Compare Lessing, *The Education of Mankind,* sections 1 ff., 32, 85, 86, 93 f.
[21] Herder, *Ideen zur Philosophie der Geschichte der Menschheit,* various editions.

and versatile. "Ever renewing its youth in its forms, the genius of humanity flourishes and comes to new expansive life in nations, generations, and races."[22] The progressive unfoldment of humanity in the course of civilization was not merely affirmed or outlined by Herder; it was traced in detail throughout ancient and medieval cultures and up to modern times.

In the divine epos of history, past and present are only beginning and preparation; the future will be ever a prospect of still greater advancement. This inexhaustible perfection is within man's powers; it is the natural self-realization of man's spirit, which is God's purpose for humanity. Leibniz's ideal of the Republic of Minds, the divine masterpiece on earth, found its fuller exposition in Herder's philosophy of historical progress.[23]

The reaction of the public to this philosophy of history varied with the temperament of the readers. The phrase *divine epos* expressed a main characteristic of Herder's portrayal of history. It was in its way a poetic vision and had both the merits and the defects of poetic insight. Herder's saga throbbed with the pulse of historical life through the ages. It appealed greatly to the more romantic of his readers, who prized lyrical eloquence above reasoned exposition, and it had unmistakably dramatic elements of truth. But it was not convincing to Herder's teacher Immanuel Kant, who demanded for the philosophy of history not poetic utterance but scientific statement: less feeling and more careful reasoning.[24] Herder resented Kant's criticism, for he felt that Kant had not done justice to the true character of his work. It would be fair to say that the fuller truth was not on either side alone, nor even between the two; it was in each of them as com-

[22] *Ideen,* 9: i.
[23] Compare E. Kühnemann, *Herder,* 2d ed. (München, 1912), pp. 377, 405 f.
[24] Compare Kant's *Gesammelte Schriften,* Prussian Academy ed. (Berlin, 1912), 8: 55.

pleted by the other. The best history must be marked
not only by factual accuracy and scientific grasp but also
by imaginative humane insight.

Toward the close of the eighteenth century Kant himself wrote several essays bearing on the philosophy of
history and the belief in progress. But Kant has been
well described as the gate into nineteenth-century thought,
and it seems advisable to consider his contribution to our
problem later, in relation to his successors in the movement of modern idealism.

Two French thinkers of the period call for more direct
attention to their systematic theories of historical progress
in the realization of social values: Turgot and Condorcet.
The continuity of thought in these two is evident, and it
has been commonly recognized. But the general opinion
of a reasoned advance from Turgot to Condorcet has been
questioned by some critics who have regarded Condorcet's
extensive work as at most an "oratorical amplification"
of Turgot's fundamental conceptions.[25] Without prejudging this issue of appraisal, we should rather consider the
leading ideas in these two outlines of history.

A distinguished biographer of great statesmen ranked
A. R. J. Turgot (1727-1781) with the ten greatest men
in the modern world, and yet judged him, by ordinary
standards, as a failure.[26] His struggles to save France
from its imminent economic and political disaster proved
unavailing. As governor of Limoges (1761-1774), then a
very poor district, he established agricultural and veter-
inary schools, planted potatoes and cotton, and started
silk, paper, and tannery works. He brought prosperity to
the entire region. He was appointed controller general
of finances (1774-1776) and started a rigorous program.
No more taxes, no loans, no insolvency but economy. His

[25] Compare E. Caro, *Problèmes de morale sociale* (Paris, 1887), p. 270;
J. B. Bury, *The Idea of Progress* (New York, 1955), p. 206.
[26] A. D. White, *Seven Great Statesmen* (New York, 1910), p. 165.

projects failed due to the opposition of the aristocratic classes whose vested interests were being endangered, and also due to the distrust of the populace. The church opposed him because of his proposed tolerance of the Protestants. But the failure of established institutions in his age did not lead him to social pessimism but rather confirmed him in his principles of the right historical course of assured progress, through emancipation from stubborn bigotries and the application of steady enlightenment to practical human problems. Like a resolute surgeon, he urged the grave need of radical reforms in the social system, but he was confident of the basic soundness of man's constitution and of eventual welfare and advance.

Turgot's works include long and detailed writings on political economy, taxation, agriculture, finances, budgetary reforms, but the reader would look in vain for an extensive treatment of the philosophy of history. Yet in his twenties he had planned to write a treatise on that subject. We do have an outline of his main principles and also two important lectures delivered at the Sorbonne, all three done in 1750, contemporary with the publication of Montesquieu's *Spirit of the Laws* and Voltaire's historical *Essay*. All these works were definitely secular in their historical outlook; unlike the providential determinism of Bossuet, they traced the course of history as an enterprise of human effort with human capacities and limitations, in a social and physical environment. This was historical naturalism. In his distribution of emphasis Turgot stressed the importance of men's beliefs and moral attitudes as determinants of individual conduct and social policy. He was not unmindful of the natural conditions of human living, but he studied with greater care man's own ways with nature, what his mind demands and exacts from his environment.

The Sorbonne Lectures traced in bold outline the course

of progress in history. In the first, Turgot expounded "the advantages which the establishment of Christianity have yielded to humanity." This was not a theological or an ecclesiastical but a humanitarian eulogy of the Christian religion. The brilliant culture of classical antiquity was a culture of the elite; it had no regard for the common people. Against this exclusiveness, the Christian gospel reached the weary and the heavy-laden. Despite repeated betrayals of its social ideals of brotherhood by corrupt tyrants, the Christian spirit has reformed the entire lives of men and nations, spreading justice and charity and goodwill. Between churchly bigotry and the airy unbelief which was so rife in his day, Turgot urged in his social philosophy of progress the high historical claims of Christian philanthropy.

This spirit of constructive liberalism in religion was expressed also in the two "Letters on Tolerance," in which Turgot maintained that sound religion is the guarantee of human rights. An atheist can recognize only a mechanism of nature and human existence. In a godless world, contesting interests and claims could be adjudged only on a basis of prevailing force. Religion alone can replace this struggle of powers and demands by a truly moral issue of justice and injustice. Above the law of might it set the divine law of right. The oppressor, despite his superior force, is condemned for his defiance of God's law and order. But just because religion and morals are thus recognized as the basis of social justice and right government, religious tolerance becomes irrefutable. Religious worship cannot be subject to royal or governmental ordinance. Freedom to worship God according to one's conscience is the essence of true religion. The spirit of brotherly love has been the great gift of Christianity to the world. This spirit has been betrayed by high churchmen in the name of Jesus Christ; but against the horrors of the Holy Inquisition and Saint Bartholomew's Night and lesser ecclesiastical oppressions, we should recognize the progressive achievement of a humane civilization by the Christian dynamic of justice and charity.

Here was thorough conviction of progress and optimism, but not sanguine laudation. In his second Sorbonne Lecture, "On the Successive Advances of the Human Spirit," and in his planned discourses on "Universal History," Turgot traced the onward course of social institutions, but he also exposed the superstitions and errors, the backslidings and frustrations which have obstructed and misdirected men's higher ideas and purposes. He sought progress, and everywhere he saw mostly errors.[27] But optimistic confidence prevailed in his reflection that men can rise to higher ground from their very disorder and injustice. Societies and nations, like individuals, learn through trial and error. For despotism is the easy first plan, to force one's will on others who are in our power. It takes long years of oppression before men turn gradually to the harder but surer road of self-control and justice and fair play.

Turgot was not content with general advocacy of the principles of progress. Even in his brief outlines he cited historical chapter and verse of specific humane achievements in enlightenment and in mastery over the rigors of nature and the hard and corrupt beastliness of men. From hunting to pastoral and to agricultural economy and then to expanding industry, men gained progressively more settled and reliable livelihood. From rude skills in devising weapons and tools and other practical craftsmanship, men proceeded to knowledge of vaster range and deeper insight, and their skill and crafts matured to artistic power. The development of language perfected the intercommunication of minds, and the preservation of men's ideas in writing made possible the mental interplay of past, present, and future generations. Through the

[27] Compare Turgot, *Oeuvres* (Paris, 1844), 2: 600.

written word humanity achieved a consciously historical life. This progressive enlightenment has had its beneficial effects in every field of human activity: first of all in the more immediate and rudimentary provisions of food and clothing and shelter, and then in the larger economy of efficiency and comfort. As men were thus learning how to live more safely and more productively in their environment, they have also recognized both the problems and the opportunities of their own personal careers and their social-institutional milieu.

Turgot did not overlook man's most immediate and intimate social institution, the family. His discussion of the gradual attainment of monogamy and the advance of women from a state of servitude to increasing freedom and social initiative was not only a liberal historical retrospect but also a forward glance to a later and more civilized day, which even now is still to come in many lands. All the way through, nature and man are engaged in productive activity. Turgot combined this dual aspect of men's lives, external-physical and inner-human, in his conception of political geography as a field of fruitful inquiry.

This outline of universal history was meant to be more than a record of the past, of facts and events. It was to be a philosophy of history, interpreting the fundamental trends of the vast historical movements and formulating those trends as historical principles. In this projected world-historical theory, Turgot was a predecessor of Condorcet and of Comte. The famous Law of the Three Stages of Thought, which Comte expounded in extensive detail, may be read substantially in Turgot's outline of "Universal History" and in his other "Thoughts and Fragments." In the progressive development of men's ideas he traced three important periods. Before learning the causal connectedness of processes in nature, men ascribed every condition and change in the world to imagined beings like themselves, gods, goddesses and other spirits. Anthropomorphism marked both their religion and their substitute for science. When philosophical reflection disabused men of this traditional mythology, their next recourse was to cosmological speculation. They explained the course of nature in terms of various abstract essences and faculties. But beyond the belief in myths and metaphysical speculation, historical progress led to the recognition and perfection of the scientific method by the direct study of the facts, the formation of hypotheses, the testing of proposed explanations by experimental control.[28]

While intellectual advance of mankind has not proceeded through these three stages in any field without deviation, nor has it ever moved full front, the overall record of history has been one of positive and varied development. The intellectual progress itself has been an outstanding aspect of the more general growth of humanity, for it has itself been a major factor in determining other forms of human advance from darkness and disorder to ever greater enlightenment and justice. "The total mass of mankind, by turns of calm and turmoil, good and evil, marches ever, however slowly, towards greater and greater perfection."[29] These confident affirmations of historical progress were eloquent expressions of a young man's faith in the future of France, despite seemingly hopeless conditions. This faith was scorned by the course of events. Turgot's career as an economic and political reformer was an initial local success followed by general failure which left no prospect for him and apparently none for his country. He died in 1781, on the eve of the Revolution which he had worked to avert.

Even more impressive is the theory of progress of Marquis de Condorcet (1743-1794) because it was the proclaimed social gospel by a man writing during the

[28] Compare Turgot, *Oeuvres,* 2: 655 ff.
[29] Op. cit., 2: 598.

darkest days of the Terror, writing his book in garrets while in daily peril of his life, fleeing from the police who finally seized him. His own death in prison saved him from the guillotine. Condorcet championed the highest ideals of the French Revolution; he saw those ideals and principles betrayed by unprincipled and cruel men; but although his vision for mankind was being flouted by bloody actualities, he reaffirmed his historical conviction of progress and eventual advance, and he wrote with unwavering ardor. Those who did not pity his pathetic faith have admired his sublime serenity unto death.

Condorcet's work *A Historical Tableau of the Progress of the Human Spirit* was written by a fugitive without access to libraries. The insufficiency of detailed documentation cannot be charged fairly under those conditions. The amazing fact was that the book was written at all. Condorcet, to be sure, was not an unpracticed writer: precisely in the field of recording great men and great achievements he was a past master. A "perpetual secretary" of the Academy of Sciences, he had written *éloges* of over sixty French academicians and also of other distinguished minds, including Pascal and Huyghens, Linnaeus and Franklin. He admired and wrote biographies of Voltaire and Turgot. He came to his principal work as an avowed biographer of humanity. He would record its meager beginnings, the principal stages of its development, its continual expansion in range and intensity of achievement, the assured maturity of its powers, and its boundless future prospects.

As a biographer of academicians, he recognized individual mastery, but he also acknowledged the genius of the race as a factor in progress. The invention of the arch, he wrote, must have been the creative act of some one person, but language was achieved by a whole society.[30] In the vast historical span of Condorcet's work,

[30] Compare Condorcet, *Oeuvres complètes* (Paris, 1804), 8: 25;

the broad features of groups and races prevailed the book was a social history of mankind and outline of civilization: "to show by reason and by factual evidence that nature has set no limit to the perfection of human faculties; that man's perfectibility is really boundless."[31]

It should be noted at the outset that Condorcet's idea of perfectibility was primarily intended to signify advance in enlightenment. This emphasis on intellectual progress, which he shared with Turgot, has been criticized as one-sided. Outrages in our modern world have been committed by the use of the most expert science and technology. Despite such shocking evidence, which his own day was providing in France and which was involving his own destruction, Condorcet was unwavering in his basic conviction that scientific knowledge and its applications to human welfare assured the final overthrow of all barriers and the rise of a better society. Insufficient knowledge and dogmatic bigotry have checked progress, sometimes for long periods; the only hope has been in more thorough and more widespread understanding.

Condorcet's history traced nine epochs in the advance of civilization. Within these nine are four important stages, three of them progressive and one a period of stagnation.

During the first stage, comprising the three earliest epochs, men achieved the rudimentary conditions and forms of organized social life. The need of cooperation of large numbers to supply the necessities of life joined families and clans into larger groups. The social bond was strengthened by the increasing continuity of men's social economy. The men of the first epoch engaged in fishing and hunting expeditions: a nomadic existence of periodic alliance. More continuous was men's common

---

Tableau historique des progrés de l'esprit humain, ed. of 1900, p. 13. The latter more readily available edition is cited in the following notes.

[31] *Tableau*, pp. 2 f.

work as herdsmen, even though they were still nomads. But when the fishermen, hunters, and pastoral tribesmen turned to agriculture, settled tribal and national life was achieved. Attachment to the soil which men cultivated, to their granaries and homes, gave them a tradition, a lore, and a history.

The development of language perfected the interplay of minds; the invention of writing enabled those early men to share their ideas more effectively and to transmit their gains to later generations. But uncontrolled desires and passions incited tribes and nations to war with each other, and their thinking and conduct were rife with confusion and superstitions. This stage of the first three epochs was also marked by men's beginnings in crafts-manship and practical mastery, the invention of tools and perfected methods of operation.

The second stage of human progress was that of classical antiquity. Greek genius flourished in a culture of free inquiry and creative activity. Dismissing traditional superstitions, the Greek sages undertook the exploration of the nature of things, perfecting speculative reason but also delaying scientific mastery of the facts by their search for some one first principle or law of cosmic order or the highest good. For all that, Greek minds also advanced positive science, geometry and astronomy, and the practice and theory of popular government. In the whole range of the arts, Greek genius set for mankind a standard of excellence.

In the progress of civilization we survey the classical age by relating and also distinguishing Greek and Roman antiquity. Condorcet preferred another distinction. His point of transition, from Athens to Alexandria and to Rome, is marked by "the division of the sciences," that is, the advancement of knowledge by specialized investiga-tion. He noted the Hellenistic progress in physics and mathematics, the work of Archimedes, Pliny's *Natural*

History, the perfection of agricultural methods, the Julian calendar, the jurisprudence of the later Roman Stoics.

The destruction of classical culture marks the beginning of the third stage of history; it is Condorcet's sixth epoch, the medieval "Dark Ages." He regarded this period as one of decadence in science and in general enlightenment; in his view it was indeed a profound night: "Theological reveries, superstitious impostures are now the whole genius of men; religious intolerance is their only morality; and Europe, forced between priestly tyranny and military despotism, waits in blood and tears for the moment when new enlightenment will lead it to a new life of liberty, humanity, and virtue."[32] The intensity and the thoroughness of this condemnation should suffice to express Condorcet's profound animosity to the whole Catholic theological tradition. What the barbarian invaders did to the structure and body of the classical world, the priests did to its spirit. Needless to point out, this is a very one-sided appraisal. From the whole medieval world of Christian-Catholic eclipse of science and free productive inquiry, Condorcet turned toward the only rays of light and promise of progress, which in his view came from the Arabs. It was in fact the spread of the Arabian treasures of classical knowledge and Arabian sciences—astronomy, optics, medicine—which aroused Western Europe from its theological sleep of a thousand years.

The last stage of our civilization is seen by Condorcet as comprising three epochs, the seventh to the ninth in his tabulation, from the Scholastic learning of the Middle Ages and the Renaissance to his own day. The revival of scientific inquiry, first on Arabian models and then gradually in more independent Western thinking, affected man's entire world-outlook. The introduction of Aristotle's works had a dual result. On the one hand, the doctors of the church used them in their own dogmatic

32 Ibid., p. 71.

systems, but on the other hand, Aristotle's methods developed and disciplined Scholastic reflection, even though adherence to some of his ideas also retarded the progress of the natural sciences.

The close of the medieval period was marked by growing interest in ancient classical literature, both Latin and Greek, by a secular spirit no longer subservient to ecclesiastical authority and by a pronounced naturalism in thinking and in practice. The invention of printing multiplied the number of books and of readers, and the available new knowledge reached the whole range of society. As the leaders of modern thought were expanding men's cosmic range, increasing multitudes were able to follow them in their modern outlook. Dismissing their traditional provincial mentality, modern minds were ready for the independence and the tolerance of critical thinking, both of them conditions of progress. From demanding and gaining autonomy of scientific thought, men proceeded to claim justice and freedom in liberal social and political institutions: a demand long resisted and slow in reaching even partial realization. The entrenched oppressors of the common people joined with the priestly bigots to repress men's struggle for a decent human livelihood and for a more truly humane life.

Condorcet signalized the advance to a more definite scientific and social mastery represented by the work of Francis Bacon, Galileo, and Descartes. In his judgment Descartes's thought inaugurated the last epoch of our civilization, which found its culmination in the revolutionary establishment of the French Republic. But he also recognized the important influence of John Locke in fixing the proper sphere and limits of human inquiry by strict adherence to the actual course of experience. As the natural sciences have expanded and deepened their view of nature, so men's self-understanding has ruled out any final reliance on rigid social forms. Condorcet shared with Jefferson the resistance to the "servile and absurd" commitment, once for all, to any inflexible constitution or system of laws. Always the better social insight will be critical of the old, always it must be ready for revision and reform. The American Revolution and the establishment of the new Republic overseas, a federation of sovereign states, opened new vistas of future social advance. A great impulse was given to the spirit of radical reconstruction in Europe, and the French Revolution was the next step of human progress. Forty years after Condorcet's death Alexis de Tocqueville pointed to the acknowledgment and the gradual attainment of the principle of human equality in the United States as marking the true direction of historical advance.

Condorcet's emphasis on intellectual growth as a condition of social progress was reaffirmed in his praise of the civilizing influence of Newtonian science, of Franklin's more special electrical researches, the greater mastery of chemical analysis, the advance in physiology and anatomy and their applications in medicine. Scientific method perfected in one field of inquiry extends its mastery to other related fields, and man's intelligence grasps better the system of nature and our own place and prospect in the world. "Thus all man's intellectual occupations . . . tend toward the progress of human reason."[33]

Under the title "tenth epoch" Condorcet draws his prospect of the future advance of civilization. He expresses his hopes in the form of three questions, which indicate his conception of the progressive human welfare. "Finally, will the human species improve itself, either by new scientific discoveries in the sciences and the arts, and as a necessary consequence, in the means of individual well-being and the common prosperity; or by progress in the principles of conduct and in practical morality; or finally through the real perfection of the intellectual,

[33] Ibid., p. 156.

moral and physical faculties which may well follow, or through the improvement of instruments which heighten the intensity and direct the use of these faculties, or again, through the betterment of man's natural organization?"[34] He answers all these questions in the affirmative, quite convinced that nature has set no barriers to man's hopes. But his social optimism, while unlimited in its eventual prospect, is not offhand and sanguine. He points out the obstacles to further progress; they are chiefly in the still persisting inequalities of different social classes: in actual wealth, in heritable property assuring the economic stability of a family, and in educational provisions. So long as some men have to live on the bare edge of subsistence and without opportunity for mental cultivation, society will still be far from its goal. Drastic reforms are required, even in the most advanced countries, to put an end to these inequities.

The revolutionary age in which Condorcet lived ruled out any complacency; yet he never lost his firm confidence. He pointed out definite reforms and social gains in public education, both in the pure sciences and in technology. Progressive education should be more than instruction in abstract knowledge and in technical skills. By schooling and legislation and political-social order, society should cultivate in the individual citizen a sense of productive solidarity and concern for the common good. It should lead men to see their own highest welfare in an equitable life of cooperation with others, without envy and without exploitation. Condorcet looked forward to more perfect communication of ideas, more thorough and varied application of scientific thought in every field of human activity. He contemplated the course of mankind in future ages, "marching with a firm and sure step on the road of truth, of virtue, and of happiness."[35] This prospect

34 Ibid., pp. 162 f.
35 Ibid., p. 189.

should console thinking men for the errors, crimes, and injustices which still sully the earth.

The most important work in social philosophy during the eighteenth century was Adam Smith's *Inquiry into the Nature and Causes of the Wealth of Nations*. Adam Smith (1723-1790) had neither the firm hope of Turgot nor the heroic confidence of Condorcet. In Adam Smith's optimistic view men needed not restriction or reform but only the freedom to realize their common welfare. Could his program be an economic version of Rabelais? It would surely be an odd surmise, considering the spotless respectability of the Scottish sage. *The Wealth of Nations* was intended as an outline of men's economic advance through the wise pursuit of their interests, with fair-minded regard for the interests of others. Men compete with each other, but there is mutuality in their respective advantages, and their fundamental relations to each other are not hostile. They naturally serve each other to their common good. Rapacious selfishness is not good business; in manufacture as well as in trade men's own decent consideration for the other party in the contract is a firm basis of sound prosperity in the long run.

The natural relations of men are thus guarantees of their eventual increasing welfare. Only ignorant disrespect for them through blind selfish greed checks social progress. If masters and their workmen, merchants and their customers understood the mutuality of their interests, the domestic economy would move to greater prosperity. Likewise with world trade and the general welfare of mankind, if all realized the wisdom of international equity and collaboration. "Progress of opulence" is assured by the release of artificial barriers to the natural economic processes, *laissez faire*. Men's growing enlightenment, as it teaches them fair play, will lead them on the course of expanding social welfare and progress. This sanguine outlook, at the beginning of the industrial revolution, was in harmony with Adam Smith's view of human affairs. His work was published in 1776, but in it he referred placidly to "the late disturbances."[36] So in good faith he was quite assured that men were bound to have always "the greatest possible quantity of happiness,"[37]—a pronouncement which, like Leibniz's "best of all possible worlds," invites a sardonic comment.

[36] Adam Smith, *The Wealth of Nations,* ed. Edwin Cannan, 2d ed. (London, 1920), 2: 79; compare the Editor's Introduction, 1: xiii.

[37] Adam Smith, *Theory of Moral Sentiments,* Pt. 6, sect. 2, chapt. 3 (London, 1892).

CHAPTER FIVE

The Problem of Progress in the Nineteenth Century

IN VARIOUS WAYS the philosophy of Immanuel Kant (1724-1804) marks and determines the intellectual transition from the eighteenth century to the nineteenth. The significance of Kant's reflections on the problem of historical progress is not to be judged by the extent of his writings on the subject. Actually these writings are very fragmentary, not to be compared with his major *Critiques.* Five essays may be cited; the largest of these, on "Eternal Peace," runs to about sixty pages, and the shortest, specifically on "The Principle of Progress," is compressed to ten pages. On this topic Kant's terseness compares with Turgot's, and so does the importance of his ideas.[1] Three of the essays are of especial interest to us.

In 1784, during the decade of the *Critiques,* Kant wrote a brief monograph titled "The Natural Principle of the Political Order, Considered in Connection with the Idea of a Universal Cosmopolitical History." Kant's exposition was ordered under nine theses. In them he developed his conviction of a natural unfolding of human capacities, in the individual's reason and more completely in the race. Men's attainments through the use of intelligence mark their perfection and happiness. Kant maintained, however, that this development is stimulated by men's mutual antagonism in society, an antagonism which at length leads to the establishment of order and law. The organization of a civil society under law becomes man's greatest practical problem, the most difficult to solve. Men have perverse misdirections of their will which reason must overcome and correct. Our nature is not spontaneously inclined toward justice and peace and perfection. Men have to learn their higher destiny, and learn it the hard way: from ruinous strife they must rise to concord and cooperation.

This arduous advance may be noted also in the international field. The higher social order depends upon the legal regulation of the external relations among states. History may be regarded as the realization of a hidden plan of nature to achieve a political order and constitution in which men's capacities can be developed fully. A philosophy of world-history which so interprets a perfect civil union as the goal of humanity may be viewed as forwarding the basic purpose, but not the easy course of nature. Kant speculates that nature may yet produce a Kepler or a Newton in the field of universal cosmopolitical history. He does not mention Herder, the first part of whose *Ideen* appeared in the same year as his own essay.

Under the topic "The Principle of Progress" (1793) Kant examined the relation of theory to practice in international law. The issue between love of mankind and misanthropy would depend upon our view of man's range and prospect, whether humanity warrants hopes of a better and higher future. Here Kant stands with Lessing and against Moses Mendelssohn, who had a negative appraisal of historical progress. Kant expressed it as his firm moral conviction that "as the human race is continually advancing in civilization and culture as its natural purpose, so it is continually making progress for the better in relation to the moral end of its existence, . . . this progress, although it may be sometimes inter-

---

[1] Compare the convenient edition of Kant's *Eternal Peace and Other International Essays,* ed. E. D. Mead (Boston, 1914).

rupted, will never be entirely broken off or stopped."[2]

This conviction strengthens our dutiful commitment to virtue, and nothing short of the complete disproof of progress can affect it. Instances of past defeat and frustration cannot undermine it, for we are not justified in admitting the finality of any failure. Dismay at our evils may be due in great measure to our higher and more exacting standard of judgment; our harsh self-criticism may itself be a ground for hope. The skeptic who dismisses the thought of historical progress should remember that international relations expose the least amiable qualities of human nature. And precisely here men need, not the traditional reliance on balance of power, but "a system of international right founded upon public laws conjoined with power, to which every state must submit."[3] This is valid on rational ground as a theory; Kant upheld it as good also in practice.

This proposal of an international legal and political system Kant developed in his essay "Perpetual Peace" (1795), which like his essay on progress was written during the terrible years of the French Revolution. Kant formulated the preliminary and the definitive articles of an eternal peace between states. The first requirement is that they should be articles of real peace, not of a provisional truce pending the next eventual war. The integrity of states should be respected: no state should intermeddle by force with the constitution or government of another state; no national debts should be contracted as a treasury for waging war. The maintenance of standing armies should be entirely abolished in the course of time; even in wartime there should be no dishonorable stratagems of hostility which could destroy mutual confidence and the future possibility of an enduring peace.

In order to assure more definitely these conditions of

[2] Op. cit., p. 59.
[3] Op. cit., p. 65.

lasting international concord, Kant held that every state should have a republican civil constitution. The representative governments thus formed should acknowledge a law of nations, as a federation of free states. In this international system the rights of men as citizens should be restricted to conditions of universal hospitality.

Kant did not regard his theses and articles of peace as mere academic notions. Writing as he did in a time of political turmoil, he reaffirmed his fundamental conviction of future progress toward a cosmopolitical order of enduring justice. "Perpetual peace is . . . no empty idea, but a practical thing which, through its gradual solution, is coming always nearer its final realization."[4]

These conclusions in the philosophy of history may be regarded as involved in Kant's ethical theory. The essence of morality, according to Kant, is in men's dutiful respect for principles of inherent worth, in their pursuit of the right, without ulterior considerations of expediency, just because it is the right. Without this essential integrity of spirit there can be no genuine moral conduct. The historical facts of men's advance from a contest and conflict of forces and advantages toward some recognition of fundamental rights and obligations provide real evidence of men's moral capacities in gradual operation. The course of history may serve to reassure us that the ethics of unconditional dutiful obligation, or in Kant's phrase "the categorical imperative," is not merely a theoretical ideal but an expression of men's actual spiritual principles. As the historical record thus provides at least some factual premises of the ethical interpretation of human life, which Kant had developed in terms of practical reason, so his ethics in turn warrants a historical prospect of a gradual and arduous realization of human progress. This mutual involvement of ethics and the

4 Op. cit., p. 127.

philosophy of history may be traced in Kant's thought. It was not worked out in his own brief treatment of the problem of progress, but it can be studied in the future development of modern idealism by some of Kant's successors.

The romantic strain in Herder's epic of history, which Kant had criticized, was reaffirmed in the literature of the period, and it found also philosophical statement. Nature was envisioned as instinct with a divine urge toward perfection which manifested itself in a native and universal progress. Among the post-Kantian idealists we may note this direction of thought, especially in F. W. J. Schelling (1775-1854), a philosopher of poetic temper and brilliant but unsteady reflection.

The sterner Kantian view of human nature as involving a tension of low inclinations and high principles, and of historical progress as strenuous, was developed in the ethical idealism of Johann Gottlieb Fichte (1762-1814). Fichte's own character was an embodiment of the categorical imperative of unconditional devotion to duty, the militant moral will. In personal life he championed an ethics of unyielding commitment to the challenge of duty, against any lure of inclination or inducement of expediency. We do not tend naturally toward the ideal; instincts, desires, and impulses drive us astray; but against them all is the stern resolution of our moral reason. The moral law does not describe our usual behavior; it prescribes our duty, and its edicts are sovereign in the spiritual life. Our dutiful respect for these ideal principles emancipates our will from servitude to impulses and inclinations. Morality is our achievement of spiritual freedom. This dutiful conviction is expressed in our conscience, which is not any kind of inclination but the rational recognition of imperative high principles of action. To Fichte, this resolute upright will was the characteristic spirit in truly moral conduct. "Act always in accordance with your best conviction of your duty; or, act according to your conscience."[5]

The elaboration of this ethical idealism in a philosophy of history may be read in Fichte's lectures on *The Characteristics of the Present Age*. Fichte interpreted the course of history as a contest of rational motives with instinctive drives and as the eventual but hard ascendency of reason over instinct. He traced five epochs of historical development.[6] The first period is that of instinctive reasonableness: as in the age of innocence, men believe in accordance with reason, but without conscious rational conviction of the will. The second epoch is that of authoritarianism: the instinct of reason assumes a powerful form in some individuals and classes, and they impose their laws on the populace, with its blind belief and obedience, in the bondage of sin. The revolt against this servitude marks the third period, an age of insurgent freedom of instinct, but negative at the outset, acknowledging no principle and no verity, rampant sinfulness. In and through this disorder, rationality comes to prevail in the fourth epoch, marked by men's conscious election of reason and its truths and principles, an age of enlightenment, the dawn of social justification. The consummation of this rational art of living, in the fifth epoch, is in the ideal self-realization of humanity, the fullness of spiritual justification.

In characterizing these five epochs we have deliberately used the present tense throughout. For it should be stated clearly that Fichte did not offer his outline as a *tableau historique*, like Condorcet's, as derived from the factual course of events in history. What he proposed was his

[5] Fichte, *The Science of Ethics*, Conclusion of Part 1; trans. A. E. Kroeger (London, ed. of 1907), p. 164.

[6] Compare Fichte, *Sämtliche Werke* (Berlin, 1846), vol. 1: *Die Grundzüge des gegenwärtigen Zeitalters*, pp. 11 f.; compare also Xavier Léon, *Fichte et son temps* (Paris, 1922), 2: 442 f.

philosophical analysis of the stages of man's rational self-realization.[7] In this spirit of speculative philosophy of history, Fichte evaluated the characteristic features of his own age. He asked: to which one of these five epochs do we belong? His own answer varied. He saw his contemporaries in revolt against the servitude to external authority but without the thorough attainment of rational self-control and conviction of imperative principles. But somewhat later he also had a patriotic vision of the German spirit as beginning its rise to the higher stage of rationality. This note of Germanic exaltation marked Fichte's clarion call to his people during the Napoleonic crisis. More fundamental in his philosophy of history was his conception of the chief marks of the progress of civilization: the subordination of individual desires to humanitarian universal principles, and the boundless prospect of man's ideal development. The latter is in full harmony with Fichte's ethical idealism. Truly understood, the ethical world-order is never an actual fact but always an ideal goal. It "never is, but eternally ought to be."[8]

The idealistic view of the history of civilization was developed systematically by Georg W. F. Hegel (1770-1831). The main outlines of his *Philosophy of History* were presented in the concluding sections of his ethical treatise, *The Philosophy of Right*. Hegel contemplated the history of mankind as the progressive realization of "Reason" or the "Idea" as the true essence or meaning of the world. In his absolute idealism both the dialectical process of thought and the historical course of human development lead to the same fundamental conviction of the spiritual character of the universe. As he declared it, the Rational is the Real, and the Real is the Rational.

[7] Compare Fichte, *Grundzüge des gegenwärtigen Zeitalters,* pp. 131 f.
[8] Fichte, *Reden an die deutscht Nation,* in *Sämmtliche Werke* (Berlin, 1846), 7: 297.

The philosophy of history and moral philosophy proceed from the self-recognition of a rational dynamic in Reality. Just as nature is not a mere togetherness in space but an intelligible cosmos, so history is not a mere succession in time but a progressive realization of values. As Hegel stated it, in a line from Schiller, "the history of the world . . . is the world's court of judgment."[9]

Hegel viewed the historical revelation and self-realization of rational spirit as man's attainment of freedom. But his conception of freedom is not one of indeterminate spontaneity. In different epochs and environments spirit achieves its various appropriate expressions. There is neither blind fatalism nor random arbitrariness in history, but developing emancipation of rational character. So at the beginning of his *Philosophy of History* Hegel declared: "Reason is Thought conditioning itself with perfect freedom," and in this sense he maintained at the conclusion of his treatise that "the History of the world is nothing but the development of the Idea of Freedom. But," he added, "objective Freedom—the laws of *real* Freedom—demand the subjugation of the mere contingent Will."[10]

In this historical perspective Hegel expressed his conception of progress. Historical progress signifies the growing realization of rational organization and freedom in human lives, "the thorough moulding and interpenetration of the constitution of society by it."[11] The salient principle in universal history is the revelation of man's real capacity for betterment, his perfectibility, the advance from the imperfect to the more perfect, but also the manifestation, in the lower or imperfect stage, of the germ or capacity for more perfect attainment. Hegel acknowledged the

[9] Hegel's *Philosophy of Right,* trans. T. M. Knox (Oxford, 1949), p. 216; compare p. 10; compare Schiller's poem "Resignation."
[10] Hegel, *Lectures on the Philosophy of History,* trans. J. Sibree (London, 1914), pp. 13, 19 f., 476.
[11] Op. cit., p. 19.

kinship of his view with the Aristotelian realization of potentialities. Like Aristotle, Hegel admitted no essential dichotomy in nature. The dynamic process operates throughout; it is natural in the fullest sense of the term; and if, in a religious spirit, we exalt it as God's plan and purpose in nature, we are reaffirming its basic role in reality.[12]

Unlike Fichte, Hegel devoted the body of his treatise on the philosophy of history to detailed historical exposition, filling out the outline presented at the conclusion of his *Philosophy of Right*. In his survey the progress of civilization was presented as moving westward, from China and India to the kingdoms of the Middle East, to Greece and Rome, and then to Western Europe, or as Hegel preferred to call it, the Germanic World, *die Germanische Welt*. In this westward course of civilization, he noted a progressive expansion of rational freedom in social and political order. In the Oriental empires, the people regarded only one man, the despot, as free, and yet because his unrestrained power of impulses and passions was not directed by reason, even he was not really free. The Greeks first experienced the spirit of freedom, but they, as also the Romans, limited their recognition of free rational self-expression only to the elite class. The acknowledgment of the fundamental and inalienable rights of man, of any man whatever, was attained through the influence of Christianity. The history of the Western world has realized progressively this Christian conviction that all men are by right free.

Fichte had regarded his ethical ideal of historical progress as eternally pursued but never completely attained. Hegel not only described his historical era of acknowledged universal freedom in Christian Europe as the Germanic World but proclaimed that "the Germanic spirit is the spirit of the new world" and that "the destiny of

[12] Ibid., pp. 56, 59, 38.

the German peoples is to be the bearers of the Christian principle" and even hailed the Germanic World as already being in "the fourth phase of world-history," the Empire of Spirit in the full sense.[13]

German idealism developed in an age of political and social reconstruction. In his youth Hegel had been stirred by the spirit of the French Revolution and had sung the "Marseillaise" in a German translation made by his philosophical friend Schelling. Fichte wrote inspiring appeals to the German nation during the Napoleonic wars. For a number of years Kant kept on his desk a portrait of Rousseau. The upsurge of romanticism which marked the turn of the century was more than a trend in literature; it swept throughout Europe in social thinking, religion, and philosophy. Revolution and romanticism were both rejections of established traditions and institutions; they were clarions of a new and better age. The new radicalism was not limited to France. Some of the early converts became conservatives in later years. The revision of ideals in French thought followed in several directions, the most important of which, for our study of progress, was that of Positivism. But the English reactions to the radical ideas and stirring events were also very significant.

An interpretation of human life and history which negated not only any specific *ancien regime* but all forms of governments and institutional frameworks was advocated by William Godwin (1756-1836) in his *Enquiry Concerning Political Justice, and Its Influence on General Virtue and Happiness,* published, like Kant's *Principle of Progress,* in "the terrible year," 1793. Godwin's intellectual genealogy has been traced to Swift and Mandeville, to Hume and Rousseau, Helvétius and Holbach. He recognized no innate and fixed major differences among men, but regarded them all as capable of unlimited development, by experience and training. Existing governments

13 Ibid., pp. 354, 115.

and other social institutions have corrupted and enslaved men. The aim of all true moral and social philosophy must be to free mankind of its shackles. In his program of philosophical anarchism Godwin himself disavowed any revolutionary aggression or violence. He would only urge and persuade, with full confidence in the eventual power of his truth. Freedom and enlightenment, he felt sure, were bound to release men's capacities and lead to progress in every field. "With what delight must every well-informed friend of mankind look forward, to the auspicious period, the dissolution of political government, of that brute engine, which has been the only perennial cause of all the vices of mankind."[14]

Godwin's influence on his younger contemporaries was strong but not always enduring. Especially notable are the various reactions which his doctrine aroused in the romantic poets. No one of them can be regarded as a mere disciple of Godwin, but his strong protest against the enslaving rigidity of social institutions was reflected in some of their poems. Shelley in particular viewed morality as realized in spontaneous acts of justice and benevolence, overcoming the individual's selfish impulses and free from the constraining bonds of institutional regime. Nature is not dull or inert but instinct with boundless spiritual potencies with which the emancipated spirit of man can commune. In the freer civilization which we should strive to achieve, men will wipe out injustice and misery and will progress to greater and greater perfection.

Godwin's influence on Southey, Wordsworth, and Coleridge seems to have been that of accentuating some of their early romantic revolt, from which all three receded later in life. Young Wordsworth hailed the new era of human freedom and progress signalized by the French

---

[14] Godwin, *Enquiry Concerning Political Justice*, 3d ed. (London, 1798), 2: 212; compare pp. 546 f.; compare also the annotated edition by F. E. L. Priestley (Toronto, 1946).

Revolution and was even inclined to find excuses for the cruelties of the Terror. Coleridge and Southey pursued utopian dreams of establishing an ideal "pantisocracy" on American shores. In later years all three mellowed, or stiffened, in various degrees of conservative conformity. This was distressing to younger liberals like Robert Browning, who wrote the poem "The Lost Leader," when Wordsworth accepted his royal appointment as poet laureate: "Just for a handful of silver he left us,/Just for a riband to stick in his coat."

Coleridge turned conservative in his social-political alignment, but in his philosophical fundamentals he pursued the course of liberal reconstruction. From romantic revolt against rigid forms and conventions in poetry and other institutional shackles, and from ventures in empirical psychology, he returned to the Platonic and Neoplatonic visions which had charmed him in his youth and which reassured his possession of the spiritual values of religion and the ideals of human progress and perfectibility.

Robert Southey (1774-1843), poet laureate and honorary academician, turned from his early pantisocratic visions to contemplate the new machine age of industrial advance. His two volumes entitled *Sir Thomas More, or Colloquies on the Progress and Prospects of Society*, covered all imaginable topics, in a manner recalling the conversational luxuriance of Coleridge. The themes of progress and prospects of society are taken up especially in the second volume. In a meandering way, turning from the landscape beauties of the rivers Greta and Derwent, Southey calls attention to a cotton mill built on a fine site fit for a monastery, and so on to modern manufactures and the steam engine which "alone, without war, and without that increased taxation which war has rendered necessary, would have produced all the distress which our manufacturing population has experienced and is likely again and again to experience." Commercial prosperity rivals educational advance in corrupting the moral fiber of men.

In an epigram that might have come from Rousseau, a petty African king is cited who would send his sons to England that they might "learn to read book and be rogue." But that mood is not the settled temper of the elder Southey, who also sees the new technology as a great power for good as well as for evil. The upward turn in social development, however, must depend upon the right moral and social principles. Southey quotes Kant's theses for the establishment of a perfect constitution of society, and he adds his own Christian emphasis. Social perfection cannot be attained "till there be a system of Government, conducted in strict conformity to the principles of the Gospel."[15]

The ideal of unending historical progress was not only the goal of philosophical perfection but also the exalted vision of poets. In this respect the nineteenth century tends to repeat the eighteenth. In both of them we can trace the issue between optimistic and pessimistic evaluations of the course of history. Before we turn to Comte and Spencer and Schopenhauer, several poets of the buoyant spirit should claim our notice.

The first of these is François René de Chateaubriand (1768-1848); although he did not write in verse, his temperament is poetic; it combines aristocratic loftiness with humanitarian zeal. His *Genius of Christianity* was a romantic eulogy of the Christian religion. In rapturous prose Chateaubriand chanted the beauties of the historical pageant of Christianity in Western civilization: its mysteries, sacraments, doctrines, homilies, its cathedrals, abbeys, sculptures, paintings, hymns; the entire Christian epic—Christian missions, Christian chivalry and charity, Christianity as the light of spiritual beauty in the progress of civilization.

While we cannot overlook the rhetorical display of

---

[15] Southey, *Sir Thomas More: or, Colloquies on the Progress and Prospects of Society* (London, 1829), 2: 243, 249, 412; compare pp. 408 ff.

Chateaubriand, it was a contagious rhetoric, magic in his sentences, which imparted, if not firm conviction, yet a wistful inclination akin to faith revived, a nostalgia of Christian piety. But though this romanticism might seek to regain in intense reaffirmation the blessed enchantment of the traditional faith, its orthodoxy was unreliable because both its thought and its sentiment were self-centered. In chanting the glories of the old saintliness it was not really resuming the venerable themes but rather cherishing its memories as sources and motives of its new self-expression. It sought to bring the old altars to itself, not itself to the old altars.

Two poets whose lives spanned the nineteenth century expressed a historical optimism, never docile but ever struggling with doubts and dire actualities, resolute thoughout. In the middle of the century Tennyson's *In Memoriam,* containing some of his best poetry, was a sustained spiritual utterance, tragically *de profundis,* ever aiming at the summit in heroic devotion: "And one far-off divine event/To which the whole creation moves."

Almost a decade before *In Memoriam* Tennyson had declared, in "Locksley Hall," his firm confidence in the ongoing progress of mankind. That poem began with a story of frustrated love which leads the spurned lover to a gloomy view of civilization. But the poet returned to new and unfaltering confidence in progress: "Yet I doubt not thro' the ages one increasing purpose runs,/ And the thoughts of men are widen'd with the progress of the suns." Tennyson's prospect and vision are not limited to ever expanding knowledge but extend to physical mastery and social order and well-being and worldwide justice and concord:

> For I dipt into the future, far as human eye could see,
> Saw the vision of the world, and all the wonder that
> > would be;

Saw the heavens fill with commerce, argosies of magic sails,
Pilots of the purple twilight, dropping down their
                                        costly bales;
Heard the heavens fill with shouting, and there rained
                                        a ghastly dew
From the nations' airy navies grappling in the
                                        central blue; . . .
Till the war-drum throbb'd no longer, and the
                                        battle-flags were furl'd
In the Parliament of man, the Federation of the world.

On a vaster all-cosmic span Victor Hugo, writing in
exile, cast an all-encompassing view in time and space
across the whole expanse of world history and portrayed
the universal ascent of man from darkness and thralldom
to light and liberty. In the preface to his epic of all
creation, the *Legend of the Ages,* he outlined his immense
design: "The expansion of mankind from age to age, man
rising from gloom towards the ideal, the heavenly trans-
figuration of terrestrial hell, the slow but supreme dawn-
ing of freedom, right for this life and responsibility for
the next; a sort of religious hymn of a thousand stanzas,
springing from profound faith and with a lofty prayer at
the summit." Neither our Western civilization nor our
planet bound his contemplation: not only all the nations
on earth but the entire cosmos will manifest the final
consummation of the divine plan:

> The nations to each other brotherly will call;
> The dawn is near, the morn of liberty for all,
> Volcanic day when justice reigns;
> And men will penetrate through their encircling night,
> Will see their bondage change into victorious might,
> And jewels shining from their chains.

Hugo envisioned mankind as sweeping through the
heavens on an aerial ship, ever higher;

Where does it go, this ship?

It soars to right and reason and fraternity,
It seeks the saintly and religious verity,
Without imposture and disguises;
It cherishes the love that binds all men in duty,
It serves the great, the good, the just, aspires to beauty;
Lo, upward to the stars it rises![16]

Our comment on this poetic all-cosmic union should not overlook Hugo's more specific advocacy of an international federation which may still appear precarious of attainment, but to which yesterday's League of Nations and the United Nations of today are definite approaches.

The expanding spiritual outlook of German idealism, the self-penetration and intimate expression of romantic poetry, and the liberalism of the post-revolutionary age which spread the new ideas in Western Europe were finding a characteristic utterance in the Transcendentialism of New England. As the leading mind in that movement, Emerson (1803-1882), pointed out, its name derived from the use of it in Kant's philosophy,[17] but its meaning in American thought outreached its Kantian connotation. "Transcendentalism" extended beyond prior ways of thought and conviction: beyond Puritan rigor and rigid doctrine, but also and mainly beyond the materialistic trends of the Enlightenment, especially in its French expression. Against dogmatic formalism in religion and the externalities of gross naturalism, the spreading American liberalism emphasized the reality of aspiring and expanding spirit and the fuller realization of it in the inner freedom of a more humane commonwealth.

The social outlook and program of Transcendentalism aimed at the attainment of more than political indepen-

[16] Victor Hugo, "Tout le passé et tout l'avenir," and "Plein ciel," in *La Légende des siècles* (Paris, n.d.), vols. 3, 4.
[17] Compare Emerson's *Works,* Concord Edition (Cambridge, Mass., 1903-1904), 1: 339 f.

dence, at the emancipation of America from colonial tutelage and traditional conformity. Two of its characteristic trends were especially noteworthy. It ranged beyond its former Puritan-biblical bounds, toward the broad cultural-historical treasury of ideas and ideals, in all lands and ages. And, while thus universal in its responsiveness to a vaster past, its present concern was intently personal and forward-looking in searching spiritual pioneering. The Transcendentalists might have spoken the words of Tennyson's Ulysses: " 'Tis not too late to seek a newer world," but to each of them the wide-ranging adventure was an intimate pilgrimage.

These pilgrims of the liberal spirit shared a community of purpose, but each held to his own individual capacity and temperament. We need here to take a closer view of their best mind and leading spirit, Emerson, and of his rich treasury of wisdom, chiefly his progressive outlook, for his age and for America, for mankind and for human nature throughout history, and for the very nature of reality under God.

The recognition of an upward dynamic at the very core of being must have been Emerson's early conviction. He set it down as the motto of his first published book, *Nature:*

> A subtle chain of countless rings
> The next unto the farthest brings; . . .
> And, striving to be man, the worm
> Mounts through all the spires of form.

Before Darwin's *Origin of Species* he responded positively to evolutionary ideas, but in his own spiritual ways. As he read Lamarck, he felt like hailing the caterpillar in a neighborly spirit: "How dost thou, brother? Please God, you shall yet be a philosopher."[18] As for the caterpillar, so

---

[18] Compare *Works*, 1: xxix.

for his Transcendentalist hermits of aspiring ideals: he
saw their thoughts as reaching upward, "to reorganize
themselves in nature, to invest themselves anew in other,
perhaps higher endowed and happier mixed clay than
ours, in fuller union with the surrounding system."[19]

Emerson's social-historical optimism was not unqualified
or altogether docile. He noted that progress in civilization is so gradual that it is not marked and, even worse,
that the advances themselves are so liable to involve backwash and degradation, that man often has only "succeeded
in making his sensuality more daintily luxurious, his
crimes more ingeniously abominable."[20] Repeatedly he
observed that progress is attained only by individuals,
that it is not realized in the social order. This view inclined him even to dismal comments: "When were not
the majority wicked? or what progress was ever made by
society?"[21] But the prevailing tone of Emerson's thought
is one of positive appraisal. The true aim in progressive
activity is expansively human, "an infinite, not a special
benefit." And it is not altogether exceptional: "There is
a blessed necessity by which the interest of men is always
driving them to the right." This conviction did sometimes
proceed to a confidence which later events have scarcely
justified. One can only quote without any marginal comment: "War is on its last legs; and a universal peace is
as sure as the prevalence of civilization over barbarism,
of liberal government over feudal forms. The question
for us is only *How soon?*"[22]

This optimistic view of the course of history found
especial confirmation in Emerson's survey of his contemporary scene. "The new conditions of mankind in
America are really favorable to progress. . . . The mind

19 *Works*, 1: 359.
20 Emerson's *Journals* (Cambridge, Mass., 1961), 2: 77; compare p. 92.
21 *Journals* (1965) 5: 194; compare p. 259; compare also *Early Lectures*, 2: 173 f., 185.
22 *Works*, 1: 214; 11: 147, 161.

is always better the more it is used, and here it is kept in practice."[23] In his famous Phi Beta Kappa oration, "The American Scholar," he had expressed in his conclusion a hope that was also a challenge, "A nation of men will for the first time exist because each believes himself inspired by the Divine Soul which also inspires all men."

So from the worm and the caterpillar up to man in America and to mankind in the cosmos, Emerson's view was centered on the universal pulse ever pointing upward. Who was ever more versatile in his repeated expression of this conviction?—"The voice of the Almighty saith, 'Up and onward for evermore! . . . That which is made instructs how to make a better. . . . There is no sleep, no pause, no preservation, but all things renew, germinate and spring. . . . Within every man's thought is a higher thought—within the character he exhibits today, a higher character."[24]

The utopian strain or background of the positivism of Auguste Comte (1798-1857), the outstanding social philosophy in France during the nineteenth century, cannot be ignored, but it should not be overdrawn. Comte's relation to Claude Henri de Saint-Simon (1760-1825) included a considerable community of ideas but a growing difference in temperament and an eventual alienation. Saint-Simon was an evangelist in thought and action, a promoter of grand projects like the Panama and Suez canals, an agitator of political and economic reconstruction, an apostle of a religion of social justice and cooperation. He preached with fervor his "New Christianity" in which "the Man-God of the Christians" was to be replaced by himself, the "Man-People" "Earth, rejoice, Saint-Simon has appeared!"[25] His firm faith in social progress rested

[23] *Works,* 11: 516.
[24] *Works,* 2: 126, 318, 319; 8: 348.
[25] *Religion Saint-Simonienne, Recueil des prédications* (Paris, 1832), 1: 597, 303.

on his confidence in industrial advance and in economic reforms to assure the promotion of the general welfare of workingmen and to raise steadily the standard of living. Comte served as Saint-Simon's secretary and collaborator, but his own initial emphasis was on intellectual, scientific reform of ideas, and he distrusted Saint-Simon's apostolic spirit. The gospel note, however, was not absent in Comte's own philosophical program, and he had his own pontifical career in his later years. These two periods in the molding of positivism, the scientific and the devotional, were not incompatible, nor even independent; but the theory of progress in Comte's system of positive philosophy may be judged in secular terms, before turning from its philosophy of history to consider the "Religion of Humanity" to which it proceeded.

The earlier modern advocates of the doctrine of progress had maintained in general terms the indefinite perfectibility of men and societies. Some of them, like Condorcet, had traced the intellectual factors in the course of historical progress. Comte undertook to formulate the principles of human advancement. While he realized the close relation of men's ways of thought to their emotions and to their activities and social institutions, he concentrated his attention on the development of intellectual processes. This approach to the social and historical problem was not due to Comte's abstract conceptual bent. He regarded the social confusions of his revolutionary age as the practical results of confused thinking. He agreed with Hegel that Ideas govern the world. "The great political and moral crisis that societies are undergoing is shown by rigid analysis to arise out of intellectual anarchy."[26] Before we could hope for social order, we must first reform our chaotic thinking.

We can see, therefore, the central importance in Comte's

[26] *Comte's Positive Philosophy*, partly translated and edited by Harriet Martineau (London, 1896), 1: 15.

philosophy of his Law of the Three Stages of Thought, and of the scientific and social reform to which it points. There has been considerable dispute concerning Comte's originality in the formulation and advocacy of this law. The reasonable view seems to be one which recognizes Comte's dependence on others for his general principle, but also acknowledges his distinct title as the one who interpreted the law thoroughly. Turgot wrote of the three stages in the development of human thought, but his brilliant paragraphs, though enlightening, do not express the full significance of his historical principle or its far-reaching implications. This mastery and thoroughness of interpretation is Comte's achievement.

The Law of the Three Stages of Thought is a portrayal of the intellectual childhood, adolescence, and maturity of men in their outlook on the world. Comte called the three stages the Theological, the Metaphysical, and the Positive Scientific. The first stage, at a low level of understanding, was the stage of superstitions and myths. The entire course of nature was viewed as the operation of so-called divine or semidivine agencies. In primitive fetishism, claws and sticks and pebbles seemed endowed with weird potencies. Polytheistic imagining felt everywhere the presence of gods and goddesses. Later theology sought beyond or above this pantheon the one supreme Deity whose providence was held to direct all creation.

From this mythology of the theological stage, the developing mind proceeded to metaphysical speculation. Nature was now explained in terms of entities and conceptual abstractions. *Logos* or *Nous*, Reason, replaced Zeus. So we were told that water rises in a pump because nature abhors a vacuum.

This metaphysical stage was transitional. It was an advance from myth-making and theological creeds and dogmas to a demand for explanation. But this demand that eventually led to science was not yet scientific. It mistook speculation for scientific inquiry. Before it could reach positive knowledge, the mind had to undertake specific investigation. The scientific revolution was fundamental. Instead of pursuing wholesale cosmic speculation, the mature mind began to trace specific causal connections. Instead of the universal questions, What? and Why? it asked its more particular question, How? By observation and experiment it discovered and formulated specific causal relations. Thus the mind in its progress reached the stage of positive science.

We have used the past tenses of historical review, but the processes which Comte examined may be observed in our own thinking here and now. The progress is not uniform or full-front. It is reached earlier in some fields of thought than in others. Even in our modern age we may note that, while the general public has reached the positive scientific stage in the explanation of some classes of events, many men are still speculating metaphysically about others, and they regard still others in strict conformity to their theological orthodoxies. Comte examined these various advances also in his survey of the history of the sciences. He noted that they reached the positive stage in the order of their generality: mathematics, astronomy, physics, chemistry, biology.

This progress of the sciences of nature indicates its next important advance, the achievement of a positive science of man, man's knowledge of his own full nature. Comte did not include in his list psychology, the professed science of the mind, for he distrusted the French psychology of his day, which used introspective methods without due account of the biological basis of mental activity. The positive scientific study of human nature must set out from a dual recognition: of man's physiological organization, and then most importantly, of man's social relations and realization. The full meaning of the true character of man can be understood only in his social involvements and activities. The positive science of man is social physics, or sociology, as Comte proposed to call it.

The achievement of sociology was regarded by Comte as the next goal of progress and likewise as an indispensable condition of the further advance in civilization, beyond the modern revolutionary age with its confusions and crises. In calling the science of man sociology Comte indicated its first principle: the basic human reality is not the human individual but humanity. The term *human* means "social." This first principle must determine the true conception of the "humanities." Comte distinguished two sociological inquiries: social statics, the study of social order, and social dynamics, the study of human progress. This science of progress is not necessarily an account of invariable improvement; it is the scientific understanding of human life as a historical process of developing order regulated by laws. But as men thus come to know their social history, they can also recognize their social destiny, the ideal goal of their life as human beings. Our true fulfillment is in living a thoroughly socialized life. Comte called it *"Vivre pour autrui."*

Comte's positivism based its doctrine of historical progress on intellectual grounds. According to the Law of the Three Stages of Thought, men were bound to advance, sooner or later and in one field of activity after another, from superstitions and speculations to scientific truths. The idea of progress itself might be considered in the light of Comte's Law. Does it not also express, in its historical development, first the restriction or even the exclusion of it by the belief in a divine Providence, then the general speculative advocacy of it, and finally the demand for a specific factual and historical evidence of its truth? This evidence would not be adequate scientifically unless it integrated man with the rest of nature, without any traditional notion of special creation or any speculative substitutes for it. If man's origin in nature could be traced so as to show the rootage of historical progress in lower animal forms of life, then the belief in progress could gain scientific validity. In any case, the right method here required an investigation of the natural "descent of man." Trace man's parentage in nature as far as possible; then confirm or revise or reject the belief in progress as the available evidence may warrant.

This turn in our basic problem was affected by the theory of evolution which became dominant in biology through the work of Charles Darwin (1809-1882). The fundamental significance of the evolutionary principle was that it ranged biology alongside the other physical sciences, by abandoning any speculative dogmas about a design in nature or special creation of each form of life, and by undertaking to explain the origin of species in nature as determined causally.

In successive layers of the earth's crust, geology and palaeontology disclosed fossil remains of more and more complex organisms, justifying T. H. Huxley's account of the stream of life as a gradual change from relative uniformity to increasing complexity. The reports of animal and plant breeders showed the successful production of new varieties by effective selection. Darwin was in search of a causal determining factor of natural selection. It is interesting to note that he got it, by analogy, from a work in social theory, Malthus's *Essay on the Principle of Population*. Thomas Robert Malthus (1766-1834) had reasoned that the growth in population rises with any increase in the available resources of food and subsistence but is kept down by the natural limits of those resources. Darwin tells us in his autobiography that this idea gave him his principle of causal explanation. The limited supply of food and other conditions of survival involve all forms of life in a struggle for existence. In this struggle any species with a variation suitable to a certain environment, or to various environments, has an advantage over other species. By this natural "survival of the fittest" new varieties are preserved and multiplied, and eventually new and more complex species originate. This in sum was Darwin's theory of evolution. Spencer formulated the evolutionary process as "a change from an indefinite incoherent homogeneity to a definite coherent heterogeneity,"[27] involving increasing differentiation and integration of structure and function. The entire range of life-forms, from amoebas to mammals, could thus be explained as a process that was not designed but occurred necessarily: the survival of the fittest in the struggle for existence.

Since man is thus to be viewed as the human animal in the zoological procession, how are our traditional beliefs in human progress to be reinterpreted? Shall we hold firmly to a conviction of the historical facts of manifold development, and in view of man's newly discovered evolutionary ancestry, look for the beginnings and early forms of progressive activities in mammals and perhaps also in other animal species? Or contrariwise, shall we proceed from a strictly physical-causal account of biological processes and of man's origin and so interpret human character and activities as only more complicated varieties of animal behavior, ruling out any recognition of truly progressive development?

The choice here would seem to depend upon the thoroughness with which our evolutionism rejects teleology and evaluation in any form—not only in its initial scientific dismissal of providential design as a principle of explanation but also in its eventual interpretation of human and other forms of higher animal behavior. At this point we may only note that the writings of evolutionists do not indicate any such unanimous dismissal of teleology and evaluation of any sort whatever.

This unsteadiness in fundamental categories may be

[27] Spencer, *First Principles* (New York, 1896), p. 407.

disclosed by an examination of the diversity of ethical and social theories that have been influenced by the doctrine of evolution. We must concentrate our discussion on the particular issue of evolution and progress. Darwin himself, both in his treatises and in his correspondence, made it clear that his theory of the evolution of species was to be the very opposite of the traditional doctrine of a providential design in nature. And yet at the conclusion of his *Origin of Species* he expressed his belief that "as natural selection works solely by and for the good of each being, all corporeal and mental endowments will tend to progress towards perfection." This may perchance be a statement of fact, but on Darwin's own theory and in his text this sort of neo-providential natural selection sounds like a mythological slip. In strict Darwinism, the use of the terms *good, progress, perfection* in the above passage is scarcely warranted. Natural selection does not work "for the good of each being"; it operates causally in various environments to determine the survival or the perishing of organisms with certain variations. In a glacial flood, the surviving and thus the fittest species would be, not mammals, but maybe some microorganisms and lichens. That would be, then and there, the alleged progress toward perfection.

This whole problem of ultimate interpretation was still further complicated when human intelligence and conduct were considered in the evolutionary perspective. Darwin acknowledged with unmistakable candor his difficulty in dealing with mental powers and the moral sense. In his *Descent of Man* the chapters dealing with these two topics were memorable pioneer work in animal psychology and also in descriptive ethics. He explored the beginnings of morals in primitive societies, but more to the point, he considered the reactions in animal behavior that seemed to him to anticipate the more definitely moral motivation and action in human conduct. Can we not trace moral evolution from animal gregariousness, herd instinct, and parental care, by group restriction and compulsion, to a growing sense of sociality, to obligation and guilt or a clear conscience, to duty and concern for the common good? Perhaps we can. Peter Kropotkin (1842-1921) pointed out and insisted that mutual aid is a major factor in evolution, to be recognized along with the struggle for existence.

If we thus acknowledge both mutual aid and "nature, red in tooth and claw" as evolutionary determinants, what warrants our choice of the former as the strain of progress in the ongoing processes of life? Darwin, and Kropotkin more decisively, sought out and found instances of the growth of sociality and philanthropy in the course of evolution. But how could evolution itself yield or validate their philanthropic ethics or their corollary view of progress? In dealing with this problem T. H. Huxley (1825-1895) was more rigorous in his analysis and appraisal. He shared in the main Darwin's philanthropic ethics, but could find no evolutionary warrant for it. Gregarious instinct and parental care should not mislead us to underestimate the outstanding reality of the struggle for existence. The evolutionary jungle is not a garden plot of conscience and justice and benevolence. Morality is in fact a resistance to the evolutionary drives. "Its influence is directed, not so much to the survival of the fittest, as to the fitting of as many as possible to survive. . . . The ethical process of society depends, not on imitating the cosmic process, still less in running away from it, but in combatting it."[28] By thus pointing out the high ethical road of true human progress, Huxley did not mean to imply that he recognized it as the highway of history. His conclusion was quite the opposite. Political economy has been called "the dismal science," and dismal also

[28] T. H. Huxley, *Evolution and Ethics* (London and New York, 1894), pp. 33, 34.

was Huxley's view of the historical record. He wrote that he knew of "no study which is so saddening as that of the evolution of humanity as it is set forth in the annals of history."[29]

Here was Huxley's sharp contrast between his moral standard and his factual report of evolutionary biology, of which as a scientist he was an eminent advocate. But while the merit of his clear discrimination between evolution and ethics was important, he did not recognize sufficiently the need of a more nearly ultimate view of nature and human nature which could account for philanthropic morals as well as for the evolutionary struggle for existence. His rejection of dogmatic theology as providing him with no convincing solution of his problem was understandable; but the agnosticism to which he then proceeded was a suspension, not a prosecution of the major inquiry. The fuller truth was, and still is, beyond Huxley.

Darwin himself had recognized the contrast on which Huxley insisted, between moral-sympathetic activity and natural selection in the struggle for existence. Civilized nations build hospitals and mental institutions, nurse and preserve the lives of the infirm and imbecile. "The weak members of civilized societies propagate their kind. No one who has attended to the breeding of domestic animals will doubt that this must be highly injurious to the race of man."[30] The ruthless inference from these observations, which was not drawn by Darwin, was proclaimed by Friedrich Nietzsche (1844-1900) in his gospel of Superman. The outstanding fact of the life-process, the struggle for existence, disclosed also its dominant principle, which Nietzsche called the Will-to-Power. On the hard ground of this principle he championed a "transvaluation of all values." Our ideas of moral values and of human progress should be revised radically. Instead of condemning and

---

[29] Compare J. B. Bury, *The Idea of Progress* (New York, 1955), p. 344.
[30] Darwin, *The Descent of Man* (New York, ed. of 1896), p. 134.

rejecting the dynamic forces of prevailing activity, we should espouse them heroically and should strive for their consummation. Against any sickly pity for the weak and any nursing of the ailing and needy, we should reaffirm the strength and the excellence which achieves mastery, which will eventually cross the limits of ordinary human nature and will rise to an order of life higher than man, as man is higher than the ape. In this heroic ascent, the laggard multitude should be of no concern. A people is only nature's roundabout way of producing half-a-dozen great men. That is nature's progress, and that is the meaning of history: from time to time to raise the summit of the human pyramid of achievement.

A morally commendatory account of evolution and a full-blown theory of progress was advocated by Herbert Spencer (1820-1903). Darwin called him "our philosopher," and Spencer's works provided the most extensive interpretation of evolutionism. But his earlier writings, published before Darwin's *Origin of Species,* supported his claim that on his own he had advocated the fundamental principle of the evolutionary view of nature, which Darwin had reasoned out and formulated with great mastery and which Darwin's researches had supported with abundant evidence.

Spencer's ethics may be called evolutionary hedonism: man's basic good is happiness, and this chief value of life is realized progressively in history. As social evolution makes the lives of men increasingly complex, ruthless conflict becomes less advantageous than cooperation; men learn the survival value of justice and benevolence. "Conduct gains ethical sanction in proportion as the activities, becoming less and less militant and more and more industrial, are such as do not necessitate mutual injury and hindrance, but consist with, and are furthered by, cooperation and mutual aid."[31]

[31] Spencer, *The Principles of Ethics* (New York, 1897), 1: 20.

In one of his first important books, *Social Statics,*
Spencer maintained his belief in progress and "the
evanescence of evil." By progress he meant not merely
improvement but advancement toward ultimate perfection. "All evil results from non-adaptation of constitution
to conditions," and this maladjustment is bound to be
rectified. Progressive adaptability, through physical and
mental modification, is regarded by Spencer as a universal
law, and from it he infers that "the ultimate development
of the ideal man is logically certain."[32] This fundamental
conviction was not the expression of docile optimism about
existing social conditions. In chapter after chapter
Spencer exposed the gross injustices, inequities, and corruptions rampant in various institutions, but while he
stigmatized particular evils he seemed unwavering in his
confidence that human nature is self-reforming.

In his historical outlook Spencer surveyed the course
of civilization as "a progress towards the constitution of
man and society required for the manifestation of every
man's individuality." And this advancement is essential
and natural to every man. "Progress, therefore, is not an
accident but a necessity."[33] In his essay "Progress," published just before Darwin's *Origin of Species,* Spencer
developed a similar thesis. Starting with his basic account
of life as organic "change from the homogeneous to the
heterogeneous," he proposed to show that the same law
applies to all progress. For it is a law that every process
involves a multiplicity of changes; in the course of nature
there has been an ever growing complication of things—
increasing differentiation and increasing integration, increasing order. From the evolution of the solar system to
the evolution of all living forms and to the development
of men and societies, the same fundamental principle
applies. Progress is the law of nature, and it is historically
necessary.

[32] Spencer, *Social Statics* (London, 1851), pp. 59, 64.
[33] Op. cit., p. 65.

Spencer's conception of progress as man's adaptation to his environment led him in the development of his ideas to the conviction that man's environment evolved progressively from conflict to cooperation and mutual aid. In his earlier views of evolution, however, as has been pointed out by Kropotkin and others, "he had concentrated his attention on the 'struggle for existence,' and interpreted it in its application to animals as well as to men, as the struggle of each against all for the means of subsistence."[34] Other evolutionists held firmly to this concentration on the struggle for survival, regarded it as unabating, and proceeded to view conflict and competition as the dynamics of progress. Benjamin Kidd (1858-1916), who advanced this view in his *Social Evolution,* did not proceed to advocate a Nietzschean ethics of the Will-to-Power. He was content to expand the common saying "Competition is the life of trade" into a basic statement not only of human affairs but also of nature generally. Wherever we look we see contending activities serving as spurs to superior development and prevailing capacity. Grasses, trees, animals, men, all vie with each other. "The law of life has been always the same from the beginning—ceaseless and inevitable struggle and competition, ceaseless and inevitable selection and rejection, ceaseless and inevitable progress."[35] This tension and contention alter only by the changing of levels: as we rise from lower to higher forms of life, "the rivalry is keener, the stress severer, the pace quicker, than ever before." To be sure, Kidd does not glorify this unending struggle; he insists on it as an unavoidable fact. These are the stern realities of human life and progress, which we cannot ignore. In this ceaseless contest, the weaker and the less capable succumb and must succumb; but the contest also stirs those of superior capacities to achieve greater and greater

[34] Prince Kropotkin, *Ethics: Origin and Development,* trans. L. S. Friedland and J. H. Piroshnikoff (New York, 1924), p. 289.

[35] B. Kidd, *Social Evolution* (New York and London, 1894), p. 39.

mastery. Without competition there would be no progress in realizing the fullest possibilities of life.[36]

Kidd's view of progress expresses in a striking way the problem of developing a convincing philosophy of life on strictly evolutionistic principles. The dismissal of teleology, an advantage which made it possible for Darwin to range biology alongside of the other physical sciences, proved also an obstacle to using evolutionism as a basis for a reevaluation of human purposes and achievements. Without the recognition of a hierarchy of values, a theory of progress becomes ambiguous or even irrelevant. This perplexity in ultimate interpretation is evidenced in several varieties of evolutionary theory. The acknowledgment of the need for a thorough reinterpretation led to some radical alternative doctrines in our century. The conception of progress in two of them, emergent evolution and creative evolution, will be examined in our next chapter.

The assurance of progress as the result of competition and rivalry was not limited to evolutionary speculation. It was advocated also in the "Hegelianism of the Left" which restated the counteraction of alternatives in a doctrine of social mechanics. This was the dialectical materialism of Karl Marx (1818-1883) and Friedrich Engels (1820-1895) and the "scientific socialism" of the Communists. They shared the conviction of an inevitable advance from conflict of opposite principles or rather forces to a new position which transcends both of the contending alternatives.

The issue here was between the prevailing emphasis on basic ideas and on forces. Marx's firm choice of the latter described also his systematic alignment. He applied the Hegelian dialectic to a materialistic cosmology. His philosophy was a fusion of Hegel and Holbach. Human life, individual and social, must be seen as a mechanism of

[36] Op. cit., pp. 55, 58.

conflicting reactions. Man's fundamental reality is not Spirit; ideas and ideologies are themselves effects or by-products of material, mainly economic conditions. Change the conditions, and your alleged "spirit" also changes. Ludwig Feuerbach (1804-1872), the pioneer in this radical shift of Hegelian doctrine, had said that he had been compelled to turn over the Hegelian pyramid, from its precarious balancing on its idealistic peak to its solid material base. Marx wrote to the same effect: Hegel's dialectic "stands on its head. It should be turned over. . . . My dialectical method is not only different from the Hegelian but is fundamentally its direct opposite. . . . I regard the ideal as nothing else than the material reality, transposed and translated in the human head."[37]

History, then, is not God's march in the world, nor is it the realization of the Idea of Freedom. History is the vast interplay of men in their material environment, in which their ways of life and social order have been determined by the mechanics of their economic environment, and in which men and societies themselves have changed as their material conditions have altered. This was Marx's materialistic interpretation of history and it dictated his conception of progress and his social-revolutionary program. So he read the historical record of the radical changes in the social economy, from the ancient production of goods by slave labor to the relations of feudal lords and vassals and serfs in the medieval system and to the modern capitalistic economy of mass production.

In each of these social transitions, an economic system, which had been outgrown by the operation of new material conditions, had been replaced with mechanical necessity by another system more adaptable to the new environment. In each case the master classes of society

---

[37] Karl Marx, *Das Kapital,* ed. Karl Kautsky (Berlin, 1928), 1: xlviii, xlvii.

might hold fast to their traditional vested rights, but the new forces must irresistibly sweep them away. The old system eventually produces the forces which disrupt and then swamp it. So modern capitalism, pursuing its maximum profits by methods of mass production, requires an increasingly large class of proletarian workers. This growing contest of a small minority of exploiters with a vast majority of workingmen, individually helpless but in their organization as a class finally invincible, set inevitably both the conditions and the outcome of the social conflict. This contradiction in the capitalistic system of mass production must necessarily progress toward the ultimate victory of the exploited masses and the establishment of a communistic society.

The messianic strain in Marxism may be regarded as a providential determinism in reverse. It was a proclamation of the inevitable consummation of the proletarian dictatorship and a revolutionary propaganda to speed the coming of the day of social regeneration. But what could be the true meaning or the justification of a radical program of reform in the perspective of dialectical materialism? If men are merely the products of material conditions and if their relations to each other were determined only by the mechanics of economic processes, just as any other things in nature, why was the exploitation of them, in slavery or feudal serfdom or capitalist employment not only wasteful but also iniquitous? Marxism might uphold its conviction of the inevitable change from a capitalistic to a communist economy, but how could it evaluate this revolutionary change as right and good and as worthy of men's devotion? What meaning could "progress" have for a thoroughly consistent dialectical materialist?

This chapter on the problem of progress in the nineteenth century should include at least a brief mention of the wave of pessimism which swept through philosophy and literature, in sharp opposition to the generally and in various ways optimistic social-historical evaluation. The mere citing of some of the poets in the chorus of negation —Leopardi and Vigny, Byron and Lenau and James Thomson—should suggest its volume and temper. Here we should consider two systematic philosophers of pessimism, Arthur Schopenhauer (1788-1860) and Eduard von Hartmann (1842-1906).

It is significant that Schopenhauer had very few specific comments about historical progress. The term itself scarcely ever appears in his writings: as if he did not regard it as having any meaning in his philosophy of life. The fundamental reality in all things, according to him, is a ceaseless drive and insatiate craving which he called the Will-to-Live. In human nature it manifests itself as desire. Unsatisfied, it is painful want; occasionally gratified, it is temporary pleasure; not seeing or realizing its aim, it is deadly boredom. This will-driven life is selfish in its usual incentives, often wicked in its ruthless abuse of others, and wretched altogether in its eventual outcome. The only good it could possibly realize must be through self-forgetting compassion for the woes of others and in saintly ascetic self-effacement. But such saints are rare and even a cosmic miracle, denying the universal reality of the Will-to-Live.

What basis could there be for a belief in progress in such a dismal world? Schopenhauer described human society as a hospital for incurables, and he denounced optimism as an insult to hopeless humanity. The chronicles of mankind "find nothing else to record but wars and rebellions; the years of peace are only short pauses," like the blank half-pages between long horrible chapters.[38]

Schopenhauer's most distinguished successor, Eduard von Hartmann, cannot be called a pessimist without quali-

[38] Schopenhauer, *Sämtliche Werke,* ed. Paul Deussen (München, 1913), 5: 318.

fication. He regarded Schopenhauer's Will-to-Live and Hegel's cosmic Rationality as the two fundamental aspects of ultimate reality. The major task of philosophy, he mtaintained, must be to recognize them both and to achieve their synthesis. As with his cosmology, so with his philosophy of life. Hartmann described himself as an eudemonological pessimist and an evolutionistic optimist. In other words, he portrayed human life as offering scope for the development and realization of some genuine values, but still he saw no prospect of real enduring happiness within our reach.

Hartmann's evolutionistic optimism had considerable limitations. He did not recognize our capacity to attain fulfillment of positive values; he did admit genuine significance in our pursuit of worthy aims, even though that pursuit involved final frustration. Our intellectual striving is never conclusive, yet we can seek and find real truth, even if it is often dismal. Moral and aesthetic values likewise engage our resolute endeavor and realize genuine worth, but they lack finality or enduring satisfaction. So in broad prospect, trust in evolutionistic optimism is a belief in some available advance toward significant goals: not utter failure, yet no conclusiveness or consummation.

Even this limited advance was regarded by Hartmann as illusory, if our basic valuation is in terms of happiness. With this hedonistic outlook he shared Schopenhauer's estimate of life as a losing enterprise. He called the quest of happiness the great illusion of mankind. As a pessimistic pendant to Comte's Law of the Three Stages of Thought, Hartmann traced Three Stages of Illusion, the illusion of attainable happiness. Classical antiquity regarded happiness as being within men's reach here and now. Ancient civilization records men's increasing disillusion regarding the satisfactions of the present life. The conversion of the classical world to Christianity was in fact a transition to the second stage of the great illusion. Men turned to the hope of happiness after death, in the life eternal promised by the Gospels. This hope dominated medieval culture; but it also was dimmed and extinguished for modern critical minds by the advance of science and philosophy. Modern humanity then proceeded to a third stage of its illusion: happiness had been contemplated as attainable socially in the future progress of civilization. This belief has been called the modern man's religion.

Hartmann undertook to expose the deceptive character of this belief in the future fulfillment of men's hopes. Across the entire span of existence he surveyed our activities and found them all self-defeating and frustrating in their final and irremediable infelicity. Even our best gestures—compassion, benevolence—prove to be finally unavailing. We are back with Schopenhauer in the hospital for incurables. We may try to alleviate the patient's wretchedness, but his case is really hopeless. Though we amputate one limb after another, the deep-seated disease would still creep closer and closer. Be it private almsgiving or public charity, it is, after all, like cutting off a dog's tail kindly, inch by inch.

During the nineteenth century these turbid undercurrents of negation disturbed the more generally even flow of the prevailing course of thought and feeling. In our own century the prophets of doom that we hear predominantly today have driven many persons to despair of the prospects of civilization.

CHAPTER SIX

Contemporary Criticism

BAFFLED MINDS may describe the twentieth century as the age of frustration. Two world wars of unprecedented destruction, and a third most ruinous war threatening, have flouted modern man's confidence in assured ongoing progress. The very conditions of modern life on which men have relied for the avoidance of war and for peaceful social advance have become incitements to conflict. Herbert Spencer had with unwitting irony used the term *industrial* to describe the higher stage of evolving civilization, when cooperation would replace strife. At the third decade of the century economic experts were reasoning that the advance in industry had brought the nations into such close relations as to reduce the threat of war on a large scale. Modern science and technology have constructed engines of destruction so terrible that common and uncommon judgment have regarded them as reliable deterrents to war. Twice already has the vanity of this hope been exposed, and for a third time our age still persists in it.

Despite this half-century of ruination, our social outlook is not utterly drear. The course of events has disabused us of our former conviction of inevitable eventual progress, but it has not turned us all, or altogether, to the other extreme of utter negation. If we could only commit ourselves to the right choice of values, if we could at least temper the strife of ideologies and the struggle for domination, if we could reach some reasonable understanding between the conflicting groups of powers, our newly attained atomic technology would yield us incredible exploitation of the resources of nature and lead us to a higher civilization. Or, resisting both dark negation and stubborn optimism, prophets of redemption in our time have admonished us to cast aside our secular illusions of self-reliance and to tread the penitent path of grace.

In the previous chapter we noted several different versions of evolutionism in its application to human and social-historical perspectives. The merit of Darwin's theory in biology was in its explanation of the origin and evolution of species in causal terms, without any reference to design or teleology. But firm adherence to this view involved difficulties in dealing with what Darwin called "mental powers" and "the moral sense," in doing full justice to human historical life. In occasional passages Darwin spoke of a trend in nature toward progress and perfection, but his theory did not provide sufficient basis for such high prospects. T. H. Huxley, a strong champion of Darwinian biology, rejected any ethically commendatory versions of the struggle for existence and declared that moral conduct and progress depend on our resistance to the evolutionary drive. But he did not indicate in his cosmology any adequate ground or source of spiritual character or moral value.

Does evolutionism admit of a reinterpretation which, while providing at one end a thoroughly justified biological account of living processes, would also be marked at the other end by a recognition of truly purposive and intelligent development, in individual life and in historical progress? We shall consider briefly two contemporary cosmologies of radical evolutionary reinterpretation: the emergent evolution of Lloyd Morgan (1852-1936) and Samuel Alexander (1859-1938), and the creative evolution of Henri Bergson (1859-1941). Both of them may be regarded as involving a proposed cosmology of progress.

The theory of emergent evolution resists any proposal to explain life and mind as merely complex varieties of mechanical processes. Lloyd Morgan described himself as a thoroughgoing naturalist, but by thoroughness he understood avoidance of oversimplification. The framework of explanation in physics and chemistry cannot do justice to the characteristic nature of life, nor can mind, thinking activity, be interpreted as mere physical and chemical or physiological process. Mechanics, life, mind are all in and of nature, but not on the same level. They represent stages in the cosmic advance of organization. Life and mind are not mere resultants; they are emergents. At a certain level of cosmic activity, life emerges; at a certain level of organismic activity, living beings rise to a higher emergent character of mental and rational powers.[1]

The question arises as to how deeply this cosmic emergence reaches in the nature of reality. Lloyd Morgan avowed his "concern . . . with integral *advance* in evolutionary process . . . with a rational order of *progress*." But his basic view is that of advance *in* reality rather than advance *of* reality. The entire process of progressive emergence was envisioned by him as manifesting the eternal nature of Mind capitalized, of Spirit or God active but not growing, above the possibility of advance.[2]

The further implications of emergent evolution were developed in the realistic metaphysics of Samuel Alexander, to whom Morgan continually refers and often, but not always, defers. Alexander's evolutionism found early expression in his *Moral Order and Progress* (1889), in which he used the basic idea of development to advocate

---

[1] Compare C. Lloyd Morgan, *The Emergence of Novelty* (London, 1933), pp. 7, 64; *Life, Mind, and Spirit* (London, 1925), p. 1.

[2] Compare C. Lloyd Morgan, *Life, Mind, and Spirit,* p. 288; *Mind at the Crossways* (London, 1929), pp. 242 ff.

an ethics of mainly utilitarian-philanthropic slant. He recognized a progressive tendency toward sociality in the historical process and also an expanding range of versatility in the higher organization of men's lives. The influence of Spencer but also of idealistic Oxford was apparent in Alexander's views, and the eventual direction and choice were still in prospect.

The mature exposition of Alexander's progressive realism was presented in his *Space, Time, and Deity* (1920). Although he did not often use the term *emergence,* he contemplated the world-process as involving the periodic rise to new and higher levels of activity. Life and mind were regarded as continuous with mechanical processes, but the continuity was viewed as an expansive manifestation of nature. Nature all the way through is a surging, rising, emerging process. Unlike Lloyd Morgan's theistic view, Alexander's cosmology recognized no capitalized Divine Perfection at the origin of things. Deity is not the creative First: it is at every level or stage of existence the Higher Next. Alexander did not believe in *a* God. "God" for him signified "the whole universe, with a nisus to deity."[3] In his philosophy, the principle of progress is not merely one of historical connotation; it is used metaphysically to express the fundamental character of reality. For Alexander, in the beginning and all the way through was and is the verb, and the verb is progress.

Bergson's philosophy is an emphatic activism: "There are no things, there are only actions."[4] Against any abstract and schematic views of nature as a system of substances in space, he concentrated his attention on processes in time. And he began by demanding the recognition of time as real duration, *durée réelle*: not clock or calendar time, not discrete ticks or minutes or hours

---

[3] Samuel Alexander, *Space, Time, and Deity* (London, 1920), 2: 362.
[4] Henri Bergson, *Creative Evolution,* trans. Arthur Mitchell (London, 1928), p. 261.

or days or ages, shorter or longer extents of time, but a real flowing change and course of direction; not a series of drops but a stream. As with time so with life, so with the whole evolutionary process. So likewise it is with human activity. Listen to the living flow of the melody; if you "cut it up into distinct notes," you will lose both the melody and its supposed parts, for you get the notes truly only in the melody.[5]

The concrete reality is not the succession of discrete biological forms but the living process itself. Bergson viewed it as a creative flood, pulsing and pressing forward, on the one hand evolving definite forms, as it were, canals for its ongoing currents; on the other hand, ever overflowing its banks into new directions. With his genius for fertile metaphor and felicitous phrasing, Bergson called the process the *élan vital*, the vital urge. No abstract causal-mechanical description could ever do justice to it: here Bergson challenged the Darwinists. The evolutionary flood of life is unpredictable in its directions, creatively ongoing throughout; it does not cause but produces, sprouts, germinates, generates; it has, not effects, but offsprings.

The theory of creative evolution is not confronted with the problem of somehow bridging the chasm between nature and spirit: it denies that there is any such chasm. Life at any stage, even at its low levels, always manifests the vital urge which has in it something analogous to conscious effort. Matter and mechanics are stiffened molds or by-products of the living flood, like tidal sand-curves on the seashore or like the bark of trees which the rising sap is ever cracking with new leaf buds. More primitive in nature than the mechanics of matter and more elemental still is the urge somehow akin to con-

[5] Bergson, *The Creative Mind*, trans. M. L. Andison (New York, 1946), p. 176.

sciousness. We might call it the soul in the life, flowing where it wills.

In the ongoing course of his creative evolution Bergson distinguished two currents: intelligence and instinct. Intelligence marks especially the higher mammals and man. It is schematic, abstractly constructive, forming concepts and patterns, systematic and general. Instinct, which reaches its perfection in insect life, perceives without understanding, unreflective but unerring in its directness, hitting its mark at which it does not deliberately aim. In human experience instinct manifests itself in various forms of intuition. In his last major work, *The Two Sources of Morality and Religion,* Bergson examined the highest manifestation of the instinctive strain, mystical insight.

From such a view of living nature, the inference of progress seems patent. Progress in the distinctive historical sense is an outstanding instance of a germinal characteristic in all reality. Our actions depend upon our character, but our character is being continually recreated by our every choice and action. In living processes "the essential thing is the *continuous progress* indefinitely pursued."[6] The progress is not to be defined in abstract terms as a progress of this or that sort. Bergson's teleology is not a teleology of ends but of strivings and pursuits and of the vital urge. He advocated finalism but not finality. The progress of justice is not to be regarded as a gradual approach toward some absolute standard. It is an advance in the standard as well as in the practical realization of it. Ideals are moving targets.[7] The ideal character or principle is in the ongoing and creative dynamism itself. "All the living hold together, and all

[6] Bergson, *Creative Evolution,* p. 28; compare p. 7.
[7] Compare Bergson, *The Two Sources of Morality and Religion,* trans. Audra, Brereton, and Carter (London, 1935), pp. 57 f., 63.

yield to the same tremendous push *(formidable poussée)*. The animal takes its stand on the plant, man bestrides animality, and the whole of humanity, in space and in time, is one immense army galloping before and behind each of us in an overwhelming charge."[8]

This account of the creative vital urge which has attained the level of man's spiritual energies moved Bergson to lofty religious contemplation. Could we say that nature has justified itself and its existence in achieving human spirits? Bergson cites it as the unanimous witness of the mystics that "God needs us just as much as we need God. . . . God undertaking to create creators, that he may have, beside himself, beings worthy of his love." Beyond biological evolution, beyond human culture and historical progress, Bergson envisioned an ascent to boundless perfection: "Men do not realize that their future is in their own hands. Theirs is the task of determining first of all whether they want to go on living or not. Theirs the responsibility, then, for deciding if they want merely to live, or intend to make just the extra effort required for fulfilling, even on their refractory planet, the essential function of the universe, which is a machine for the making of gods."[9]

Pragmatism, as a theory of knowledge and as a philosophy of life, emphasized instrumental principles of fulfilled prediction and realization of purposes in action. A leading advocate of it, William James (1842-1910), opposed any view of a set and wound-up universe and urged unambiguous recognition of ongoing activity and novelty throughout the world process. Intellectual values are not abstractly inherent attributes but qualities achieved or frustrated in our course of active experience. This is the process of veri-fication, as James liked to write that term: ideas *made true* in our venture with them.

[8] *Creative Evolution,* pp. 285 f.
[9] *The Two Sources of Morality and Religion,* pp. 218, 275.

Likewise with the other values: they are not essentially constitutive but always instrumental and impending on our use of them. In all human affairs, personal or historical, we must steer resolutely between the two errors of dark fatalism and idle complacency. This was James's proposed strategy in dealing with the baffling problem of evil. The moral struggle is not futile, but neither is it superfluous. There is something really wild in the universe, but it is not hopelessly our fate to be its thralls. The struggle with it is our moral career, and on a historical plane it marks the high road of progress. Between docile optimism and pessimism, James advocated meliorism, the conviction that though the best is never realized and even the good is not a foregone conclusion, the better is ours to pursue and to achieve in some measure, though never completely. The higher goal is ours to approach but not to possess altogether. And well it is so. "The great use of a life is to spend it for something that will outlast it." This philosophy of heroic endeavor had a religious meaning for James. "Let us cheerfully settle into our interminable task. Everywhere it is the same struggle under various names—light against darkness, right against might, love against hate. The Lord of Life is with us, and we cannot permanently fail."[10]

John Dewey (1859-1952) preferred to call his pragmatic philosophy "instrumentalism." In his development of its principles evolutionistic ideas were influential, and his later statements had a positivistic emphasis on social processes and factors in thought and behavior. Philosophy as Dewey used it was a program of action, of education, of social reform. No other philosopher of his day stood out more convincingly than he on the frontline of constructive liberal advance. An essay titled "Progress," published during the First World War, presents in brief

[10] Compare R. B. Perry, *The Thought and Character of William James* (Boston, 1935), 2: 289, 313.

but clear terms his view of progress, not as an abstract idea but as men's real alternative in the historical process. Progress, in his view, is not mere change, although it does require as a condition a certain "ease of social change." It depends upon the direction which men give to changes in the social process.

Modern history has registered increasingly greater possibilities of progress through the scientific mastery of the resources of nature for man's use. This has been the great war and conquest of humanity, but whether this victory is to become assured would depend upon men's choice and resolution. Progress, Dewey maintained, must be viewed "as a responsibility and not as an endowment." The means to great human advance are within our reach, but we need critical intelligence to recognize our greatest needs and to provide the social order an implementation that would best satisfy those needs. Dewey was not content with a general statement of his principle. As he put it, progress is "a retail job," and he proceeded to a detailed outline of specific high priorities in his social program of progress.[11]

Pessimism has often been induced from, and by, personal misadventure or social adversity. Critics of the doctrine have regarded it as affliction or rancor dignified into a philosophy. They have reminded us of Vigny's "vulture of Prometheus" (cancer of the stomach), of Leopardi's catalog of ailments, lampooned sometimes with cruel irony ("I am a hunchback, therefore there is no God!"). Schopenhauer's pessimism met with dismissal or indifference during the placid quarter of the nineteenth century, after Europe had squared her accounts with Napoleon. But when the revolutions of 1848 had been smashed and had been followed by a wave of social dis-

11 John Dewey, *Characters and Events,* ed. Joseph Ratner (New York, 1929), 2: 820 ff., 824, 830.

trust and depression, Schopenhauer's philosophy of world denial came to the fore.

This sort of critique exposes a plaintive and even a peevish strain in some pessimistic reasoning, but itself fails to take due account of the conditions which provoke the vehement reactions. Job was not aroused to his tragic quandaries about divine justice until he had been laid low by his many disasters; but does this fact dispose of the real question: What sort of divine Providence dumps a man like Job on the trash-heap?

The Roman adage "*Vae victis!*—Woe to the vanquished!" has its overtones of meanings. It is the vanquished that cry Woe! but the inference that their defeat or their woe warrants any basic pessimism would depend upon our estimate of them. To the Free World, the final defeat of Napoleon or of Hitler has sustained rather than upset confidence in some sort of cosmic or historical justice. To Napoleon's marshals and grenadiers or to Hitler's devotees, the inference was bound to be radically different. We have heard of the "Impartial History of the Civil War, from a Southern Standpoint."

These aspects of some contemporary historical works may be noted in the two massive volumes *The Decline of the West* by Oswald Spengler (1880-1936). His writings do reflect a certain German state of mind as it varied with the changes of our tragic half-century. There is the depression or even the skeptical strain in the historical relativism which he unfolded in that main work, completed toward the close of the First World War. There is the upsurge of imperialist will-to-power in his *Years of Decision,* just before Hitler's rise to power. There are also bitter unpublished pages of scorn for the Nazis and their un-German, "Asiatic . . . invasion of Tartar will into the Western world."[12] But Spengler's worth is in his

---

[12] Compare Oswald Spengler, *Jahre der Entscheidung* (München, 1933),

systematic inferences. He explored the central character
of historical processes and the sort of knowledge and
likely prediction which they warrant. We may here
readily pay tribute to his incredibly vast erudition in all
fields of history, and we may defer to competent historians
in their exposure not only of his frequent errors in details
but also of his more general misdirections. What interests
us in our present inquiry is Spengler's conception of historical judgment and his outlook on the course of history.

Spengler contrasts history and science as two ways of
looking at the world and at human life. Science deals with
the world as nature, conceived as a causal mechanism of
things and processes, necessarily determined, calculable,
measurable, formulable. History, on the other hand, sees
men in the world as organic, living agents, not merely
existing but pursuing goals, having careers of achievement
or frustration. The contrasting principles of Causality
and Destiny mark the different world-outlooks of science
and history. Only confusion results if we import either
one of them into our interpretation of the other. Scientific
explanation must rule out purposiveness, "design in
nature," as rigorously as historical interpretation must
exclude mechanism. Within science, teleology is the
"nonsense of nonsense"; but likewise "the materialistic
interpretation of history . . . kills all that is organic and
fateful."[13]

In rejecting causal mechanism as a category of historical
accounting Spengler does not reject determinism. The
connotation of his principle of Destiny scarcely inclines
toward free initiative or spontaneity; it has rather some
overtones of fatalism. The life of mankind is living nature;
it has its rootage, its budding and blossoming and fruition,

Pt. 1, pp. 14, 165; H. J. Schoeps, *Vorläufer Spenglers* (Leiden, 1955),
p. 97.
   [13] Compare Spengler, *The Decline of the West*, trans. C. F. Atkinson
(New York, 1929), 1: 120, 121.

and then its decline and decay. It has its seasons or cultural epochs, each of them evincing a distinctive character and career: a heroic springtime of creative urge, a summer high tide of dominance and achievement, an autumnal decline and withering of productive energies, and then a bleak wintertime of sterile practicality or futile dogmatism, with a freezing of the creative powers of man.

Spengler distinguishes strictly two terms which are often used synonymously: culture and civilization. By culture he understands the living character, texture and design of a certain epoch or field of history, manifested in all its aspects and activities—language, folklore, art, and tradition as well as social-institutional order. Cultures are the historical varieties of human living. So we may note the varying patterns of mankind: Egyptian, Arabian, Indian, Chinese, Classical, Western European. These principal currents of historical life may be explored in each of the characteristic fields of human activity, and a major part of Spengler's work is devoted to this exploration.

In the course of history Spengler distinguishes three patterns which he names Apollinian, Faustian, and Magian. The Appolinian soul, manifested in classical culture, "recognized as actual only that which was immediately present in time and place." The Faustian soul "strove through all sensuous barriers towards infinity." The Magian soul "felt all happening as an expression of mysterious powers that filled the world cavern with their spiritual substance."[14] We may trace in the history of our Christian world the contending interplay of Faustian and Magian motives.

Every culture in its historical course, like every living thing, sprouts and grows and matures and eventually reaches its *finis*, its goal and its end. The "inevitable destiny" of a culture is to become what Spengler calls a

[14] *The Decline of the West*, 1: 247.

civilization. "Civilizations are the most external and
artificial states of which a species of developed humanity
is capable, . . . a conclusion, the thing-become succeeding the things-becoming, death following life, rigidity
following expansion."[15] Irrevocably and repeatedly the
course of history has brought human societies by different
directions and turns to the end of their road. Our own
Western culture, according to Spengler, like those before
it, has come to its end in the civilization of the nineteenth
century. This, indeed, is "the decline of the West" in
our modern life, a life of metropolitan concentration,
materialistic rigidity, spiritual wilderness, impending confusion: a civilization of money not of men, of goods and
gold not of good, of having not of being: a senile dead end
of the road of personal creative upsurge.[16] A civilization
like ours, which no longer has a future, will before long
lack a real present: "In a few centuries from now there
will no longer be a Western culture, no more be German,
English, or French than there were Romans in the days
of Justinian. Not that the sequence of human generations
failed; it was the inner form of people . . . that was no
longer there."[17]

The contemporary collapse of so many foundations of
our civilization has discredited any suave optimism and
has stiffened the thinking of our age in a skeptical philosophy of history, of which Spengler's work is a dour
expression. But this swing of the pendulum of historical
valuation, from complacent assurance to barren distrust
or even cynicism, has not proved convincing to steadier
thinking. Unlike Condorcet, who even during the years
of the Terror in the French Revolution remained unshaken
in his conviction of the ever forward march of mankind,
we have been forced to recognize the false premises of

[15] Op. cit., 1: 31.
[16] Op. cit., 2: 485 f.
[17] Op. cit., 1: 167.

the lofty doctrine of straight line progress. "But does this admission compel us to accept the Doctrine of Doom?"[18] This question is raised and answered negatively in the most impressive interpretation of the entire course of civilization undertaken in our day, the treatise in ten volumes, A *Study of History,* by Arnold Toynbee.

Between bland optimism and skeptical dismissal, Toynbee's philosophy of history is marked by a spirit of heroic resilience, a rebound in adversity. He finds nothing in man's racial endowment or in historical environment that either guarantees his uninterrupted progress or condemns him to inevitable frustration and futility. Our every experience is an urge or a check; we rise by surmounting our barriers, but we also succumb. Dominion or disaster depends upon what confronts us and how we confront it. The course of history, in this perspective, is marked by a periodic series of challenges and responses.

Is this the proverbial wisdom that gold is tried by fire? We are reminded of a saying attributed by Herodotus to Cyrus, that "soft countries invariably breed soft men."[19] We recall the concluding words of Spinoza's *Ethics*: "All excellent things are as difficult as they are rare." But can we say, the harder the trial, the better the outcome? Hardly so, for while a challenge may be too weak or incidental to arouse an energetic forward reaction, it may also be overwhelming and beyond our competence and capacities to resist. The bright pages of progress in history have been marked by "the most stimulating challenge, . . . one of mean degree between an excess of severity and a deficiency of it."[20] This sort of golden mean in the historical life of mankind must also have a propulsive factor. "The real optimum challenge is . . . one which

[18] Arnold Toynbee, A *Study of History,* abridgment by D. C. Somervell (New York and London, 1957), 2: 311.

[19] Toynbee, A *Study of History,* unabridged edition (London, 1934), 2: 21.

[20] Toynbee-Somervell, A *Study of History* (1947), 1: 187.

not only stimulates the challenged party to achieve a single successful response but also stimulates him to acquire a momentum that carries him on a step farther: from achievement to a fresh struggle, from the solution of one problem to the presentation of another, from momentary rest to reiterated movement."[21] This is the progressive rhythm that marks the march of history.

This ascending pendular or spiral rhythm which can be traced in the course of history is evident also in the lives of "creative personalities when they are taking the mystic path which is their highest spiritual level, . . . passing first out of action into ecstasy and then out of ecstasy into action again . . . in a new capacity and with new powers."[22] While on the one hand Toynbee compares historical process and individual experience and is ever ready to turn from the broadest historical surveys to specific episodes or biographical comments, his main concern is with the larger pattern, for it is by appeal to the whole that he seeks to understand the parts. We cannot comprehend the history of any particular country or epoch by itself; we must see it in its all-historical context or pattern. *A Study of History* is a most erudite inventory of historical details of all lands and ages, but the decisive purpose of the inventory throughout is the hope of understanding the nature and the prospects of the human enterprise.

In interpreting the course of civilization Toynbee distinguishes and also undertakes to relate a singular and a plural use of the term: civilization and civilizations. Of civilizations he distinguishes over a score; some of them can be combined and others redistinguished. Most of them are now entirely or largely past history; they are either dead and gone or have become arrested. Only five survive as ongoing civilized societies: our modern

[21] Toynbee, *A Study of History* (1934), 3: 119.
[22] Ibid., p. 248.

Western civilization, Russia and Southeastern Europe, which Toynbee calls the Orthodox Christian society, the Islamic civilization, the Hindu, and the Far Eastern civilizations (Chinese and Japanese).

In studying the nature and growth of civilizations Toynbee also examines and diagnoses the breakdown of so many of them. Breakdowns are not all of one kind; some societies collapse into disintegration; others stiffen into petrifaction, fossilize. We cannot undertake here any review of Toynbee's varied, detailed, and richly erudite analysis of the external and internal conditions which lead to the disruption and dissolution of civilizations. Some of these conditions have been overstressed by other historians; some have not received due emphasis. Our attention is called to the dangerous failure of self-determination, but also to the "nemesis of creativity": in idolizing its great pioneers a civilization may become complacent and, worshiping its past, may find itself without a future. Militarism may prove suicidal; in surfeit of power and consequent outrageous behavior, a society may sweep itself into destruction. Civilizations decline and fall through loss of integrity, through schisms and inner disruption.

On the constructive side, the principal forms of institutional order are examined in their role in the ongoing life of civilizations. We may note especially the estimate of religion, a stubborn shell of superstitions and a drag on progress, but in its loftier function, a vision of a higher order of society. Toynbee's philosophy of history proceeds unmistakably toward a religious-spiritual conclusion, for religion has two ground notes, one tragic and the other a note of undying hope. Religion is ever *de profundis,* but from its dark depths it aspires toward the luminous heights of divine perfection. Despite doctrinal conflicts, the higher religions seem to point to the same City of God, the spiritual ideal of civilization. In the light of this ideal, the law of progress is proclaimed as the divine law; the world is seen as "a province of the Kingdom of God."[23] Here the skeptic may rejoin: you have shown so many civilizations, and their religions with them; they decay and disintegrate, pass away: what reasonable hope can you entertain for ours? Toynbee is not a docile optimist here, but he refuses any supine surrender of his reliance on our higher values. What really matters is that we recognize clearly the directions of the higher life for man and the conditions of our advancing toward it: "Progress in the improvement of our social heritage in terms of the spiritual life of mankind, . . . the one thing of manifest and abiding values in a world in which all other things are vanity."[24]

A very disturbing aspect of our age of crisis has been the unsettlement of intellectual assurance. We have exposed the unsoundness of earlier proposed solutions, but the critical problems still engross us and despite our incertitude require of us decisions. These decisions cannot be abstract logical conclusions. They must come out of a self-penetrating conviction of our total commitment. To meet the issues which confront us in an existential crisis, no rational doctrines or principles are of final avail; we can only yield ourselves in faith and consecration. This sort of resolution-in-uncertainty marked the *Pensées* of Blaise Pascal (1623-1662), and two centuries later it found expression in the writings of Søren Kierkegaard (1813-1855). Largely neglected in his day, Kierkegaard has gained prominence in our times of unsettled beliefs. A very significant aspect of his existential dialectic may be seen in the different directions in which his influence has proceeded in our time: to unyielding theological dogmatism on one side and to atheistic moral negation on the other.

23 Toynbee, *Civilization on Trial* (New York, 1948), p. 260.
24 Op. cit., pp. 262, 263.

According to Karl Jaspers, no scientific description or explanation of human nature can do full justice to the concrete immediate reality of ourselves. A self is truly recognized as a unique commitment to certain values. "As I value, so am I, and so shall I become."[25] My true self is in my ongoing career, in what I am to become and what I ought to be. This personal prospect is a task and an obligation, and it involves me in communion and participation with other selves. My self-realization is a social experience. I am immersed in a historical process, of which, as of myself, I am bound to ask the questions, whence, whither, and to what purport? These are questions about our origin, our goal, and our significance.

In his work *The Origin and Goal of History,* Jaspers explicitly proceeds on "an article of faith: that mankind has one single origin and one goal." Confessedly symbolical in his account, he contemplates the life of humanity as a growth in lucid consciousness, the consummation of which will lead men to mutual love and understanding as "members of a single realm of everlasting spirits." But, to repeat in his own words, "all these are symbols, not realities."[26] Reviewing the actual historical record, Jaspers finds that four times in the past mankind has taken a new start. From rude prehistory, men began with the devising and use of tools, the discovery of fire, and the attainment of language. Then they established the ancient civilizations. Then their spiritual potentialities unfolded. Finally, in our civilization, the mastery of science and technology has been achieved. This series of four periods does not represent a straight line of development but a succession of "leaps," a self-thrusting forward and upward to fuller self-realization.

If we try to explain the specific direction and reach of

---

[25] Karl Jaspers, *Philosophie,* 3d ed. (Berlin, 1956), 3: 84.
[26] Jaspers, *The Origin and Goal of History,* trans. Michael Bullock (New Haven, Conn., 1953), p. xv.

each leap, we may realize that the historical process does not admit of adequate abstract formulation. Thus, Jaspers asks, why did science and technology come to fruition in our Western civilization and not elsewhere? He is prepared to cite a number of predisposing conditions but can claim no scientific adequacy for his explanation. Nor does he regard the fourth historical stage, of our scientific and technological mastery, as a stage of unqualified progress. His basic principle should apply here: we are and we become as we value. Science and technology are neither good nor bad ultimately. They are only means; their worth depends upon what we make of them. Progress *of* science and technics does not necessarily signify mankind's progress *through* them. Nor are we assured of progressive historical stability or satisfactory humane existence. Repeatedly in the past "cultures were destroyed by barbarians." Our conclusion is not bound to be one of despair, but easy confidence is also ruled out. We can only put our hope in a growing unity of understanding. Even this hope is not enough. "For understanding only links understanding as a whole, not men. It brings no genuine communication and no solidarity."[27] As at one end Jaspers finds the scientific account of men abstract and inadequate, so at the other end his historical prospect is dubious and precarious. In the symbolic speech of faith he contemplates a sublime consummation, but in actual existence he sees imminent crises.

The belief in historical progress has been called the modern man's religion. Like other forms of religion, its hold on men's minds has been unsteady, and skeptical renunciation has been tinged with regret. But is the conviction of future social progress, as a justification for so much past and present evils, itself justifiable? In raising this question, the Russian philosopher Nicolas

[27] *The Origin and Goal of History*, pp. 252, 253; compare p. 125.

Berdyaev (1874-1948) undertook a radical criticism alike of philosophy of religion and philosophy of history.

Unlike the usual historians of the belief in social progress, who regard it as a modern alternative to Christian medieval doctrines, Berdyaev considers the idea of progress as Christian in its origin. He calls it "a secularized form of the Christian idea of movement towards the Kingdom of God as the basic theme of world history."[28] Divorced from its Christian faith in life eternal, that is, in its secularized form, the belief in progress is not only illusory but tragically unworthy. We are asked to believe that countless generations of men and women would have perished in irretrievable gloom, to prepare the way for some lucky people in some unspecified future age. "Somewhere on the peak of historical destiny, on the ruins of preceding generations, there shall appear the fortunate race of men reserved for the bliss and perfection of integral life."[29] What is lacking here is the Christian conviction of the unique and irreplaceable worth of the least of these our brethren. Without the vision of the Kingdom of God, the course of history loses significance and spiritual direction.

Messianism is thus essential to a meaningful philosophy of history, but it must be a messianic expectation that can be realized neither within history itself nor altogether outside of history. It must not be a change in this world but a change of this world, a living consummation of eternity over the events of time.[30] The drama of true progress is not the secular historical play of men's projects and achievements in specific periods of time. We need an eternal outlook and prospect in which past, present,

[28] Nicolas Berdyaev, *The Divine and the Human,* trans. R. M. French (London, 1949), p. 170.

[29] Berdyaev, *The Meaning of History,* trans. George Reavey (London, 1936), p. 189.

[30] *The Divine and the Human,* pp. 181 f.

and future are caught in one divine glance, in "the true
era of eternity." History as a mere factual series of events,
as a succession in time, is meaningless. "History has
positive significance only when it has a culmination."[31]
But this means that it is not endless, that it transcends
itself in its superhistorical goal and consummation. So in
the fullness of time, time itself is fulfilled in eternity.

The existential note has become definitely pronounced
in some directions of present day religious thought,
owing to the strong influence of the contemporary theologian Karl Barth. His conception of history is resolutely
providential. He recognizes a history of mankind only
when we consider human life as more than a mere process
in nature. The idea of history has a realized significance
only when we recognize that something transcendent en-
counters and enters human life. History consists just in
this divine providential activity, God-in-us.[32] Deep within and also beyond all our histories of secular outlook is
the one true history, the history of salvation: not a history
of men's progress or failure but of God's grace.

In Barth's judgment this emphasis on divine Providence,
on salvation and grace, is all-important and must direct
all our other valuations. He is not unresponsive to secular
needs or problems. He regarded unwavering resistance
to Hitler as a religious duty. His socialistic bias has been
interpreted by some of his critics as accounting for his
rather ambiguous reaction toward Communist totalitarianism. Basically Barth resists any social-reformatory conception of the Christian faith. The tendency to secularize
the Christ is regarded by him as hateful, a betrayal of
the Saviour.[33] The gospel of our Lord cannot be for him

[31] *The Meaning of History*, pp. 195, 204 f.
[32] Compare Karl Barth, *Kirchliche Dogmatik* (Zürich, 1948), vol. 3,
pt. 2, p. 189.
[33] Compare Barth, *The Word of God and the Word of Man*, trans.
Douglas Horton (London, 1928), p. 277.

a sort of "Christian Marshall Plan."[34] Ethics and social philosophy alike must be rethought in truly Christian terms. Christian ethics is not simply the ethics of a particular period or type of society in our Western tradition. Christian ethics is the very negation of common secular ethics. Morality, as Barth sees it, is in truth obedience to God, and this obedience is not man's work but the working of God's grace in man. For grace is not grace if it is in any way attainable by man himself.

In such an unyieldingly salvational view of human life, the idea of social progress loses meaning. Our plans and systems, successes and defeats are in and of their time. They do not advance us toward our true goal, for that goal is not really ours. It is God's goal for us, and it is not in any specific time and place of ours. It is "the summation of the history of *God* in history. . . . The synthesis we seek is in *God* alone, and in God alone can we find it."[35]

Existentialism had its earlier intense expressions in the intellectual quandaries of deeply religious spirits—Pascal and Kierkegaard. But the conviction of commitment despite incertitude has possessed also minds of decidedly irreligious attitude. Atheistic existentialism, in its bearings on the problem of social progress, may be studied in the works of Jean-Paul Sartre, contemporary philosopher, novelist, playwright. He has declared explicitly that existenialism expresses for him the full conclusions from thoroughgoing atheism. There is no God who made me and on whom I can rely; so I must start with myself alone. I am what I choose to make myself, in utter and unavoidable freedom. In this free choice and action is my being, but my freely chosen being is also the ground of nothingness, for my free choice, undetermined by anything else, might have been different. There is no real reason

---

[34] Barth, Niebuhr, Daniélou, *Gespräche nach Amsterdam* (Zürich, 1949), p. 13.
[35] Barth, *The Word of God and the Word of Man*, p. 322.

for my being what I am not or for my not being what I am. This final, inexplicable fact or act of existence—insipid but also anguishing and nauseating actuality—what meaning, what value and prospect of personal achievement and social progress does this view of reality afford?

Sartre avows genuine social regard; in the great national crisis he manifested it in action. Each man's responsibility for his free choice "concerns mankind as a whole."[36] What I choose to act and to be is my "commitment on behalf of all mankind. . . . In fashioning myself I fashion man." Sartre writes almost in Kantian terms of legislating for all mankind.[37] But he cannot proceed far that way, for there is no standard to which he would appeal. He recalls Kierkegaard's "anguish of Abraham," committed despite all reason to obey God's command. How could he know that it was really the command of God? How can I be really convinced about my right commitment? Wasn't that also Hamlet's perplexity after his encounter with the Ghost? Perhaps it was only the devil's lure.

Sartre has grasped firmly the truth of the unique quality in each person's values, but their other aspect, social and universal, eludes him. Where only the bare actuality of utterly free choice can be recognized, what judgment can there be of growth or decay of men and societies, of a historical career and a direction of progress? Sartre does not believe in progress, for progress involves amelioration, betterment; "but man is always the same, facing a situation which is always changing, and choice remains always a choice in the situation."[38] Surely, we say, a man should not act in bad faith. But why not, if that is the way he chooses to act? We may call him a coward or a stinker, but on what ultimate ground are we warranted in con-

---

[36] J. P. Sartre, *Existentialism and Humanism,* trans. Philip Mairet (London, ed. of 1952), p. 29.

[37] Op. cit., pp. 30 f.

[38] Op. cit., p. 50.

demning him? Actually Sartre sees little prospect that social life can be ordered on a reliably sound basis. There is in us a sense of fellowship; there is also a resentful or hateful sense of others being in our way. Sartre's play *No Exit (Huit Clos)* portrays a chamber in hell, the hell of one's being permanently locked up with others.

A radical approach to what have been called the discontents in civilization has been that of the psychoanalytic movement in contemporary thought, represented by its pioneer and leader, Sigmund Freud (1856-1939). His psychopathological inquiries led him to conclude that cases of hysteria were due to deep-lying emotional disturbances which had been repressed in the unconscious. His psychoanalytical method was aimed at rousing the patient to recall the submerged emotional data which, once brought up to the level of consciousness, would ease and cure the hysteria.

Freud's probing of the repressed emotional disturbances convinced him that they were mainly sexual in character, and this conviction directed his thought to far-flung speculations. Only some of them can be mentioned here. He advanced a theory of the so-called Oedipus complex in infantile sexuality, regarding the child as erotically attached to its parent of the opposite sex, with animosity toward its other parent. Furthermore, he saw human personality as in a tension between two instinctual counterimpulses, one of them aggressive and destructive, the other sexual, loving, and constructive. Man's life, according to Freud, is in a contention between the *id* of instinctual dynamics, only partly allayed in his *ego* by the daily course and relations of his experience and the guidance and judgment of its higher mentor, the *superego.*

The startling character of Freud's psychoanalytical theories, which aroused wide popular interest but also emphatic and even bitter professional resistance, was his preoccupation with the basically sexual dynamic in mental life, especially at subconscious levels, what he called "the sexual etiology of the neuroses."[39] The stimulating effect of his speculations on sexuality may be noted in their widespread influence on literary and social contemporary trends. In professional psychology and psychiatry the enduring power of his ideas has been questioned by his critics on both sides of the Atlantic. According to a report of a specialist in one of our large medical schools, the number of psychiatry students concentrating on Freudian psychoanalysis during the past fifteen years has dropped from almost one half to about 10 percent.

From this necessarily very brief statement of Freud's general theories we should turn to consider his contribution to our special inquiry regarding the relation of the course of civilization to human progress. He pointed out two aspects of civilization: "on the one hand all the knowledge and capacity that men have acquired in order to control the forces of nature and extract its wealth for the satisfaction of human needs, and, on the other hand, all the regulations necessary in order to adjust the relations of men to one another and especially the distribution of the available wealth."[40] We may recognize directly the inevitable counteractions in civilized life with which Freud is concerned. They are expressions in a social-historical perspective of the deep-lying tension between men's aggressive-destructive and their erotic-constructive drives. "Little as men are able to live in isolation, they . . . nevertheless feel as a heavy burden the sacrifices which civilization expects of them in order to make a communal life possible. Thus civilization has to be defended against the individual, and its regulations, institutions and commands are directed to that task."[41] The achievement of

[39] "The History of the Psychoanalytic Movement," in *The Basic Writings of Sigmund Freud,* trans. and ed. A. A. Brill (New York, 1938), p. 936.

[40] *The Standard Edition of the Complete Psychological Works of Sigmund Freud,* trans. and ed. James Strachey (London, 1961), 21: 6.

[41] Loc. cit.

civilization requires "coercion and renunciation of instinct."[42] Man needs civilized life for his fulfillment, yet
while it expands his range of activity it also cramps his
instinctual urges; man is thus hostile to that on which he
depends for his complete humanity.

According to Freud, man's chief purpose in life is the
attainment of happiness, but "its programme is at logger-
heads with the whole world."[43] The experience of pleasure
is "episodic" and unreliable. Far more commonly, distress
threatens us from many directions in the various human
relationships in which we are involved, yet self-isolation
is no cure, for so many of our satisfactions require social
cooperation. In a historical outlook we may note on the
one hand the extraordinary recent advance in science and
technology which has tightened man's control over nature
and unlocked its formerly unimaginable resources for
human use; but on the other hand we have to admit that
all this progress in externals has not made men's lives
really happier. Scientific and technical advances seem to
involve us in new evils or to aggravate older ones. Modern
medicine and sanitation have reduced greatly infant
mortality, and the resulting population explosion threatens
mankind with mass starvation.

Along with the greatly increased control of nature Freud
notes other gains due to civilization: a deeper sense of or
for beauty, personal cleanliness, a more settled order in
daily affairs; above these he calls attention to a growing
"esteem and encouragement of man's higher mental activities"[44] and, furthermore, a more reliable social organization which largely replaces the earlier unregulated
individual demands by communal restriction of willful
indulgence. In this last respect man has lost many of his
early freedoms but has gained more reliable assurance
of others. Yet while the assurance of greater security is

[42] Op. cit., p. 7.
[43] Ibid., p. 76.
[44] Ibid., pp. 93, 94.

enjoyed, men chafe under the cramping and the impediments of civilization, and the conflict is in some areas irreconcilable. Freud's preoccupation with sexuality gives him here an interesting turn of argument. Women, whose need of protection for themselves and their children "laid the foundations of civilization by the claims of their love" in their concern for "the interests of the family and of sexual life," find their mates and providers compelled by the complexities of civilized existence to find their active lives away from home. "Woman finds herself forced into the background by the claims of civilization, and she adopts a hostile attitude towards it."[45]

Freud shows great reluctance about expressing an opinion upon the value of human civilization: whether "the whole effort is not worth the trouble." As he states candidly, "my impartiality is made all the easier to me by my knowing very little about all these things." But he centers his attention on the basic problem. "The fateful question for the human species seems to me to be whether and to what extent their cultural development will succeed in mastering the disturbance of their communal life by the human instinct of aggression and self-destruction. . . . Men have gained control over the forces of nature to such an extent that with their help they would have no difficulty in exterminating one another to the last man. They know this, and hence comes a large part of their current unrest, their unhappiness and their mood of anxiety."[46] This concluding passage of Freud's work *Civilization and Its Discontents* was written some fifteen years before the bombing of Hiroshima.

In closing our review of the idea of progress in Western thought from classical antiquity to our times, we may note the approach to the problem by two contemporary

45 Ibid., pp. 103, 104.
46 Ibid., p. 145.

thinkers who combine grasp of modern scientific ideas and historical scholarship with spiritual-religious insight.

In his work *God and the Common Life*, Robert L. Calhoun has pursued a path of theological reflection which would avoid both easy assurance and drear skepticism. He finds in the rough "unfinishedness" of nature at every stage, and likewise in our human ongoing career, evidence of an ever emerging progressive trend—a revelation of an infinitely higher, divine guidance.

A major part of Calhoun's discussion of the limits but also of the prospects of religious faith is concerned with the interpretation of man's work at its different levels and grades of significance. Martin Luther taught that the husbandman at his plow and the housewife with her looms or kitchen pots could serve God as truly as the priest at his altar. So Calhoun explores the problem of the moral-spiritual significance and achievement of men's work. He resists both the smug secularism which would trace the progressive attainment of the better and higher life through men's own insight and effort and activity, and on the opposite side the theological "nullification of everyday human concerns" as altogether unavailing, and of our daily work as of no intrinsic importance for moral-spiritual advance. Against optimists and pessimists and skeptics, Calhoun's "religious realism undertakes to criticize and endeavors to change the actual, in the conviction that it ought to be and, in principle, can become better than at any specifiable moment it is."[47] Productive work, evidence of progressive activity, may be recognized in various perspectives. It reforms situations so as to make them more satisfactory not only in supplying elementary needs but also in perfecting patterns and designs, in more enlightened workmanship, in opening vaster and higher outlooks. Labor involves cooperation; in the common life

[47] Robert L. Calhoun, *God and the Common Life* (Hamden, Conn., ed. of 1954), p. 75; compare p. 49.

men may gain mutual understanding of minds. But all the way through, in all men's work, there is no final accomplishment. Their aims are self-projecting, their conclusions raise further problems. Calhoun's reflections on this ever unfinished character of activities leads him to wide-ranging inquiries in the physical and the biological sciences, which incline him toward the theory of emergent evolution. Repeatedly he is led to his view of an unfinished universe. There is here a kinship with Aristotle's doctrine that every actuality discloses a potentiality of a higher realization.

In this expanding cosmic prospect man may be considered as a product of the world process but also as critic, creator, and worshiper. His felt present inadequacy may distress him, but it may stir him to a deep awareness of the reality of a greater good revealed in the ever higher prospect beyond all particular attainments. Himself always active, how could he regard the ideal perfection as static? The words in the Gospel should ring true to his spirit: "My Father is working still, and I am working" (John 5:17). Calhoun's cosmic and human-historical reflections thus proceed toward religious conviction: "The world is not yet fully made nor wholly good; and now at least, however it may have been in the unimaginable beginning, other factors than God are at work in it too. But God is primary, central, and sovereign in them all."[48]

John Baillie's historical review of the various doctrines of progress serves to fortify his guiding conviction that, far from being explicitly secular, the idea of progress is religious and more definitely Christian in its source and motivation. He quotes Gilbert Murray's declaration that progress is "a truth that lies somewhere near the roots of our religion," and also Dean Inge's conclusion that "no other religion before Christianity ever erected hope into a moral value."[49] So, Baillie maintains, progressivism

---

[48] Calhoun, op. cit., p. 179; compare pp. 241 f.

grows in Christian soil. "If any man is in Christ, he is a new creation; the old has passed away, behold the new has come" (2 Cor. 5:17). But one may persist in asking, is progress certain and inevitable, by nature or by divine dispensation, or is it fully assured "only *if* the race takes reasonable advantage of the opportunities at its command?" Here firm or wavering conviction would both have a religious motivation. Even when it may be considered to be false, the doctrine of progress would be "a Christian heresy."[50] On this basic ground of interpretation Baillie proceeds to further critical inquiry. There is no strictly naturalistic assurance of progress. With regard to the argument from evolution, he is not impressed by the optimistic note in the well-known penultimate paragraph in Darwin's *Origin of Species* and inclines rather to T. H. Huxley's resistance to a morally commendatory view of the evolutionary process. While he would not dismiss men's own efforts and achievements as entirely pointless, he regards them as finally unavailing. Moreover, Baillie agrees with Berdyaev in seeing a disturbing or a morally callous view in the secular reliance on future social progress: in the "willingness to sacrifice the earlier to the later generations." "We can take final comfort neither from a history that is never consummated nor from any consummation that earthly history itself could conceivably contain."[51] Sound conviction of progress requires an advance from a secular-earthly to an eternal-heavenly outlook. And it is the Christian faith that offers us "a very confident hope for the future course of terrestrial history." This hope can only be in "the progressive embodiment in the life of humanity of the mind that was in Christ."[52]

---

[49] John Baillie, *The Belief in Progress* (New York, 1951), pp. 210, 39, 71.

[50] Baillie, op. cit., pp. 89, 95.

[51] Ibid., pp. 183, 184.

[52] Ibid., pp. 220, 235.

CHAPTER SEVEN

Utopian Visions of
the Perfect Society

IN APPRAISING OUR COURSE of action, our judgment as to whether we are advancing or lagging or going astray would depend upon our view of the goal, where we are aiming to arrive. Actuality is evaluated in the perspective of ideals. So our belief or disbelief in social progress may be tested by considering men's visions of the ideal society. In the history of thought these visions have sometimes expressed optimistically the consummation or fulfillment of men's positive achievements; but more often they have been seen as in tragic contrast to the sorry actualities of human lives. Sir Thomas More's term *utopia* had this double connotation of "the blessed land" or "no land."

The authors of the principal utopias expressed their different visions of the perfect society according to their choice of the ideal values. In this respect they may be studied in their revealing character; they bespeak the various achievements or satisfactions which have dominated men's minds and hearts during certain eras in the course of history.

Our study in this field has required a gradual and then a severe restriction of choice. More than one hundred utopian works line the shelves of our libraries—and most of them have been written during the last hundred years. From this mass of blueprints for the land of the heart's desire a small number stand out as expressions of men's social ideals during principal epochs in the history of civilization; classical antiquity, medieval-Christian culture, the Renaissance, the expanding modern world, and our own times.

The Renaissance gave us the term *utopia,* but the word is of Greek derivation; classical Greek likewise is the first and in many respects the greatest of all utopias, the *Republic* of Plato (427-347). Plato's ideal state was intended to express a social realization of the basic principle of his philosophy, which may be stated as aristocratic rationalism. Plato was convinced that the source, the test, and the ideal of knowledge and of perfection should be sought in our rational activity. The reliance on the data of sense perception was in his judgment misleading, for the senses give us only shifting impressions of phenomena, appearances not realities. The real world is not a random togetherness of greens and blues, hots and colds, wets and dries; it is a cosmos of what Plato called Ideas, that is, a system of forms, laws, principles, types of structures and relations, and these are disclosed only to rational inquiry and analysis. We may take an example from geometry. The theorem which we are proving is not valid of the triangle which we have drawn on the blackboard, for no one has ever drawn or could draw a triangle or a straight line. The triangle of the Pythagorean theorem is an Idea of rational definition, and of this Idea alone is the conclusion valid. So likewise in other fields of knowledge. All of us experience the particulars of sense perception, but we proceed to knowledge and can attain it only as we rise to rational contemplation of the Ideas of the cosmic order.

Plato viewed the rational world of Ideas as a hierarchy. The various types of Ideas manifest the structure of nature at different levels of realization. The highest of all Ideas in the hierarchy of nature, according to Plato, is the Idea of Good, or as we may translate it, the Principle of Value or Dominant Perfection. The most important knowledge that we can attain is insight into relative worth. For Plato the most decisive question about anything is this: "Is it for the best?" Thus regarding value judgments as the highest expressions of reason—in logic, in aesthetics, in ethics, in social philosophy—Plato sometimes gave his Idea of Good a religious version, to signify God or the Principle of Divine Perfection.

Plato's rationalism was aristocratic in its outlook on nature. It was aristocratic also in its practical directive, and that is centrally important for our purpose. The perfection of life, its wisdom and fulfillment, demand our recognition of the relative worth and rank of human capacities and activities and the achieved dominance of the highest and best of them. In Plato's philosophy, psychology, ethics, and social-political theory sustained each other. His analysis of human nature showed its tripartite character. We are creatures of appetites and desires. We are driven to action by a dynamic power in us, will-energy or "mettle." But we also have a rational faculty of insight and judgment. If we let our sensual nature have its way uncontrolled, our desires and appetites would lead us to corrupt and ruinous excesses. The impulsive drive to action, if not wisely directed, may sweep us away to disaster. We must acknowledge the rightful rule of our highest faculty, reason, which alone can guide us according to principles of wisdom and justice. It can allow our appetites and desires their temperate satisfaction, but by proper control avoid their evil indulgence. It can direct our will-energy in the right course to the right kind and degree of activity, without impetuous abandon. In every situation we can give each side of our nature its due expression, and in this practical expression of all-round "justice" we can realize the virtues of our harmonious fulfillment or self-satisfaction.

This principle of aristocracy, or rule of the best principle, which is central in Plato's rationalism, is decisive in his social philosophy. It dominates his Idea of the perfect state. We can understand Plato's *Republc* better if we keep in mind the intended contrast between the heavenly pattern of his utopia and the various actually existent forms of government. Their defectiveness or degenerate corruption is due to the usurpation of authority by the lower faculties of human nature. In each case Plato portrays a type of individual or social degradation, low in itself and dragging the soul to still lower levels. Thus timocracy is a rule by generals and strong men; it exalts honor, martial drive, and renown as the highest values of human life. But renown and valor are apt to seek material evidence in external possessions; the strong men tend to become men of substance and property. This is the political course toward oligarchy, a state where men are rated by what they have rather than by what they are. This oligarchy, rule by wealthy men, however, is precarious, for the rich are indeed the *oligoi*, the few. The many, poor but not powerless, may well seize their chance to overthrow and dispossess their masters and establish the rule of the masses, the *demos*, democracy as Plato used the term in a derogatory sense. This is the state without any standards of higher or lower, in which the prevailing numbers are dominant. It is most unreliable, for where principles are lacking, any demagogue who can catch the ear of the populace may lead the multitude to do his bidding. Thus the state sinks to its lowest level, tyranny.

The variety of Greek city-states provided examples of all these three stages of political corruption, and it is against this exposure of actualities that we should consider Plato's portrayal of the ideal society. It was to be a realization of his principle of aristocracy, the rule of the highest principle of human nature, reason. In it a class of artisans—farmers, mechanics, tradesmen—are engaged in the production and distribution of material goods. We may call them the provisioners of society. Plato recognized their service to the state in making available men's needed food, clothing, shelter, and the other commodities required in the social economy. But while the class of artisans have a great variety of accumulated skills, astuteness in amassing goods, and always a keen eye for profit, they lack insight or right judgment of relative values; they have no vision of men's highest reach and destiny. By no means should political dominance or the direction of state policy be entrusted to them.

The state that should be well provided with material goods by its artisans must also be assured of security from domestic riot or foreign aggression. It needs a second class, warriors or soldiers. This class, the strong arm of the state, must be the embodiment of disciplined valor. While it must be ever ready to carry out the orders of the government in any public emergency, it must never assume or usurp the authority of ordering state policy. It must execute public decisions, not make them. The commands that proceed from generals to lieutenants to the troops must conform to the initially decisive principles of those in supreme authority. The state needs defensive and aggressive power but it must be power directed by rational statesmanship.

It is clear, therefore, that the highest and in fact the prime need of the state is reliable rational direction. Plato's ideal republic must have a class of guardians or judges, rationally enlightened men and agents of enlightenment. They should be men marked by preeminent intelligence and sound judgment, whose native endowment has been perfected by long training and tested through a progressively more responsible and important public service.

The effectiveness of rational statesmanship requires the assurance of its continued stability. Without any menace of upset or revolution, it must maintain its rational course, generation after generation. In order to safeguard this stable and continued dominance in the state, his principle of aristocracy, Plato was ready for radical measures and proposed a plan of life for his ruling guardian class which has aroused severe criticism. His guardians and states-men, despite their rational power, were liable to have their human limitations and frailties. The state should therefore remove from them any temptation of private gain, and it must protect itself against any misjudgment of theirs due to private family favoritism. If they are to exercise chief authority in the state, their entire mind and heart must be devoted to the public good. So Plato proposed economic and family communism for his guardian class. Those who control the entire course of the social economy should have no property of their own. And the children that are to be born to them must not be known as their own sons or daughters. They should be brought up in public nurseries and educated as children of the state.

The process of public education of the youth of the guardian class is regarded by Plato as a condition and guarantee of the stable rational aristocracy. The school program itself is definitely aristocratic. By a schedule of progressive training of the higher and still higher faculties of the mind, Plato seeks to discover superior rational power, to elicit and perfect it, and to give it effectual expression in reflection and in action and eventually in public service. The entire training must aim to lift the soul ever upward. The pupils begin with gymnastics and music; this early instruction in harmony of body and soul is to prepare them for the higher harmonies and principles of intelligence. The intellectual education is to proceed from arithmetic to geometry and astronomy, and thus upward toward dialectic, the science of ultimate truth, insight into first principles.

The students who show rational excellence in these

studies are assigned to various civil and military service. Those who demonstrate preeminence in their offices are then chosen to succeed their guardian teachers and masters. Like them they are to give the state rational direction and to educate the youth of their own generation of the republic. Their closing years are to be devoted to consultation when they are needed and to philosophical contemplation.

Plato portrays his ideal state as a heavenly pattern of perfection and also as a crucial standard by which all forms of government are to be judged. Without the effective supremacy of reason there can be no hope of reliable social order and welfare. "Until philosophers are kings, or the kings and princes of this world have the spirit and power of philosophy, and political greatness and wisdom meet in one, and those commoner natures who pursue either to the exclusion of the other are compelled to stand aside, cities will never have rest from their evils—no, nor the human race, as I believe—and then only will this our State have a possibility of life and behold the light of day."[1]

Plato's *Republic* was a philosopher's utopia. His decisive concern was to attain and preserve his aristocratic principle of the dominance of rational intelligence in individual lives and in the social order. This imperative concern led him to neglect the importance of avoiding maldistribution of emphasis. His proposed communism of the guardian class has been condemned as in effect denying to his best and most mature citizens the full range of personal experience and activity. Plato's utopia has been criticized as advocating a stratified hierarchy of classes and values. In our day fascists have denounced Plato's communistic policies, while communists have branded him as the first philosopher of a fascist ideology.

As in the social-political aspects of his perfect state,

[1] Plato *Republic* 5. 473, trans. Jowett (Oxford, 1892).

so likewise in his aesthetic outlook, in his treatment of art, of music and poetry, Plato has been judged as constricting unduly the life of the creative imagination. He was himself a supreme artist of philosophical utterance, and he grasped the great power of the arts. But that great power which could ennoble man's spirit could also corrupt him, if misdirected to low sensual ends. So Plato proposed strict censorship of all the arts to assure their conformity to ideal truth, to the demands and standards of rational intelligence.

In the critique of Plato's treatment of the arts, we should keep in mind the supreme rational values which he was resolved to preserve, and we should not overlook the actual artistic corruptions which he was denouncing. In his severe criticism Plato would expurgate the polluted strains not only in the arts of his day but even in the greatest masters. The old epics misrepresented the ideal realities. Homer "told lies about the gods." Can there be anything more disastrous than to have false and unworthy views of the highest realities? Corrupt art and superstitious religion must both be reformed, if our lives and our social order and institutions are to realize harmoniously their highest aims and capacities.

The transition of Western civilization from the medieval to the modern period was marked by a radical shift in world outlook and in social philosophy of life. Men became keenly aware of themselves and of their daily experience, of their needs and opportunities and prospects. The revolt against ecclesiastical authoritarianism during the Renaissance expressed itself initially in a classical revival. But the Humanists did not remain content with Platonic wisdom and Ciceronian Latinity. Their zeal for Greek and Roman antiquity inspired them to face their own problems with classical freedom of inquiry, self-reliant and forward-looking.

The release of men's minds from the rule of ecclesiastical authority, which marked the Renaissance and which expressed itself in the classical revival and in the secularism and naturalism of scientific inquiry, led to a spirit of untrammeled worldliness and to a demand for entirely unhampered freedom of thought and action. This was the age of the great unloosing, and its visions of the perfect society may be read in the uproarious book of François Rabelais (1495-1553), *Gargantua and Pantagruel.* Its enormous popularity—sixty editions before 1600—was no doubt largely due to its earthy obscenity and its inexhaustible comedy, but also to what it derided and what it championed. Against stodgy, pedantic, and sanctimonious conformity of any sort, Rabelais glorified the utter release of all inhibitions and traditional scruples, the unconstrained and unshackled élan of men's thought and passion and will.

Rabelais's utopian Abbey of Thélème expressed his spirit of jolly freedom in its motto, "Do what thou wilt, *Fay ce que vouldras.*"[2] It was to be without walls. Free to enter and free to leave, men and women could join it and abide at their pleasure together, without any vows of chastity, poverty, and obedience. Youth was the only condition of admission, and fine looks and a joyous spirit the terms of preference. Gargantua planned for his Thelemites an abbey of delight. Its close to ten thousand chambers were designed for ease and comfort. The apparel, the diet, the daily round of activities of these fine young men and women were to bespeak not their withdrawal from worldliness but their thorough and expert enjoyment of life. No stern rules were to govern their conduct; rather they were to have a spirit of complete relaxation. Rabelais was convinced that such a program of utter freedom would evoke the full expression

---

[2] Rabelais, *Gargantua and Pantagruel,* Book 1, chapt. 57, trans. Thomas urquhart (London, ed. of 1901).

of men's and women's energies and talents and eventually would bring out the best in them. "Men that are free, well-born, well-bred, and conversant in honest companies, have naturally an instinct and spur that prompt them unto virtuous action."[3]

Against Rabelais's worldly blast at priestly and monkish repression, we should note the tragic utopian admonition of the monastic reformer Girolamo Savonarola (1452-1498), who tried to establish a Christian theocracy in Florence. His pulpit eloquence had gained him the devotion of the populace, and he resolved to use his influence in rebuilding the city of the Medicis on a gospel plan, a government of Christ. The immediate results of this citywide conversion were astounding. Moneylenders returned their usurious profits to their victims; gamblers and idlers earned their bread in honest labor; highborn ladies discarded their fine apparel and jewelry and served the Lord in plain dress and frugal living; luxury and penury disappeared together, and the destitute sick were fed and nursed in public hospitals; lewd books and pictures were thrown to the flames; austere living and penitent worship replaced the former drunken and profligate revels of the Florentines. While Savonarola was thus translating his Christian visions into daily practice, he also defied and denounced the worldliness and corruption of the ecclesiastical hierarchy and of Pope Alexander VI.

The theocratic utopia of contrite piety proved too stern for Florentine practice. A reaction set in, and it grew in force and violence. The populace itself whom Savonarola had nursed like a good Samaritan turned against him and abandoned him to his enemies. The prior-reformer of San Marco was burned at the stake, and the Florentines returned to their erstwhile ways of life.

The Protestant Reformation expressed in its own de-

[3] Ibid.

velopment the immediate self-concern of men. The radical stand against the papal hierarchy sought to bring the layman's soul directly to God's throne, without the intermediation of priest or bishop. In this more intimately personal Christian communion of faith, as the traditional gulf between clergy and laity was spanned, the godly life no longer found its perfection in monastic withdrawal but affected all men whatever in their daily activities: not only the monk in his cell or the priest at the altar, but also the farmer at his plough and the housewife in her kitchen. The reformation, in its advocacy of a more directly personal and weekday religion, was undertaking to infuse spirituality into the modern secularism. But the secular spirit was seeking also its own individual and social outlets. Within the church, or outside of it, though not always in conflict with it, men were drafting their programs of social reform. Three outstanding examples of these early versions of the perfect society claim our attention.

The earliest of these three, Sir Thomas More's *Utopia* (1516), was the work of a famous humanist who was also a devout Catholic. His resistance to the Anglican revolt against the pope led by Henry VIII ended in his martyrdom. In our century Rome has canonized him. The complex interplay of motives in the personality of More— a friend and colleague of Erasmus, a devotee of ascetic austerities, a severe critic of the existing social systems, an eminent lawyer, a statesman of heroic integrity—this versatile mental activity was itself an expression of the crosscurrents which marked the Renaissance.

While it may be debated whether More intended his *Utopia* explicitly as a program of radical social reform or merely as an idealistic and ironical speculation on a Platonist pattern, the work itself was an exposure of rampant evils and a portrayal of a proposed blessed society. Perhaps More drew his ideal chart first and then surveyed in disdain the actual conditions in Europe and more particularly in England. In his published work the exposure comes before the revelation. Inequity and corruption blight the lives of people, and the laws and courts that should have protected men in their natural rights seem rather to flout them and to work injustice. The ruling powers protect the rich in their affluence and scorn the poor in their struggle to earn a pittance. Soldiers returning from the fields of battle find no fields of peace in which they can make an honest livelihood and so they turn to beggary or robbery. The death penalty for theft does not deter desperate men from stealing but only tempts them to avoid detection by murdering their victims. The laws tread hard on the delinquent poor instead of giving them a chance of gaining their subsistence. Amidst all this misery of common folk, opulence and luxury, gambling and garish profligacy stain the lives of the lords of earth, both laymen and clergy. Baron and bishop revel together with tyrannous royalty, despising a beggarly people.

This wretched and iniquitous state of society can never be ended so long as its fundamental cause remains, namely, the institution of private property, which incites men's oppressive greed and defeats social justice. So More's *Utopia* is premised on his first principle of economic communism. Where there is no longer any chance of private gain, citizens will tend to concern themselves with the general welfare, and society will become a true commonwealth. In a state of public cooperation, where money, the handling of it, usury, and theft would be of no further avail, the energies of all people would be engaged fairly in the common work of society, without grinding labor and without idleness. More's blessed island of Utopia prospers on a six-hour working day. Add eight hours for sleep, and all men still have ten hours of the twenty-four for relaxation and culture. Public entertainments as well as public education are recognized functions of the state. The schools impart manual training as well as intellectual discipline; the cultivation of the arts is aimed at perfecting the general taste rather than at mere popular amusement. Economy and convenience are secured by public refectories, and dinners become also social gatherings. While thus easing the daily drudgery of household work, the utopian state is directly concerned with safeguarding homelife by strict regulation of marriages to prevent contamination of the race or unsuitable matches. Socialized medicine, preventive and curative, protects the health of young and old.

For the political order of his ideal society More advocated a government of elective monarchy. The people are to exercize control by choosing their king and by reserving the right to depose him if he abuses his authority; but while each city governs itself, there is no direct popular rule in the state. In its relation to other governments Utopia, having no thought of aggression or conquest, always prefers negotiation to the use of force; yet it keeps itself ready for untoward hostilities. The devotion of the citizens to their country is a strong bulwark, but the Utopians prefer to engage mercenaries to fight their battles rather than to spill the blood of their own young men. Even the hiring of assassins is not excluded from their strategy.

The economic and social equality of the citizens of Utopia would not be compatible with requiring any of them to do the scavenger's or other similarly low and menial labor, which nevertheless must be included in the order of the day. For these services More demanded a class of slaves, and he would make his demand serve two purposes by enacting enslavement as the penalty for crimes. In cases of adultery, for instance, the innocent party may remarry, but not the guilty one, who is condemned to slave labor.

In view of More's own strict religious devotion, his treatment of faith and worship is significant. Utopia practices religious tolerance, for without the imposition of conformity men would have a better chance of reaching true belief and worship. The Utopians frown on bigots and on zealots. In religion as in all secular pursuits, men's lives on the blessed island are to be guided by fair-minded concern for the general welfare and happiness.

Tommaso Campanella (1568-1639), like Bernardino Telesio and Giordano Bruno, was an Italian of the South. He studied under Telesio and, like Bruno, entered the Dominican order and early showed resistance to established authority, theological and social. A stalwart champion of freedom, he aroused the hostility of the Spanish despots in Naples. His chosen motto was "*Nunquam tacebo,* I will never keep silent," and he paid for his radical speech by some thirty years in jail. The beginning lines of one of his sonnets describes his life: "To fight three mighty evils I was born:/Tyranny, sophistry, hypocrisy." Only during the closing years of his life, when as a refugee from Spanish rule he gained the protection of Richelieu in Paris, did Campanella enjoy freedom and recognition.

In his defense of the new methods of research, in physiology and more especially in the astronomy of his great contemporary Galileo, whom he championed in a treatise, Campanella took his stand in looking to modern science as the guide to progress. Even more important in his view was the need of complete reconstruction of existing social institutions. His utopian program was presented in the work by which he is best known, *The City of the Sun.*

Campanella's ideal society shares main features with Plato's and More's and is more radical than either of these. Like Plato he would enthrone reason and calls his chief ruler Metaphysicus. This metaphysical monarch governs through three deputies, whose names indicate Campanella's principal hopes for a just and progressive society: Power, Wisdom, and Love. In the portrayal of his ideal government, he is not satisfied with generalities but punctuates his demanded reforms in detail. First and foremost for him, as for More, is the outlawing of private property not only for the ruling guardian class, as in Plato's *Republic*, but for all without exception. But unlike More, Campanella would not have a class of slaves in his state. Every man and woman in his solar city does his work whatever it be, without partiality or prejudice, and by avoiding any superfluous production of luxuries and by encouraging perfection of skills the working day is reduced to four hours. Thus energetic but not overworked, in frugal living with simple natural diet, young and old grow in health and strength. Their way of life prevents most ailments, and proper care checks any exceptional disease.

Plato had advocated family communism for his guardian class chiefly in order to prevent the succession of worthy rulers by their unworthy sons through parental favoritism. More's own patriarchal household exemplified his high regard for the social dignity of homelife in the perfection of human values. But monastic Campanella regarded the family institution as cramping and unsocial. His citizens "deny . . . that it is natural to man to recognize his offspring and to educate them, and to use his wife and house and children as his own."[4]

We should expect from our Dominican a more significant religious view than that presented in his book. The Solarian worship includes an elaborate system of confessions of sins and absolutions, volunteered but never executed human sacrifices, for "God does not require death." We read of perpetual prayers and supplications, psalmody, and dancing rituals. The articles of the Solarian

[4] *Ideal Commonwealths*, by Henry Morley (New York, 1901), p. 156.

creed include belief in God "under the image of the Sun," and "beyond question" the immortality of the soul. Campanella's speculations are a strange blend of scientific alertness with astrological muddle, and they affect his religious visions.[5]

Campanella is quite expert and even amusingly detailed in his utopian imagination: in the variety of improvements and new appliances produced by inventive genius and by the more general training in science and technology. He describes the skillful tactics of his Solarians in waging war and their practical efficiency in all their daily occupations: farming, clothing, public eating places, schools. Men plough and sow, harvest and thresh and press their vintage; women milk the cows and make cheese, spin and weave, barber and sew, and fiddle and pipe at the public concerts, but not blow the horn or beat the drum. Both sexes wear the same garments, but men's togas reach above the knees, and women's, below. The borders of their undergarments are fastened with globular buttons and caught up here and there with chains. The common public dining rooms are like monastic refectories. Men and women sit at the same tables but on opposite sides, and there must be no noisy talk during meals; instead, they all listen to a young man reading a book from a high platform, "intoning distinctly and sonorously."[6] All this was duly envisioned by the Renaissance radical monk in his prison cell.

These sundry details are parts of Campanella's utopia, but they should not divert our attention from his main reform purpose. He would design a new social order in which men's minds would be freed from the fetters of bigotry, in which economic exploitation and oppression of the common people would be abolished, and men and women would enjoy together the fruits of universal labor

[5] Op. cit., pp. 175, 178, 179.
[6] Ibid., p. 154.

in healthy, vigorous, and simple livelihood. He does not recognize the personal values of intimate homelife which were evident to More; neither of them considers the alternative of a social reform that would correct the abuses of economic exploitation and inequity while preserving the worth of productive initiative and material satisfaction in private ownership and operation.

Francis Bacon (1561-1626) outlined a complete reorganization of intellectual productive activity to understand the laws of nature, utilize its resources for man's advantage, and achieve a new and expansive civilization. He called his vast encyclopedic project "The Great Instauration," under six heads; it included mainly four undertakings. First, he exposed the stagnation of knowledge through the long medieval centuries, as due to the use of dogmatic syllogistic reasoning about nature instead of direct examination of its structure and processes. We must recognize the main misleading preconceptions—as he called them, the Idols of the Mind—which obstruct scientific advance: common prejudices, individual biases, confused use of words impeding scientific communication, and varieties of professional and traditional dogmatism. We should rid ourselves of these as completely as possible; we should come to nature with a clean slate, ready to learn, not to debate. The outline of a new method of investigation, inductive logic, was Bacon's second main proposal. After extensive observation, without any initial commitment and speculation, the inquiring mind which has noted certain repeated events and forms of behavior in nature should probe more carefully to discover some one factor that accounts for the behavior. It then observes or experiments to see if the absence of that factor eliminates the behavior, or if the variation of that factor increases or decreases the phenomenon. This sort of observation or experimental inquiry Bacon proposed to apply throughout nature. A third grand project, requiring a large staff of scientific workers, was to yield some 130 "histories" of as many fields of nature. On the basis of this immense variety of investigations he could foresee the progressive achievement of a scientific philosophy of nature, the fourth and crowning achievement of his intellectual reform of civilization.

All the way through, Bacon combined in his encyclopedic prospect pure and applied science. Mastery of nature requires understanding of nature's laws, but this understanding and mastery is most rewarding in its practical results. Knowledge is power. More important and more fruitful than any question of government must be the organized promotion of scientific research. In this conviction Bacon portrayed his ideal society, the *New Atlantis*. The preeminent department of this utopia, the "Salomon's House," was praised by Bacon as "the noblest foundation . . . that ever was upon the earth, and the lanthorn of this kingdom." We can recognize in it a vastly expanded form of our research institutes and foundations. Its purpose is stated concisely, but the implementation of it is extensively ramified. "The End of our Foundation is the knowledge of Causes, and secret motions of things; and the enlarging of the bounds of Human Empire, to the effecting of all things possible."[7]

The program of state-supported researches indicates the vast range of Bacon's utopian prospect. Even a brief summary will suggest its boundless scope. New Atlantis has extensive and deep excavations, even to six hundred fathoms, in which men study "all coagulations, indurations, refrigerations and conservations of bodies"; it builds towers up to half a mile in height set upon mountains, likewise used for "insulation, refrigeration, conservation," but also for weather observation and reports of winds, rain, snow, hail, and fiery meteors. There are artificial wells and lakes, both fresh and salt, used for fisheries, mineral springs and baths "tincted upon vitriol, sulphur, steel,

---

[7] *Philosophical Works of Francis Bacon*, ed. J. M. Robertson (London, 1905), pp. 721, 727.

lead, brass, nitre, and other minerals," where various medicinal researches are pursued. In botanical gardens and biological laboratories, plant and animal breeders seek to produce new and better stocks. Large chemical plants are devoted to the discovery of new metals and the production of better alloys and also to the compounding of drugs for the cure of sundry diseases. Machine shops of all sorts, furnaces of great diversity, some of them producing heats in imitation of the sun, laboratories of research in the varieties of light, institutes of tool and instrument manufacture of great precision and delicacy: there seems to be no end to the ramification of the projects of Salomon's House. All this work is organized on a statewide plan; the workers in the various fields of investigation report to the central office; experts edit their materials, appraise their likely practical applications, propose further inquiries. Traveling fellows inspect any promising lines of research pursued in other lands, for testing and use in the New Atlantis.[8]

Bacon's work was left unfinished; but fragmentary as it is, it expresses his spirit as the champion of scientific investigation that was to achieve a new civilization through mastery and use of the resources of nature. Bacon was a promoter of science rather than a productive scientist. He was deficient in his appreciation of the scientific works of his contemporaries; he failed to do justice to Harvey or to Galileo. Nevertheless his spur to organized research may be traced in his influence on the establishment of the Royal Society of London, the Paris Academy of Sciences, and similar institutions in Berlin, Bologna, and elsewhere.

Utopian plans of the perfect society have expressed the self-outreaching spirit of confidence in periods of intellectual and social revival and advance and also the resolute

[8] Op. cit., pp. 727 ff.

persistence of men in times of revolution and unsettlement. So during the Renaissance the awakening of European minds to the vast prospects of humanism and naturalism stirred the men whom we have been considering to much vaster outlooks of social realization. They expressed the pioneering zeal of early modern thinkers in various directions of progress: intellectual, political, economic, religious. Alongside of the liberals and radicals, there were also conservative visionaries who would refashion the new social order in conformity with old patterns to which they were accustomed.

The early modern age was itself providing instances of new worlds and new ways of life overseas. On American shores, the Pilgrim Fathers aimed to establish God's kingdom on earth: "Know this is the place where the Lord will create a new Heaven, and a new Earth in new Churches, and a new Commonwealth together."[9] The European utopians looked westward across the Atlantic: the narrator in More's *Utopia* was a voyager with Amerigo Vespucci; Bacon's New Atlantis was a remote island "beyond the Old World and the New": Campanella's City of the Sun, in Taprobana, was also vaguely and distantly overseas.

While Europe was embroiled in political and religious conflicts—the Thirty Years War in Germany, the struggle between king and Parliament in England, the civil war in Holland, the exploitation and oppression of the common people by the centralized monarchical regime in France— the American colonists were building new ways of life and before long were to plan for still fuller initiative and complete independence. The release of the European mind during the Enlightenment, especially in France, stirred the demand for political and social-economic emancipation. The *philosophes* of the *Encyclopédie* were

---

[9] From Capt. Edward Johnson's *History of New England, or Wonderworking Providence of Sion's Saviour* (1654), quoted here from H. W. Schneider's work, *The Puritan Mind* (New York, 1930), p. 8.

doing more spreading abroad the new knowledge. They have been rightly named "the fathers of the Revolution." The achievement of American independence, in which French sympathy and assistance played a role, had its prompt repercussions in France: the Fourth of July was followed by the Fourteenth.

These two revolutions, beyond their actual results, stirred men's dreams of more extensive realization of human life as it should be lived. The post-revolutionary age, in Britain as well as in France and America, bred many utopias, some of them only plans on paper, others actually tried out. The increased tempo of contemporary life and its continual transformations inside and out, with boundless prospects but also dire threats challenging men's minds, have aroused both heralds of incredible progress and prophets of doom. More than any other period of history, our atomic age is an age of utopia indeed, but in its double meaning of incertitude: "the blessed place" and "no place at all."

The great multitude of contemporary utopias precludes any detailed review. Even a brief catalog description of them could scarcely be attempted. If a widely sampling reader's judgment may be trusted, the neglect of many of them would matter little. But it is of interest to consider some characteristic purposes and ideals which have found expression in these utopian writings, for they serve to accentuate the values and also the problems which engross contemporary social thought.

The principal modern utopian projects of reform, as might be expected, concern the main social institutions. First and most extensively considered is the economic and political reconstitution of society. Many modern utopias manifest a communistic trend, which we noted already in More and in Campanella. The root of social evil is exposed as the maldistribution of property. Some utopias have followed the proposal of James Harrington in *Oceana*

(1656) in urging the "agrarian balance" in land ownership and general equalization of property. But other utopians have denounced the institution of private property as inherently evil and have traced the high road to human betterment in various forms of communistic economy. On the eve of the French Revolution Rousseau stigmatized as the founder of corrupt society (or author of inequality) the man who first enclosed a piece of ground to call it his own and found people deluded enough to believe him. During the Revolution Babeuf urged the abolition of all ranks and inequalities, the complete social and economic leveling of all citizens. Étienne Cabet, in his *Voyage to Icarie* (1840), would put all persons and all types of work on a par, scientists and scavengers.. Everyone was to do his share of the work in the social economy and receive from the state warehouses whatever he needed, on the same terms with everyone else. Across the Channel, Robert Owen (1771-1858), both by his proposals and by his actual trials of them in Scotland and in America, inspired a series of utopian ventures. He was a pioneer in the modern cooperative movement, but beyond this elimination of middleman profits, he would abolish all exploitation by organizing small social colonies on a basis of community of labor and of its fruits, without the evils or the miseries of inequality.

The emancipation of men from economic servitude, which was the basic purpose of the utopian abolition of inequality, promised still further realization of freedom. The motto of Rabelais's Abbey of Thélème, "Do as you will!" was shared by many modern visions of the ideal society. An outstanding protagonist of the release of men in all directions, very contagious in its day, was Charles Fourier (1772-1837). The first article of his creed seems to have been Rabelaisian: the root of all evil in human life is repression. Break the institutional shackles which hamper the free release of men's ideas and energies and

passions alike. Replace social control by free social communion in all respects; replace exploitation or competition
by free cooperation, and men will find their fulfillment.
To realize this ideal, Fourier proposed the establishment
of small *phalanges,* communities of some 1,600 or 1,800
persons who would live together in unrestrained spontaneity, like butterflies, *papillons,* enjoying continuity or
else change in their programs of life as they might prefer:
different work, different mates, without any restriction.
Fourier was prepared to practice what he preached, without any concessions to traditional scruples or inhibitions.
Pending the establishment of his Eden of free work, free
play, free love, his societies of propaganda tried it out
as far as they could, within or without the law, and in
some of their excesses matched in practice the license
which sullies some of Fourier's pages.

Despite the mixture of the maudlin and the prurient
in Fourier's gospel of unrestraint, his influence may be
traced in the establishment and in the understandably
brief histories of several utopian communities. The most
noteworthy of them on American shores, Brook Farm,
was not started as a Fourierist *phalange* but as a settlement of Christian cooperation, led by the liberal clergy-
man George Ripley. The advocacy of Fourier's ideas by
Albert Brisbane affected Brook Farm vitally but also
aroused the opposition of some of its best members—
Hawthorne, Charles Dana, Bronson Alcott—and sorely
disturbed its founder who had firm trust in common honest
work without exploitation and in Christian brotherly love
and who cherished pure family loyalty and loathed
license. In the end Brook Farm collapsed, although Hawthorne, its most distinguished member, declared that it
had "struck on what ought to be a truth."[10] The wisest
man of the Brook Farm days, Emerson, visited the pro-

---

[10] Compare Katherine Burton, *Paradise Planters: The Story of Brook Farm* (London and New York, 1939), title page.

jected ideal society but would not join it. He could not visualize true emancipation by the simple course of moving to another community. Freedom must be won in one's own inner life. "I wish to break all prisons. I have not yet conquered my own house."[11] Mrs. Browning agreed with Emerson:

> . . . Ah. your Fouriers failed
> Because not poets enough to understand
> That life develops from within.[12]

The dissolution of monogamous family life, which was the most radical and objectionable article in Fourier's creed of human liberation, has been advocated by other utopians, though by none more flagrantly than by him. There has been widespread criticism of the rigid enforcement of the bond, especially in Roman Catholic lands, without the relief of divorce, even in cases of family chaos intolerable to the parents and ruinous to the morale of children. In more extreme opposition, family communism has been advocated as a replacement of the tight home unit, with its stiff bourgeois conformity to customary ideas and institutions, by a looser cohesion that would allow the freer and unbound attachment of individuals in new and better social relations.

Closely related to utopian criticism of traditional home-life have been various eugenic projects for the improvement of the human race. Plato first of all advocated selective mating in the guardian class of his Republic to assure the bearing of the best and most gifted children. With a similar purpose Sir Thomas More insisted on the most thorough physical examination of all who planned to marry. Campanella put all family unions under the strict control of state officials. Modern utopias have shown

---

[11] Emerson, *Journals* (Boston and New York, Oct. 17, 1840).
[12] Cited from Harry Emerson Fosdick, *Christianity and Progress* (New York and Chicago, 1922), p. 90.

similar concern for the successful breeding of an improved human race by eugenic regulations. It may be noted that some of these utopian projects have urged not release and free range of individual inclination, but on the contrary stringent control in the interest of future generations and the destiny of the race.

The utopian provisions for the upbringing of children concern the problem of public education. A number of modern utopias have followed Plato's proposal to remove children from the liable hazard of prejudicial influences of their own parents by bringing them together under the care and guidance of mentors selected by the state. By sharing a similar well-chosen bodily and mental diet, pupils can show fairly their aptitudes or special capacities. They will thus be given the right opportunities not only to follow their characteristic bent but also to serve society to the best advantage. By the right course of training of its youth, men can avoid the two vices of idleness and drudgery. Utopians have been assured that, in an educational system thoroughly organized for social service, science and technology will flourish and resources of nature will be used to the increasing advantage and prosperity of the state. Actually modern technical advance has repeatedly outstripped the dreams of Bacon or the modern utopians. In 1892 Ignatius Donnelly prophesied the day when aerial vessels would fly between New York and London in thirty-six hours. The fundamental ideal of a society directed by expert technicians has been proposed in our time as a definite plan for immediate social reform.

It is not easy to draw a sharp borderline between the utopian visions of the perfect society and what have been called the "pseudo-utopias," that is, definite plans of specific social reconstruction fortified by severe exposures of existing injustice and corruption. Along this indefinite margin may be noted two modern schemes of the better life, the "Freeland" of the Austrian economist Theodor Hertzka and the American Edward Bellamy's *Looking Backward*.

Hertzka brought to his proposed reconstruction of society the reputation of mastery in his science of economics. The title of his main work, *Freeland: A Social Anticipation* (1890), was meant to express his conviction that he was drawing the picture of an actually realizable future. He proceeded to direct promotion of his project. About one thousand societies were formed for the establishment of the new colony. Suitable land was made available for the settlers in British East Africa, near Mount Kenya, but difficulties complicated the initial start and finally the plan had to be abandoned.

"Freeland" shared with Brook Farm the same optimistic conviction that men and women will readily undertake the hard work of collaboration in building a new social order. The African jungle and the equatorial humid heat were not the only obstacles to the persistent strenuous labor of the Freelanders. The ideal "basis of perfect liberty and economic justice," recognizing "no exclusive right to property" but securing to each worker "the full and uncurtailed enjoyment of the fruits of his labor" was announced on the first page, but the realization of it in the sequel was another matter. Hertzka appealed candidly to the normal self-interest of his prospective citizens, but he could not be assured of their loyal cooperation when the finances of his proclaimed "Eden Vale" became straitened and men could no longer see their own way to any likely advantage.

Bellamy's *Looking Backward: 2000-1887* was published only two years before Hertzka's *Freeland*. As indicated on its title page, its purported viewpoint forecast a century of social progress. As Bellamy reports the future Boston of the year 2000, the American social order will have been reformed inside and out. Perhaps this feature of immediately realizable social transformation accounts for the great popularity of the work.

The chief feature of the new life, in Bellamy's utopia, is a system of universal labor, operating without exception, but in each case in a field freely chosen by the individual. Bellamy's America of the year 2000 may be described as a land of industrial militarism. By abolishing all private industry or business of whatever sort, all private buying and selling, the utopian state has become the universal and the only employer of all labor and supplier of any goods. Service to the state, then, has become an inevitable condition of survival. Boys and girls receive their preparation for life and enjoy their youth until they reach the age of twenty-one; men and women past the age of forty-five are "honorably mustered out" to retirement and leisure. During the intermediate twenty-four active years each person must choose freely his own line of work. To insure the doing of the less congenial and even disagreeable labor in the social economy, the government officials reduce the hours of labor in it to attract the needed volunteers. Bellamy is prepared for extreme measures in this matter. "If any particular occupation is in itself so arduous or so oppressive that, in order to induce volunteers, the day's work in it had to be reduced to ten minutes, it would be done. If even then, no man was willing to do it, it would remain undone."[13]

In Bellamy's Boston of the year 2000 money has been removed from circulation; the state's payment for all work is in the form of labor credit cards, which each person may use to procure whatever goods he needs or desires from the government supply stores. The state provides not only agricultural and industrial products but also books, works of art, entertainment, music. Bellamy's

[13] Edward Bellamy, *Looking Backward: 2000-1887* (Boston and New York, ed. of 1889), p. 68.

cultural anticipations include many appliances and services which we already have: broadcast musical programs and other forms of mass cultivation or diversion. The detailed planning of this social economy and the effective operation of the system of universal labor require a highly trained body of public officials, and Bellamy has elaborate plans to serve these ends. His work inspired a number of more-or-less similar schemes, but it also evoked much criticism of his sublime confidence in the social panacea of universal labor army discipline.

An outstanding characteristic of our twentieth century has been the contrast between its incredible advance in scientific-technical mastery and its lagging moral development, especially in international and interracial relations. We have already swept far beyond the fondest utopian dreams of the past in probing and exploiting the forces and resources of nature, but so much of our social life is still barbarian in thought and action. We have split the atoms but cannot unite men to live together in justice and peace. Catalogs of twentieth-century utopias list over three score titles; some of them are diagnoses of present corruption rather than visions of future perfection. The appalling waste of humanity in two world wars, the dismal eruption of excesses and atrocities among the presumably advanced and cultured nations, the spread of ideologies promoted by men disdainful of the most elementary human rights and expert in most vicious propaganda: all these have shaken people's confidence in the soundness of our civilization and men's hopes of any likely restoration and advance toward social sanity.

Our age has produced even "utopias in reverse," exposures of further alarming spread of social cancers that threaten the very life of civilization, and not at some remote time but at a menacingly near date. Against Bellamy's *Looking Backward: 2000-1887*, we may read George Orwell's *Nineteen Eighty-Four*, published in 1949, some of whose forecasts sound like present-day journalistic reporting. Even those optimists of our day, who portray tomorrow's marvels of atoms-for-peace, are aghast at the threats of the book and wonder if we shall have any civilized tomorrow, or any tomorrow, to record. It is not a perverse pessimistic choice but the looming darkness of our age which forces this utopian chapter to end on a dismal note. Nevertheless our choice is still open, between catastrophic downfall and the upward advance toward incredibly greater fulfillment of personal and social values. We shall try to explore the various crossroads of history on which this basic choice of destiny has confronted men in the past, and which still confronts them.

PART TWO

Social Confidence
and the Despair of Progress:
Alternative Judgments of Civilization

CHAPTER EIGHT

The Evolution of the Family and the Emancipation of Women

IN THIS SECTION of our work we return to the consideration in our introductory chapter of the agelong controversy between optimism and pessimism in their contrasting accounts of the human enterprise. Each of these counter-appraisals is impressive in its own way, with considerable historical evidence to support it, but neither one is really convincing in final judgment. An alternative view, proposed in our introductory chapter as a more adequate interpretation of the historical process, has for its basis the idea that the history of civilization is marked by an increasing range of human capacities *for good or for evil*. The historical process cannot be described truly as an upward curve of progress or by a downward curve of degradation, nor yet by a random line of meaningless activity. The entire scale of values is spread on an ever widening range. The course of civilization shows how much higher men can rise—or how much lower they might sink. Both fulfillment and frustration depend upon their right or wrong choice between contending values.

The following chapters undertake to test this proposed interpretation of civilization and progress by an exploration of the various fields of social activity both in the past and in the immediate situation of our own days of crisis. The present century illustrates most strikingly our basic principle. Atomic science and its technical applications have made available for us hitherto unimaginably vast resources of nature, the wise peaceful use of which can enable us to achieve unprecedented cultural perfection. But these atomic energies are also engines of destruction, and we are on the verge of blowing our whole civilization to extinction.

Our proposed view of the problem of progress in the history of civilization may be tested most directly and intimately by examining the evolution of the family. No other institution concerns individuals so vitally for good or for ill; no other touches so closely the relation of basic human groups, men and women, children and adults; no other bond of union affects so thoroughly the social texture of more and more humane living. It is not a matter of accident that family kinships have provided the symbols or ideals of right order and spiritual perfection. The example of religion may suffice, with its apotheosis of family bonds: Father Dyaus or Zeus and Mother Earth, *Magna Deum Mater*, Our Father in Heaven, the brotherhood of man. If our proposed interpretation of the relation of civilization and progress is right, the evolution of the family should yield evidence of historical advance in the realization of high values but also of corrupting strains on expanding fields of social complexity. The related problem of the emancipation of women is of imperative importance; it concerns half of the human race.

Fair inquiry here has been helped by the extensive modern studies of the history of marriage and family institutions at all levels of social development throughout the world. The available knowledge of the facts should warn us to avoid offhand generalities about primitive universal promiscuity.[1] We can also understand better the motivation of many cruel or even unspeakable savage practices.[2] At the other end of the historical scale, we

---

[1] Darwin, *The Descent of Man* (New York, ed. of 1897), pp. 590 f.; compare Edw. Westermarck, *The Future of Marriage in Western Civilization* (New York, 1937), p. 16.

[2] L. T. Hobhouse, *Morals in Evolution* (New York, 1915 ed.), pp. 340 f.

should recognize the high attainment and the still higher prospects of modern monogamy, but also the confusions in which it has become embroiled by the very complex social order which has made its attainment possible. So our inquiry should seek a reasonable course between romantic idealizing and unwarranted scorn of primitive societies, and likewise between complacent domestic modernism and woeful dirges on the decay of Western family life.

The basic role which marriage and family life played in the structure of tribal societies had economic involvements. Tribal marriage was more than sexual mating. Through its expected offspring it was a source of power for labor and for war. It bound together families and clans, but it also aroused contests for priority and possession. One settlement of this issue was in the so-called group marriage, which should not be confused with promiscuity. In this form of family life all the men of a certain family group are recognized as husbands of all the women in another family group, often with converse relation, in what thus becomes a marital alliance of two clans. Less elaborate variations of this form of family sometimes indicate economic motivation. The eldest brother in a family may gain a bride by purchase or service or stratagem or with the help of his brothers. He is then her chief or principal husband, but his brothers are also admitted to her as auxiliary mates and are thus provided with a wife that they could not otherwise obtain or afford.

The marital aspects in the relations of clans and tribes determine the individual's range of choice, which is definitely limited for the groom and scarcely or not at all available for the bride. Inquiries into these marital-tribal relations disclose deep-lying horror of incest which find expression in religious beliefs. Two types of primitive marriage have been distinguished, marrying-in and marry-

ing-out, endogamy and exogamy. In endogamy the prevailing motive is that of tribal cohesion. Families form
new kinship bonds but always within the tribe, to
strengthen the tribal solidarity. Marrying an alien is not
allowed. Within the tribe there are kinships of con-
sanguinity which may not be violated by intermarriage.
Even endogamous tribes loathe incest.

The revulsion to incest has been interpreted variously.
The doctrine of Freudian psychology, of filial-parental
hostility owing to a son's incestuous love for his mother
and of a daughter for her father, has met strong opposition
from some sociologists who have collected their mass of
evidence from all races and ages. Edward Westermarck
considered filial-parental frictions, but saw "no evidence
whatever to attribute them to sexual jealousy." In our
day Pitirim Sorokin sharply dismisses this and other related Freudian theories as "pseudoscientific fantastic nonsense."[3] Some investigators have regarded the horror of
incest as an intense expression of normal emotional reactions. We are told that familiarity breeds contempt; at
any rate we may add that familiarity leads to indifference.
Brothers and sisters or other close kin in the family circle
who have played and fought together since earliest childhood are not so likely to arouse each other when they
reach adolescence. They take each other for granted.

We should note in earlier societies the definite restriction of individual initiative and final choice in marriage
unions. This restriction exercises effective control on the
young men, but it generally involves the utter subjection
of women. A tribesman's daughter is his to dispose of as
he wills. A woman is not a person; she is the property of
her father or, after him, of her eldest brother. She may
love some youth and elope with him, or despite her resistance she may be acquired by rape or capture. In

---

[3] Westermarck, op. cit., p. 97; Pitirim Sorokin, *The Reconstruction of Humanity* (Boston, 1948), p. 147; compare p. 146.

either case her menfolks, resenting the violation of their property rights, would demand compensation. If in more regular and tribally decent manner she is obtained by purchase or by the young man's service to his bride's family, the transfer is a transfer of possession. Petruchio's boast in Shakespeare's *Taming of the Shrew* will be recalled:

> I will be master of what is mine own.
> She is my goods, my chattels; she is my house,
> My household stuff, my field, my barn,
> My horse, my ox, my ass, my anything:
> And here she stands, touch her whoever dare.

These dark chapters of history recording the subjection of women are not relieved by the institution of the so-called mother-right family. There is clearly a distinction between "mother-right" and "father-right." It is not the same as the distinction between a matriarchal and a patriarchal social order. In a father-right family system, the bridegroom took his bride to his hut in his tribe, and the children that were born to them belonged to his tribe. In a mother-right society, the bride remained with her tribe, and her husband through the years had access to her, but their children belonged to her tribe. Mother-right, however, did not signify the right or freedom of the women. In both types of society woman was subjected to male control: in father-right families she was ruled by her husband and his menfolk; in mother-right families, she was subject to her father's or her brother's rule.

The emancipation of women, which is a major part in the attainment of progress in family life, has been a slow process, and its long story is not quite told even in our day. Here also are some striking variations due either to changing social customs even in early societies, or else to the exceptional capacities of some women to win and to hold their ground by dint of charm or guile or by superior strength of character. In some societies the mother's practical direction of her household and her authority over her children and her hold on her husband have been so dominant as to justify the descriptive term *matriarchy*. More generally, however, the historical tendency has been toward a father-right family order and then toward a definitely patriarchal system. The mother-right family order lacked many elements of permanence. Man, generally master over women, demanded mastery in his own house. This demand could not be resisted effectively by the brothers of his mother-right wife, who like him sought mastery over their own wives. This growing ascendancy of husbands in family control had important consequences in affecting the structure and the relative permanence of the family.

We have been considering so far some features of a primitive monogamy which is fairly general but often so crude as scarcely to warrant the name. It was vague and unreliable just because it lacked the essential respect for the personal dignity in the marriage relation. For where a woman was her husband's acquired property and the producer of still more property through her children, it was natural that men of means should proceed to polygamy or concubinage. The chief, the lord of the manor, could afford a number of women to glut his passion or expand his family of servitors.

The term *polygamy* is used here in its common meaning, but it is not quite accurate and needs revision. In opposition to monogamy, polygamy signifies a family system in which a person has more than one spouse. But that person may be a man or a woman, so clearly two types of polygamy have been distinguished, with a plurality of wives or a plurality of husbands. Sociologists speak of a family where one husband has several wives as polygyny, and of a family where one wife has several husbands as polyandry.

Polyandry is not common. It is due to the paucity of women or to the extreme poverty of men, or to both conditions. Where girls are killed or sold in slavery, or where life is barely sustained, a man who managed to enter a marriage might admit others to share in its satisfactions and obligations; or several men might venture to live together with one wife. The plural husbands are apt to be brothers, and usually one of them has a preferred status as elder and chief, the others being auxiliary. Of this type of family it may be said, just as of the mother-right family, that it is not necessarily matriarchal. The one wife is still usually subjected to the will of her several husbands. But there are also forms of polyandry in which the one wife directs the common household, including the men.

While polyandry is found mainly among low primitive tribes, there are evidences of it among more evolved societies, among the Tibetans and some Arabs. In early India it stirred even epical imagination. An episode in the *Mahabharatta* tells of an incomparable celestial maiden who prays five times to the god Mahadeva to grant her a husband possessed of every accomplishment. Mahadeva promises her that in a future rebirth she would have a literal fulfillment of her fivefold plea. So as Draupadi she is finally married to the five valiant Pandava brothers, with their golden crowns and heavenly garlands.

The story of polygyny, or polygamy in its more common meaning, is much longer. It has ramified through many societies and periods of history, and it still persists as a recognized type of family life outside of Western civilization. Closely related to polygyny and often hard to distinguish from it is concubinage. The difference in rank of a plurality of recognized wives, where priority of marriage but also a husband's preference may set one wife as chief and superior to the others, becomes in concubinage a basic difference in status. The concubine is a mate but not a spouse; she may be the recipient of favors but does not have a claim to rights of estate or inheritance.

While there are no instances of recognized polygyny in our modern civilization, except the temporary Mormon aberration, and while bigamy is criminal under Western laws, European tradition does record plurality of wives or concubines on the royal or aristocratic level. The first instance is from the Iliad, beginning in its opening lines with the wrath of Achilles, whose beloved captive Briseis had been taken from him. The Germanic races provided divided evidence on polygyny. The common tribesmen were generally monogamous, but not the Gauls. The chiefs had several wives, and this practice continued even after their conversion to Christianity. The Meroving-ian kings indulged in it; Charlemagne had two wives and two concubines, the same number as the Irish king Diarmet. Charlemagne's example seems to have been followed by some of his clergy. Peter the Great (1672-1725) distributed among his boyars the women captives in his campaigns.[4]

Plurality of wives as a recognized institution is mainly Oriental. In biblical tradition Abraham and David may be mentioned, but the outstanding polygamous prac-titioner was, of course, Solomon, with his swarming harem. The social program of the *Koran* turned largely upon Mohammed's establishment of polygamy as a reform of the loose domestic disorder of Arabian life. Plurality of wives could be maintained only among the mighty and wealthy. Modern evidence indicates that in Iran and Pakistan scarcely more than 2 percent of the families are polygamous. Similar accounts of traditional Chinese polygamy and concubinage likewise seem to limit them to the ruling and rich classes. In general survey harems have been luxuries of those who could afford them.

[4] Compare Westermarck, op. cit., pp. 172 f.

A flagrant feature of early marriage and family relations has been the general disregard for personal freedom and dignity. This disregard, on primitive levels, subjects both husband and wife to tribal restrictions. One's mate is not chosen but assigned; the initiative belongs to the family elders who themselves follow tribal customs of exogamy or endogamy or whatever group tradition may dictate. But even more settled and seemingly hopeless is the subjection of woman. In whatever way she may be obtained by her future lord, there is no recognition of her personal rights. These distressing conditions are not limited to primitive and barbarian societies. The emancipation of women is a story of very slow development. Prior to the Reformation English marriage customs included shocking practices. We read of the case of Elizabeth Paston who, "when she hesitated to marry a battered and ugly widower of fifty, was for nearly three months on end beaten once in the week or twice, sometimes twice in one day, and her head broken in two or three places."[5]

He who acquired a wife acquired property of which he might dispose as he wished. He could order her labor and enjoy the fruits of it. Even if he did not multiply wives or concubines, he could be as profligate as his fancy or his funds might carry him, but adultery on her part was a crime of which he was judge and executioner alike. He might return her to her family or even kill her and her lover *in flagrante delicto*. Should she prove childless, her husband, as an alternative to casting her away, might order her to bear him a child by another man. And should he die childless, both the Manu law in India and the Mosaic code required her to yield herself to his brother so as to provide an heir to her dead husband. In polygamous families the eldest son might inherit his dead father's entire harem except his own mother.

[5] G. M. Trevelyan, *English Social History* (London and New York, 1942), p. 65.

Whenever he willed a man could offer his wife's body to a guest. This grand gesture of hospitality is customary among African savages and elsewhere, but it is disturbing to find Greek and Roman examples of it. Plutarch related Cato's extended loan of his wife Marcia, pregnant, to his friend Hortensius, with the approval of her father. Socrates lent his not so dear wife Xanthippe to his young friend Alcibiades.[6] And we may come nearer home and remember that the plot of Thomas Hardy's novel *The Mayor of Casterbridge* turns upon the sale of an English wife.

The thralldom of wives did not entirely preclude attachment. Customs and individual temperaments vary, and even low primitive family life has always afforded instances of considerate regard in family relations. Eskimo natives on Baffin Island have been described as showing not only devotion and patient goodwill to their children but also conjugal love and loyalty. But most of the evidence points the other way throughout the world as far as the servitude of wives is concerned. The Chinese *Book of Songs, Shi-Ching,* is very frank on the subject: How do we proceed in taking a wife? . . ./Why do you still indulge her desires? We are told that on the day of her wedding a Chinese girl's father would order a palanquin, lock his daughter in it, and hand the key to her bridegroom. A woman's servitude was not limited to her immediate relatives by birth or marriage. Like other valuable property, she was under the strong hand of the liege. The king's or the lord's power over his subjects was especially strong in ordering or prohibiting the disposal of a maiden. At our weddings we hear the traditional formula: "Who gives this woman away?"—but it was no mere formula in earlier days. English peasants had to pay their lord a fine or a tax, *merchet*, for permission to

---

[6] Compare Plutarch's *Lives,* "Cato the Younger"; Letourneau, *Evolution of Marriage* (New York, 1891), pp. 53, 201 f.

marry. Louis XII of France compelled Alain d'Albret to have his daughter marry Cesare Borgia, to reward the latter for bringing him Pope Alexander VI's bull annuling the marriage of Louis to Jeanne of France, so that he could marry Anne of Britanny.[7]

The proprietary view of wives was manifest on every occasion. A woman was living property and the producer of more living possessions. An adulteress cheated her owner of his rights, but she might also add to his estate. He might kill her and her lover, but he might also accept compensation and eventually keep the bastard addition to his increasing labor force. In other ways also there was no recognition of woman's personal rights. A wife was not admitted as a witness or a claimant in court. She had no individual rights of grievance against her husband. A shiftless drunkard, whose children were supported by his abandoned wife's toil, could go to her employer and legally collect and drink up her wages. Not until the late nineteenth century was an Englishwoman protected in this regard, and in some parts of the United States the remedial legislation was even later.

In our day, though a woman may be admitted to employment, she still receives on the average lower compensation. These very days our news media report demonstrations in our cities by thousands of women who are protesting against this wide and increasing pay gap between women and men. Despite the spread of coeducation in our colleges and graduate and professional schools, we are told that "few women have been able to enter the professions. Only 1 percent of federal judges, appointed by the President of the U.S., are women. Only 1 percent of engineers, 3 percent of lawyers, 7 percent of physicians, and 9 percent of scientists are women. . . . Even in the teaching field . . . the gap seems to be widening."[8] In

[7] Compare Hobhouse, op. cit., pp. 194, 216.
[8] *U.S. News and World Report* (April 13, 1970), p. 36.

business or industry, available statistics indicate various obstacles to women's rise above subordinate employment and gross inequality in their compensation for comparable work. The present "women's rebellion" is a widely organized resistance to these various discriminations. On many fronts American women are banded against their present economic disadvantages.

The historical record of women's agelong servitude exposes the double standard in judging licit and illicit sexual relations. In Greece and Rome the adulteress faced rigorous conviction, but her husband's profligacies, even when flagrant and censured, were not regarded as crimes from which she had any right of redress. As late as 1930 the laws of Italy distinguished between a wife's *adulterio,* always criminal, and a husband's *concubinatio,* punishable only if notorious or if he brought his mistress into his family domicile. Likewise in Spain; in France the adulterous husband had to reckon only with a liable fine.[9] In British and American legislation we may note a slow but eventually plain recognition of wives as claimants to release from their adulterous husbands. Protestant influence has been on the woman's side, but its effect has been slow. Only in 1923 did English law finally acknowledge the equality of men and women in domestic suits.

The servitude of married women has been a major expression of the general derogation of the female sex. Folklore abounds in praises of wives who bear their husbands sons, not daughters. Ask a Turkish peasant how many children he has, and he is likely to answer: "Four, and two girls." This sharp partiality for male offspring is not altogether extinct even in our society, and its defenders are not slow to cite reasons. A family established in solid substance, in business or profession, cannot continue through daughters who depart when they get married.

---

[9] Compare Edw. Westermarck, *Evolution of Marriage in Western Civilization* (New York, 1937), pp. 62 f., 68.

Only sons can preserve and advance the family name. Is it owing to some regard for this condition that Spaniards retain in their names their maternal as well as their paternal lineage? In Czechoslovakia, when Thomas Masaryk married he adopted as a part of his own name that of his bride, Charlotte Garrigue.

Islamic tradition praises marriage and the abundance of offspring. Among the great prophets Jesus was exceptional in remaining single; but we are told on good Muslim authority that when he returns at the end of days he will marry and have children. Islam has few good words for women: "Most of them are in hell." Still there is a way upward even in servitude. Woman's one virtue is her submission. A good wife is one who, when her husband utters a foolish oath, fulfills it so as to defend his honor. A wife's submission, which is her status, becomes a virtue when it is loyal. In India this ideal of unwavering wifely devotion found expression in the heroine Sita of the epic *Ramayana*. Boccaccio used the same theme with variations in his *Decameron,* in the familiar story of patient Griselda. The laudation of wifely loyalty was bound to affect the whole estimate of womankind. When in Greek legend Alcestis laid down her life to save that of her lord, King Admetus of Thessaly, Hercules brought the heroine back from Hades. Undying loyalty evokes undying love. Without heroics Confucian canon stipulated that husbands should be devoted and wives affectionate. Mutual personal attachment becomes less and less exceptional, and it finds expression and portraiture in lyric and dramatic poetry.

The emancipation of women in history has been gradual, occasional, and not always permanent. The Roman matron of the imperial period, in contrast to her earlier subjection, gained explicit recognition of her rights in law and in fact: unprecedented and unmatched by later epochs until our own. She could not be married without her own consent. She could hold private property and dispose of it; she could be a plaintiff in court. She had become like her husband a legally acknowledged person. This great gain in freedom, however, became also a release of license. Women could freely go their own way, and they did, through the abuse of easy separation and through flagrant profligacy. Seneca referred ironically to women who kept track of past events not by referring to the consuls in power but to their own various husbands.[10]

In its estimate of womankind, the Christian tradition marked both a recession and an advance. The Gospels spiritualized the old commandments; the Sermon on the Mount is the classic of the most initimate personal religion. This worship of God in spirit and in truth, as it subordinated all externalities and all worldliness, condemned carnal indulgence. It did not exalt marriage but admitted it as a concession to man's frailty. It had an ascetic trend and naturally sought the higher perfections of the godly life in monastic withdrawal, with its threefold vow of chastity, poverty, and obedience. This view of life regarded woman as the unclean vessel of sex. Tertullian stigmatized all womankind: "You are the devil's gateway!" A sixth-century bishop even questioned whether women were really human.[11] The church condemned the surrender of the spirit to the flesh. In its judgment the great lovers of popular lore were polluted sinners.[12] But just because it branded lust as a mortal sin, the church held both men and women under heavy judgment. There was high promise in that stern verdict. If marriage was regarded only as a concession to human frailty, and carnal union justified only by childbearing, then that relation must be a sacrament for both man and

---

[10] Compare Hobhouse, op. cit., p. 211.

[11] Compare Westermarck, *The Origin and Development of the Moral Ideas* (London, 1906), 2: 663.

[12] Compare R. B. Perry, *Realms of Value* (Cambridge, Mass., 1954), p. 368.

women, both of them sinners in need of salvation and both of them children of God. The judgment that had condemned woman, the temptress of men, exalted the wife, the mother of men, even as it adored the Mother of the Savior of men. The spiritual emphasis of Christianity had a dual expression, first in monastic asceticism not only of men but also of women in nunneries; and then in moral elevation of family life, with gradual and very slow emancipation for women and respect for their moral worth in the sight of God.

When lust is stigmatized and sex admitted only as a medium of propagation, when the body is viewed as a temple of the Lord, bodily life itself, as a vehicle of the soul, may gain in dignity that must not be violated. Immemorial practices such as infanticide and abortion were rejected as heathen abominations. It should be noted that in savage societies infanticide was commonly due to the economic stringency of people ever on the verge of starvation, utterly unable to feed any more hungry mouths. The killing of the crippled and the aged was likewise often an emergency measure; they had to be abandoned by the wayside on the long nomadic marches so as not to endanger the survival of all. In the gradual advance beyond savage indigence, as the killing of infants and the abandonment or disposal of the infirm and the old could no longer be regarded as imperative, both practices were censured and then condemned as criminal. Christian condemnation of infanticide has been traditionally most severe. Legal codes in Western Europe have sustained popular judgment. While the dire penalties—burial alive or burning at the stake—have been discontinued, infanticide is still adjudged as murder.

Abortion and castration have been other ways in which distraught savages have tried to ward off the threat to their survival. By the use of dangerous drugs or by unspeakable mutilations they might risk health and life to thwart the results of passion which they could not control. Under civilized conditions of medical advance these two practices have been subjected to a twofold change. They have tended to yield to safer and more widely spread means of birth control, by the use of contraceptives. With the perfection of surgical treatment, abortion and vasectomy have generally become legalized procedures.

The problem of birth control cannot be settled by off-hand condemnation or advocacy. It confronts us as we study the statistical curves of population increases during the past century, especially in countries like India or China or Latin America. The very advances of modern civilization in checking or eliminating certain plagues, in sanitation or improved child care, which have reduced infant mortality and lengthened the span of human life, have been multiplying children beyond any available or prospective means of subsistence even in our modern greatly improved economy. Even in the days of the Roman Empire, when the world's population has been estimated to have doubled once in a thousand years, the church father Tertullian, in the third century, viewed the existing situation with alarm: "We find in the records of the Antiquities of Man that the human race has progressed with a gradual growth of population. . . . What most frequently meets our view is our teeming population; our numbers are burdensome to the world, which can hardly supply us from its natural elements; our wants grow more and more keen, and our complaints more bitter in all mouths, whilst nature fails in affording us her usual sustenance. In very deed, pestilence, and famine, and wars, and earthquakes have to be regarded as a remedy for nations, as a means of pruning the luxuriance of the human race."[13]

At the end of the eighteenth century Thomas R. Malthus

[13] Quoted in *Population in Perspective,* ed. Louise B. Young (New York, 1968), p. 3.

(1766-1834), in his *Essay on the Principles of Population*, pointed out that population growth runs ahead of the food supply and jeopardizes human welfare. As is well known, Malthusian researches suggested to Darwin his basic evolutionary principle of the survival of the fittest in the struggle for existence. The dire social implications of Malthus's *Essay* did not assume the priority in nineteenth-century thinking which they have today. William Godwin (1756-1836) tended to dismiss the problem: "Three fourths of the habitable globe are now uncultivated. The parts already cultivated are capable of immeasurable improvement. Myriads of centuries of still increasing population may pass away and the earth be still found sufficient for the subsistence of its inhabitants."[14] Godwin's myriads of centuries have already proved to be far short, and the view of the population explosion in our time is radically different.

This problem of exploding populations has thrust itself into the midst of any discussion of modern family life with a shock of frightful emergency that brooks no postponement or delay. In public concern it shares top priority with only two or three other problems in our social system, and in the judgment of many competent social critics it is more alarming than any other, for it confronts everyone; it menaces mankind with imminent famine and possible extinction. These dire forecasts have been supported with extensive detailed statistics, but their meaning can be made unmistakable by a bare terse statement of the awesome facts.

Charts of world population growths record a steady and then a more and more furious rate of increase. At the beginning of our Christian era mankind included some one hundred million souls, and it did not reach a total of six hundred million until 1700. But during the follow-

14 William Godwin, quoted by J. B. Bury, *The Idea of Progress* (New York, 1932), p. 228.

ing century and a half the world population doubled, and then more than doubled during the next hundred years, and now it numbers over three billion, an increase in a single century equal to that of all previous ascertainable time. Even more alarming, it threatens to double again during the next generation.[15]

Confronted with these staggering facts, expert students differ only in the degree of their forecasts of universal doom. Some of them seek hope of staving off famine and mass starvation by greatly increased agricultural production of food, or else by the comforting news that people, many people, do not really require so many calories. But other competent judges, and not at all in minority, with Paul Ehrlich in the vanguard, see no ground for any future but total disaster, unless the present rate of human fertility is altered drastically. There is no possibility of feeding the ever sweeping glut of hungry mouths. India, whose famine is today being partly allayed by American mass-shipments of food, promises a great rise in her production of crops, but how can that added supply nourish its inconceivable human crop which will tomorrow be hurdling over the half-billion mark?

Even beyond the inevitable threat of mass starvation, the population explosion statistics shock us with the dire forecast of the congestion of the hungry multitudes which the surface of the earth literally could not contain. A distinguished witness before a subcommittee of the United States Senate cited "a long-range projection by the National Academy of Sciences . . . that in about 650 years there will be one person per square foot throughout the United States."[16] This dire projection calls our attention to a dismal aspect of the population problem. In the not very distant future we are menaced with literal starved

[15] Compare Stanley Johnson, "All about Food" in *Vista,* the magazine of the United Nations (March-April 1970), p. 28.

[16] Compare *Population Crisis: United States Senate Subcommittee Hearings,* Washington, D.C. (January 26, 1966), Pt. 1, p. 156.

extinction; but in the immediate future we are drifting toward conditions of life which are less and less humanly tolerable. The disaster which confronts civilization is not only how many billions can literally survive on earth, but how many more can live a really human life.[17]

In more immediate projection and in less catastrophic terms, birth control, a problem of the gravest emergency in Asia and Latin America, is important also in our Western civilization of the North Atlantic regions. It is clear that as of this day we in the United States at least face no threat of starvation. Our productive capacity far exceeds our present demands and should meet any immediate needs as our population increases. In fact, our present problem has for some time been that of overproduction of food; it is a problem to our farmers which the government has tried to meet, and also America's opportunity to feed starving millions overseas. But even if our agricultural rate of production could be matched the world over, it still could not check the crisis of the ever inundating glut and plethora of hungry mouths. In 1965 thirty-five American scientists, all of them Nobel prize winners, sent a petition to Pope Paul VI, asking him to reconsider the Roman Catholic Church's ban on artificial birth control. And according to a Gallup poll that summer, 61 percent of American Catholics believed that their church would eventually approve some method of birth control; more than half of them expected such an approval within five years,[18] an expectation that has not been realized. There is a general and unmistakably growing demand for education in planned parenthood. Along with its provisions for birth control and with proper medical advice and direction, we require social reforms to provide better assurance of adequate hospital care to the indigent

[17] Compare Joseph Wood Krutch, "A Naturalist Looks at Overpopulation," in *Our Crowded Planet,* ed. Fairfield Osborn (Garden City, N.Y., 1962), pp. 211 ff.
[18] Compare *Population Crisis,* op. cit., Pt. 1, p. 18; Pt. 2, p. 456.

and protection of working mothers before and after childbirth.

There are other sides to the problem of population and planned parenthood. Fair judgment should recognize a spreading social evil in our so-called higher classes: well-to-do and educated men and women who have the means to bring up fine children to expand our cultured population but who, though by no means ascetic, spurn the cares and the responsibilities of parenthood. This resulting reduced self-repopulation of our cultured classes cannot be regarded as very recent or as due to the present loosening of traditional moral values and induced by the perfected and more readily available use of contraceptives. According to a sociologist's record of 1941, over 40 percent of American families were childless or had only one child.[19] Our civilization raises contrary population problems for opposite social groups; birth control calls for different judgments in dealing with different personal and group conditions. The good and the evil are not the same at the two sides of the scale, and the needed reforms must vary appropriately.

It is important to recognize that some of the most distressing conditions in modern family life are to be found among our "best people" and that they have been the result of the very advance in the emancipation of the modern woman. This emancipation which has made possible manifold fulfillment of personality in all the various relations of homelife has also released irresponsible self-indulgence and license. The basic probem is that of individualism, which may be morally productive but also unprincipled and corrupt.

The old traditional family was not an autonomous union of a man and his wife and their children. It was a link in the chain of tribal solidarity, tribally ordered and

---

[19] Compare Pitirim Sorokin, *The Crisis of Our Age* (New York, 1941), p. 188.

controlled. Within the range of group control a man acquired his wife, sometimes by capture but more commonly by purchase. On barbarian levels this plain business transaction still persists. There was also resitance to it, due to family pride and also to a gradually developing parental devotion. This growing sense of personal regard finds expression in customary sanctions and in legislation. The Manu code in India prohibited marriage by purchase, and the *Mahabharatta* condemned it sternly: "He who sells his daughter goes to hell."[20]

Early Greek tradition sanctioned marriage by purchase and, even after it was forbidden by Solon's laws it still persisted as late as the age of Demosthenes and Aristotle. Gradually, however, the purchase ceased to be a sale. A father would expect some solid evidence of the value which a suitor for his daughter set on her, but on receiving the proffered sum or goods he gave them to his daughter as a dower. The former purchase price became a part of the bride's estate. The father even added to it, as a gesture of ample provision to assure the girl's maintenance of her accustomed way of living in her new home. This available ample provision for one's daughter made her more desirable and more likely to win a fine husband. So by a reversal of economic considerations the purchase price which bought a good wife was replaced by the dower which attracted a good husband.

It is interesting to note in this evolution of marriage customs a growing regard for the personal welfare of one's marriageable daughters, but also a calculating view of family interests which settles the eventual choice and to which the young woman's own preference was regarded as quite subordinate. Even in our Western civilization the conventional marriage in established families of substance did not consult primarily the preferences of

[20] Alexander Sutherland, *The Origin and Growth of the Moral Instinct* (London, 1898), 1: 217.

individuals, and scarcely at all those of the prospective
bride, but rather sought a satisfactory alliance of solid
names and estates. This professed substantial good sense
was not limited to the aristocracy. The opening lines of
Tennyson's "Northern Farmer: New Style" come to mind:

> Dosn't thou 'ear my 'erse's legs as they canter awäy?
> Proputty, proputty, proputty—that's what I 'ears
> 'em saäy. . . .
> Thou'lt not marry for munny—thou's sweet upo'
> parson's lass—
> Noä—tho'lt marry for luvv—an' we boäth on us thinks
> tha an ass.

What marks the modern marriage is its release from
any family or group dictation, its individualism in profession and in practice. Our young people may not be
unresponsive to economic motives; a young man may
aspire to marry the boss's daughter, and a girl may hope
to marry into a good solid family. But most of them
regard their marriage as their own concern, their own
choice in marrying and their own decision if they separate
or are divorced. And fundamentally they are right: it is
their business; but it should be a stable business, not
precarious and bankrupt.

We should do better justice to the contemporary family
if we note carefully some features of its threatened disintegration. Our American record is certainly dismal. For
years on end we have had an increasing divorce rate; in
1956, one divorce for every four marriages. The average
duration of the marriages before divorce has been
reckoned as a little over six years. A study of divorce
statistics shows that there are today five times as many
cases of broken marriages annually as a hundred years
ago. Lamentable as this condition is on the face of it,
even more distressing is our gradual change of attitude
toward divorce. We have accepted it as a matter of course.

Young people of prudent foresight may even provide for their eventual separation by agreeing in advance on the acceptable terms of settlement, so as to avoid later unpleasant disputes.

The problem of divorce exposes the conditions for good but also for evil in the greater individual freedom allowed by modern civilization. Rigid prohibition of divorce will not cure the evil. There are families in hopeless discord of body and soul, where husband and wife and children face only misery and moral chaos. All of us know people who have made every effort of patience and goodwill to save their home, yet in the end found it wrecked beyond recall. But all of us in fairness should admit that the usual divorce calls for a different description. Families break up mainly owing to wayward self-indulgence, selfish stubbornness, and irresponsibility, without patience or a sense of duty or a reasonable temper. Modern freedom has released this selfish license, but modern freedom is likewise the essential condition of the moral fulfillment of personality in productive interplay and interpenetration of lives, conjugal, parental, filial.

Our modern society, with its shocking divorce rate and its corruption of human lives, is also a society in which the moral values of lifelong monogamy are being realized in millions of homes. The economic emancipation of modern women has made it possible for their choice of marriage to be a real and free choice. Women's political enfranchisement required long hardship of pioneer work in Great Britain and the United States; its success there has been followed by adoption of it with less resistance in other lands. Electoral rights have enabled women to take their stand effectively in the various activities and measures aiming at a better democratic future. It cannot be said that women have had a faultless record in the democratic process, but it has been remarked significantly that the League of Women Voters has become probably the most alert and best informed body of responsible citizens in our country. The opening of all the avenues of higher education to women has raised professional standards and has improved the care of children, provisions for public health, and general social welfare. Over against the loose free love in our time, we should recognize the far more common free responsible marriage in uncounted millions of homes where husband and wife live in harmony and mutual respect, where parents and children work and play and plan together for a fuller life.

CHAPTER NINE

Household Economy and Bodily Well-Being

OUR PREVIOUS CHAPTER was concerned with the historical evolution of the home; it naturally leads us to consider the physical setting of homelife. Our first topic here is that of housing, men's long journey from caves to huts to cottages or mansions. Primitive men's early dwellings were shelters of refuge from inclement weather and safety from predatory beasts or enemies. The savage imitated the animals in seeking some shade from the day's heat and at night burrowing or crouching in some cave where he felt protected from attack. He expanded the rude housing which nature provided him; he explored the deeper recesses of his cave or scooped out the tuff or rubble inside, to stretch out more comfortably; he piled up rocks at his entrance to obstruct any untoward intrusion. He sought out less accessible and safer dwelling. Tribes then stepped out to open ground, circling their chosen site with walls, and against them built their rude houses on the inside. Nomadic herdsmen needed mobile shelters and gradually mastered the craftsmanship of tepee and wigwam and yurt.

With the use of tools and skill in using wood and stone and adobe and later fired bricks, men proceeded to more ambitious building. Chimneys and windows replaced the holes in the roof and the small openings in the walls. Ladders became stairways; the roof of the hut became the floor of the second story, and cellars were dug for the storage of foods and other supplies. As the outward house thus grew in size and shape, the interior planning disclosed a more highly developed household economy. Bed and board and cooking pot that had huddled together in the cave or hut now had their separate rooms, with all the resourcefulness of design and building in seemingly boundless prospect. And even at this level of progress in building we have scarcely traversed the barbarian stage in housing development.

As men advanced to multiple housing, some of the acute modern difficulties confronted the builders. From the Great House of Indian cliff dwellings to the apartment skyscrapers of our metropolitan canyons, as from the oriental caravanserai to the mammoth hotels of our day, or from the chains of huts of older days to the widely ramified suburban development on different economic and architectural levels, the span is stupendous and the range of problems is as varied. Urban crowding of workmen's families in dingy tenements, which was one of the results of the industrial revolution, has not yet been corrected, but automobile transportation has made possible residential expansion in suburban areas of green lawns and woodland. This cultural sweep brings likewise radical changes in the household economy and in the programs of daily living.

In appraising residential progress, comparisons of present dwellings with those of bygone ages, even of earlier modern days, may be made on more than one standard. In terms of structural size and majesty, the royal palaces or lordly manors of old may rival our modern magnificence. The ancient Tibetan monastery of Lhasa housed 7,500 lamas. The front façade of Versailles stretches to almost a quarter of a mile. As for the living, so for the dead: what modern mausolea reach the magnitude of the Pyramid of Cheops or the beauty of Taj Mahal?

If we turn to the other side of the evidence, a comparison of modern with ancient hovels would not be so informing as the contrast of the household equipment of the modern home not only to ancient dwellings of the corresponding social level but also to the castles and palaces of bygone lords and kings. We find examples in the Western world. Look at the old kitchens of noble castles and colleges; visualize the daily household program of Holyrood. When Peter the Great visited the old Hanseatic city of Danzig in 1711, the citizen deemed most worthy to entertain him was Schopenhauer's great-grandfather. The weather turned very cold; the prosperous banker-merchant warmed his guest chamber by burning bottles of brandy on the stone floor. At the chateau of Malmaison, the bathroom provisions included a tank full of water above the tub, which was heated when required.

The mention of kitchens and bathtubs raises the whole problem of plumbing and household sanitation. In structure and in equipment alike peasant houses and stables were joined in common filth and stench. But nobility and even royalty were not much cleaner or more sanitary. Lord and lady were perfumed but seldom bathed. To be sure, hot springs had always drawn invalids in search of a cure, and the Baths of Caracalla still recall the magnificance of Roman public bathing as a social institution. Despite isolated instances like Japan or Finland, the usual program of mankind until very recent days did not include provisions for daily personal cleanliness. Tolstoy describes the elaborate preparations for a grand ball, when a particularly fussy princess washed not only her face and ears but also her feet.

The related topic of latrines and toilets taxes the resources of decent exposition. The peasant might step into his stable or outdoors to relieve himself, even as the highborn lord did behind the gate of the courtyard or castle or palace. When servants were slow in bringing

chamber pots, the Dauphin of France used the corner of
his room. Slops were emptied through the windows onto
the street with no concern for the heads of passersby.
Great cities as well as small hamlets reeked with filth.
Measures of sanitary reform sometimes ran open sewers
in the middle of the street. These pestilential conditions
may still be observed when one crosses the borders of
modern civilization. But even in our lands memories still
reach beyond the days of modern plumbing. Tourists
visiting ancient manors or monasteries are doubly impressed by their outward majesty and by their unsanitary
equipment. In the early years of this century a German
crown princess refused to live in her appointed palace
which lacked the decent provisions of the common modern
apartment.

As to kitchen equipment, gray-haired housewives may
recite the progress from open fire cooking to kitchen wood
or coal stove and to the modern gas or electric range. It
would be trite to point out the complete transformation of
cooking made possible by our present-day appliances of
reliable, controlled, and clean heat. Equally or even more
important is modern refrigeration which has not only
prevented spoilage of foods but has preserved for use at
all seasons the greatest variety of foodstuffs in the common household. Sociologists remind us that we civilized
Westerners have discovered scarcely any of our basic
foods; we owe them to primitive folk or to Orientals:
corn, rice, sugar, and so many meats and vegetables and
fruits. What we have learned is how to preserve and
use them at any time.

While modern kitchen appliances and food provisions
have increased beyond comparison our bill of fare, applied
science and the progress of medical knowledge have provided us with expert advice on diets for the various needs
of health and bodily welfare. Food chemistry serves
preventive medicine; the better understanding of the

alimentary properties of fats, proteins, and carbohydrates, and more recently of vitamins, has enabled millions of those whose knowledge can influence their practice to stay healthy.

Scarcely any other exhibit in the chart of historical progress is more impressive than the statistics of the greatly improved public health and lengthened life-span in the modern Western world. Better medical care and greatly improved sanitary conditions have not only decreased the frightful infant mortality but have also contributed to the general extension of the average life-expectancy. These radical changes have been the achievement mainly of the past hundred years. It was reckoned in 1833 that four-fifths of the children born on the island of Saint Kilda did not survive beyond their first fortnight, largely due to the storing of manure in the peasant huts, causing tetanus. Detailed unspeakable and scarcely readable accounts of noisome British workmen's tenements, as late as 1840, are matched by a foul page in a letter by Erasmus describing some better-class houses during the Renaissance. Without such accounts we could not grasp the full meaning of the differences between the early modern and the more recent mortality tables. According to the records of the city of Geneva, the average length of life prior to 1600 was eight years, and even as late as 1700 it was twenty-seven. The figures for England rose in one hundred years, 1840-1940, from forty-five to sixty-three. In less than a century England reduced her death rate by half, France by almost a half, and Italy by two-thirds. Our American death rate in 1901 was 15.7 and in 1949, 9.7 per thousand. Our Western span of life has been twice as long as in India,[1] but during twenty years the average length of Hindu life also has increased by one-fourth.

[1] Compare F. Sherwood Taylor, *Science and Scientific Thought* (New York, ed. of 1963), pp. 191, 200 ff.

Exceptional longevity can be noted in every land and age. Chinese tradition honored the ancient wisdom of Lao-Tsze, "the old Sage," so highly that legend described him as being seventy years old at birth. History also records the almost centenarian Sophocles completing his Oedipus trilogy, and during the Renaissance Titian still painting in his nineties. The Old Testament reckoned the years of man as three score and ten. But these instances do not affect the wholly contrary general statistics. Pope Innocent III in the twelfth century remarked in his book on the misery of human life that few in his age lived past their thirties.[2]

Studies of these vital statistics impress on our minds the astonishing progress in medicine and surgery, both theory and practice. Medical research, in discovering the causes of numerous diseases and curative agents and methods, has lessened the gravity of many former banes of young and old and has virtually eliminated some of them. As late as 1847 one half of amputation surgery patients died from septicemia. In 1865 Lister began designing his technique for aseptic surgery, and within two years was almost entirely successful in preventing the fatal results. Not only cure but prevention of disease may be cited from British statistics of deaths from typhoid fever, which decreased during 1871-1941 from 400 to less than 10 per million.

In the forefront of achievements in this general field has been the gradual wiping out of malaria and yellow fever, not only in temperate zones but also in the tropical regions. When a noted parasitologist was asked about recent United States malaria statistics, he replied simply that there were none to record. The history of plagues which had ravaged whole countries both East and West is

---

[2] Innocent III, *De Contemptu mundi, sive de miseria conditionis humanae*, cited from Migne, *Patrologia latina*, vol. 217 (Paris, 1855), 1: 10.

a dismal record of "the black death." Athens during the Peloponnesian War, Jerusalem and Rome at the beginning of our era, Constantinople in the reign of Justinian, and epidemically across the map of Europe during the Middle Ages, in England during the fourteenth and fifteenth centuries and again most violently in the seventeenth century, when one-seventh of the population of London perished—these are the most disastrous instances. In the Orient, especially in India, the plague is still a deadly menace, but the discovery of its causes and modern preventive measures have banned the scourge from countries with modern sanitary provisions and controls. Within our own memory diseases like diabetes, diphtheria, and mastoiditis have yielded to medical treatment; the check of poliomyelitis is still a headline newspaper item. The timely discovery of potent drugs saved Winston Churchill's life from pneumonia in faraway Cairo during the Second World War. A number of great killers, tubercular or cancerous, though still unsubdued, are strongly besieged. And without further reference to specific diseases, the general standard of hygienic hospital care, especially in the Western world, is in amazing contrast to the pestiferous lazarettos of earlier days.

But the very progress along many lines in our household economy and in our conditions of public health has had also its counteraspect in the deleterious effects of the modern ways of living. Uncontrolled appetites can be more readily indulged in our days of boundless varieties of food and drink, and multitudes are ruined by intemperance. We are just now seriously grappling with the pollution of our air and water supply. How are we to advance the very industry that furnishes our modern conveniences and yet cope with its destructive smog and sludge? While the health benefits of suburban living are steadily extending to manual and white-collar workers, uncounted millions are still packed in the slum districts of our cities.

The suburban idyll itself has not come up to its advertised perfection. The commuter's daily schedule has often reduced to a minimum the intimate contact of fathers and children. For millions it has produced a new kind of drab routine existence.

Despite the marvelous advances of medical science, the strains and corruptions of modern life are overtaxing our hospital provisions. Even more distressing is our record of mental breakdowns. The widespread and rising standards of our psychiatric services have their obverse and depressing aspect in the increasingly grave need of multitudes for restoration of normal behavior.

A specific and very grievous instance of this problem is the spreading use of narcotics and other drugs, some of them extremely noxious. This alarming abuse has not been limited to delinquents and street gangs; it has invaded colleges and universities and even our public schools, upsetting normal responsible conduct and releasing morbid and lawless excesses. It is spreading appallingly among juveniles. The number of arrests in New York for drug-related offenses by young people aged eighteen or less increased 1,860 percent in eight years. According to a reported interview with the director of the Federal Bureau of Narcotics, during 1969 almost 1,000 persons in New York died due to heroin-related causes, a number "greater than those caused by any other factor among people between the ages of 18 and 35. . . . Incredible as that may seem, it is true."[3]

Heroin is reportedly the terminal and most destructive of a long list of drugs on the addict's line, which usually begins with marijuana and proceeds to LSD and other synthetic products. A derivative from opium, heroin has its chief source in the poppy fields of Turkey; the refining of it is being done in illicit French laboratories; its transportation across the Atlantic and its distribution in Amer-

---

[3] Compare *U.S. News and World Report* (May 25, 1970), p. 38.

ica is a most ramified international operation. It is a feeder of crime in two ways. It is so fantastically profitable that trafficking in it has become a main concern of criminal syndicates. And the far-gone heroin addict turns to burglary or worse in order to procure the money for the highly priced drug.

Abuse of drugs in some form has been traced back to very primitive social levels, as in the present use of peyote by Indian tribes in Mexico and in our Southwest. But modern chemistry has multiplied the variety of toxic products; the tensions and also the inducements of modern life have spread the drug distribution throughout our social system, deleterious in different ways to our social welfare. At one end of our social scale, the drug use is menacing the normal development of reportedly 15 to 20 percent of our college and university students and is seeping down into the public schools, thus imperiling the intelligent leadership essential to our future welfare. At the other end, heroin traffic and addiction, in the entire process of production, distribution, and use is so closely bound up with organized crime in the underworld that the suppression of it is a major factor in assuring any real progress in personal security and social well-being.

The most shocking aspect of this whole modern problem is the pollution of our natural environment, most flagrant in the leading industrial countries but not at all limited to them. "For the first time in the history of mankind, there is arising a crisis of worldwide proportions involving developed and developing countries alike—the crisis of human environment. . . . It is becoming apparent that if current trends continue, the future of life on earth could be endangered."[4] The daily news media, panel discussions, and more extended surveys by experts are piling up the woeful evidence: of our foul air, tainted by smog

[4] George F. Kennan, "To Prevent a World Wasteland: A Proposal," in *Foreign Affairs* (April 1970), 401, quoting U.N. Secretary-General U Thant.

and noxious gases, of rivers and lakes and seas contaminated by sewage and industrial refuse, of land eroded and devastated and turned into junk heaps, of the mass destruction of fishes and birds by toxic effluents and pesticides—the list seems endless. We read of a tuna fleet working off some coastal refineries near Marseilles and having to dump its catch which reeked of crude oil. The air polluted by the industrial plants in the Ruhr Valley of Germany is blown northeastward and falls down as "black snow" over the Scandinavian countryside. In faraway Siberia limnologists are warning the government authorities of the threatened befouling of Lake Baikal, the deepest body of fresh water in the world, by the discharged refuse from cellulose plants. The Soviet conservationists would save Lake Baikal from the pollution which has already contaminated the Volga River, poisoning sturgeon life, the source of caviar.

Nowhere in the world is the problem of environmental pollution more flagrant than in the United States. We are the foremost industrial nation in the world, foremost in our extraction and use of the resources of nature—and also in the abuse of our environment. This "galloping consumption" has gripped our minds these latter days with a sense of immediate and utter disaster. The sources and areas of pollution are various and they complicate the proposed methods of control. The mass production and distribution of insecticides and pesticides has helped our farmers to save their crops. But the indiscriminate use of many of those highly toxic chemicals has spread their deadly effects at large, poisoning our land areas and the rainwater that washes the deadly sprays and powders into the rivers. Rachel Carson was among the first to arouse us to a sense of our peril by exposing the resultant wholesale destruction of fish and bird life and of lasting danger in our use of tainted plant and animal food supply.

Every year some hundred and fifty million tons of

smoke and fumes are discharged into the air that we Americans have to breathe. Seven million automobiles are junked annually over our countryside; twenty or thirty million tons of paper trash and more than seventy billion cans or jars or bottles. Our coasts and waterways, lakes and rivers are being contaminated, some of them seemingly past reclamation. We read that Cleveland's Cuyahoga River has a thick top layer of oil waste which burst into flames recently and burned two bridges, and that "to restore Lake Erie to its purity of twenty-five years ago will require 40 billion dollars and 50 to 500 years, provided all pollution is stopped now."[5] But a writer in Houston should not merely cite examples from Ohio when a television broadcast from New York tells him that Buffalo Bayou in his Texas metropolis is rated as among the filthiest rivers in the country.

Our threatened environmental disaster is not limited to the land surface and to its waters and air cover. We are fouling the oceans east and west of us and the Gulf to the south. Oil drillers off the California coast have released uncounted tons of their black discharge onto the beautiful beaches of Santa Barbara. Inadequate valve protection on oil well pipes is menacing the coastal strips of Louisiana with the black flood, deadly to marine life and to the subtropical beauty of the South.

The contamination of our waterways and air by discharged sewage and industrial waste and by smog and toxic fumes is not the only kind of our environmental pollution. The enormous power plants which generate the electric supply needed for our expanding industry and private use suck in the cooling flow of our rivers through their pipes, to discharge it hot and destructive to fishes at the other end. Some two hundred jet planes cross the Atlantic every twenty-four hours, each of them

[5] Robert Humphries, "The Imperiled Environment," in *Vista* (March-April 1970), p. 17; compare p. 18.

blowing off a hundred tons of carbon dioxide over the ocean. The effect of this inordinate discharge threatens to disturb the entire heat balance of the earth. But these warnings by our scientists are confronted by counter-protests: What then? Shall we stop producing the needed electric power, and shall we reduce our aviation services? These counterprotests surely do not close the discussion of the pollution emergency problem, but even this brief survey points out the truth that advancing civilization in the course of history manifests the expansion of human activities, for good or for ill, with better and higher prospects but also with graver perils.

CHAPTER TEN

Economic Values, Technology, and Human Progress

OUR PRECEDING CHAPTER was concerned with shelter, nourishment, health, and general vitality. These aspects of men's well-being are themselves largely affected by or even the result of their material welfare. They depend upon the degree to which men can utilize the economic means to effective and satisfactory activity. The expression "economic means" is appropriate, for economic values are distinctively means to the realization of the other values in which human life finds effective expression. Ethical analysis has distinguished two kinds or rather aspects of values: intrinsic and contributory. All values have a contributory or instrumental aspect: they affect or enable us to realize other values. While in this way all values reach or point beyond themselves, most values have also intrinsic worth; we cherish them for themselves. Whereas all values are contributory and most values are also intrinsic, economic values are exceptional in this respect: they are only contributory or instrumental; they have no intrinsic worth. To be sure, we do value them, as conditions for the realization of other values.

Economic values are only means. Mistaking them for ends and making the mere accumulation of them the goal of human activity is the folly of the miser's or the plutocrat's crass materialism. But we should not err in the opposite way, as much traditional religion has done, and glorify holy poverty. The economic values are not only important; they are often indispensable means to the realization of the other values. Material resources are required for the fulfillment of men's and women's capacities in a satisfactory homelife: for the education of children, for intellectual and aesthetic cultivation, for security, for long-range planning, and for the other individual and social goods of humane living. Reasonable balance of judgment is needed here to recognize the right place of economic values in the integral and harmonious self-fulfillment of men's lives. That recognition should enable us to acknowledge the moral basis of the demand for social-economic justice and to trace the historical lines of economic progress.

The idea of property or ownership involves the social recognition of a person's rightful claim to the exclusive possession or use of certain things. Regarding the ground of proprietary claims, opinions have varied. Referring strictly to fact, men have reasoned that possession is nine-tenths of the law. Wordsworth's ironical lines come to mind:

> . . . The good old rule
> Sufficeth them, the simple plan,
> That they should take, who have the power,
> And they should keep who can.[1]

Against this sort of disposal, men have sought just ground for upholding, but also for resisting individual claims to exclusive ownership and use of various commodities. Labor has been regarded as the source and basis of property, but in ways, not always clear, which would disqualify the probably hard working robber or extortioner or pirate. Some utopias have condemned private property as the root of social injustice and misery. Ownership has

[1] Wordsworth, "Rob Roy's Grave," ll. 37 ff.

also been viewed as essential to man's self-realization. Appropriation, that is, acquiring possession and use of things, was judged by Hegel as a step in the expansion and fruition of human personality.[2] Social justice and welfare, then, would seem to demand not the abolition of private property but the extension of its personal benefits to as many persons as possible. We may thus see at the outset the various issues of the social-economic problem which engross our present discussion.

The firm conviction of ownership has been regarded as having its roots deep in human consciousness. Some psychologists have even traced it back to analogous reactions in animal life. A fox protects its burrow; a mocking bird defends against invasion not only its nest but also the area around the tree on which it has settled. Sociologists in their studies of primitive tribes have noted the claim and the recognition of ownership, but they have noted also a certain disregard or even unawareness of exclusive possession. Both individual property and the absence of it reflect the organization of primitive life. Nomadic tribes obviously cannot have our ideas of real estate. Hunting or fishing or herding were traditionally communal activities. The Eskimo's whale, or in other tribes the lesser catch, could not be preserved and were available only for immediate consumption, tribally. Sundry personal belongings were one's own, likewise one's ax or spear, paddle or fishing net; still, if they were not in actual use, another member of the tribe might be free to use them if needed. The man who killed the bear would have first claim to the fur, but if he had killed a deer, another hunter coming upon it might well help himself to the game, leaving the rest of the carcass for the returning hunter's use.

Among pastoral tribes proprietary rights are not very

[2] Compare Hegel, *Philosophy of Right*, trans. S. W. Dyde (London, 1896), 1: i.

definite. A choice pasture may be occupied by the same herdsman season after season, yet the unfenced range was at the disposal of the firstcomer. Should he have ventured too far afield in quest of lush herbage and found himself on land commonly used by strangers, he would find his holding precarious. Within different limits of territory, land ownership in primitive societies is not uniformly stable. The tribesman cultivates fields that are traditionally tribal. Custom may grant him or his family or clan continued access to certain tracts, or the elders may periodically redistribute the tribal land for individual cultivation. This unsteady character of land tenure marks also the produce of land cultivation. Neither of them was reliably individual initially; both were communal in disposal. Planted and harvested and gathered, corn and beans or rice would be heaped together for tribal distribution, and one would get not one's own produce but what was tribally judged to be one's need and share. Division was likely to be uneven. The weak tiller might get a meager portion, and a leader of a stout clan would grab and hold far more than his fellows.

Kings and chiefs have maintained overall possession, allowing grants to their selected vassals and treating the common workers of the soil as their slaves and serfs. This black tale of slavery concerns more than property rights. The slave could hold nothing as his own, for in no sense was he his own but altogether another's. Even if they were not downright slaves, the common run of tribesmen owned or cultivated land by the king's grant: his the initial consent and his the eventual tribute.

The primitive emphasis in tribal property rights is reflected in the various ways in which ownership has been respected or flouted. Insight into the typical tribesman's attitude should enable us to clear up conflicting views of savage honesty or thievery. Neither of them, in our sense of the terms, was characteristic to any extent.

The property rights which a savage is apt to respect are rights sanctioned by his tribe, his fellow tribesman's rights. His "domestic" honesty is a part of his general tribal conformity. The tribe chastizes its thieves as it punishes any other transgression of tribal mores. Theft is punished the more severely the higher the owner's rank. Stealing from a chief or priest is fatal.

Not only tribal control and punishment deters one from stealing, but also religious fear. Magic and taboo doom the thief. In a violent thunderstorm the Bechuana savages spit on the ground and vow that they have not robbed any of their neighbors. In old Tonga the king's property was regarded as taboo. Stealing the king's property was believed to cause scrofula, which could be cured only by the thief's kissing the king's heel. (The old English name for scrofula was "the king's evil"; kings of England were touched by sufferers of the bane, in a healing ritual attended by Christian chaplains.) Of course, primitive behavior includes much indiscriminate thieving as well as some honesty.

The record of general practice, as it enforces respect for tribally sanctioned ownership, might allow common or even complete disregard for the property of aliens. A stranger is a likely enemy—*hostis*, hostile—and in any case he has no rights and may be stripped of his goods. Robbing an enemy tribe might endanger one's own people, and if it failed it would be condemned, but if it was successful it was praised. Not only among Arabs was the word *robber* a personal boast. The straying traveler, especially if he rode alone, was risking peril at every turn of the highway: a state of affairs that the word *highwayman* should recall to us. Despoiling the stranger was the order of the day, unless he were alert and fortunate enough to reach the tribesman's threshold with a rightful claim to hospitality. Then he would have a welcome and the protection due to a guest. He could sleep in peace without any worry about his belongings, and his host, who would have plundered him on the road, would defend him and his goods under his hospitable roof. Aside from hospitality, the dread of a tribesman's taboo may protect the stranger from theft. On stopping at some Polynesian island without intent to trade there, New England ship captains used to invite the king or chief to come aboard and, for value received, to touch the deck or the top of the ladder. The whole ship then became taboo to the islanders and so safe from pilfering.

For long primitive ages a man's wife was his property, at his disposal. Was this virtual enslavement of women general, implying that they never had any ownership whatever? This has been commonly held but has also been disputed by leading sociologists. Among peoples of higher culture, in Jerusalem and Rome and much later in London, a married woman was partly or altogether the economic ward of her husband. The European record is that of the very slow recovery of women's proprietary rights.

Where mothers had no recognized ownership, children obviously failed to qualify. If fathers had the right to do away with children judged to be infirm, or more often with too many girls, any consideration of children's property rights would be out of the question, with the exception, not very clear, of their claim to their own earnings. Children's proprietary claims come into clearer focus in considering inheritance customs and regulations, and these have varied greatly.[3] Among very low savages, where there is little that could be called private property, the question of inheritance could scarcely arise. Somewhat higher up the scale, a dying man would leave his goods and his wife and children to the care of his nearest kin. The widow's share of inheritance is not reliably hers, and the children's lot is often very precarious. Tribal

[3] Compare Henry Maine, *Ancient Law* (London, ed. of 1913), p. 117.

custom is hard on bastards unless legitimated by later marriage. Orphan daughters in China and in ancient Israel could inherit only in the absence of sons. In Babylonia, in Rome, and in India the status of daughters improved in the course of time, but Scandinavian and even very late English law did not recognize clearly a daughter's rights. The succession of a princess to the throne would be unquestioned, and in the inheritance of large aristocratic domains, as matters of dynastic order, traditional customs have been strict, but they vary. Laws of primogeniture which keep the noble family estate and title in the line of the eldest son are familiar, but there are also laws of ultimogeniture, where the youngest son of the family inherits all.[4] Russian traditional practice in Tsarist days distributed titles and estates among all the children: thus a great many princes of some ancient names would be living at the same time.

Many of the conditions described here have been largely discarded in our modern days; the survival of some of them in recent Western culture should remind us of the short historical span of machine-age industry and agriculture. Despite the impact of our economy on the rest of the world, a large part of mankind lives still under primitive or barbarian conditions. The changes in the social-economic structure have been amazingly rapid in many countries partly modernized under colonial regimes and now bursting forth in newfound nationalism. The student of economic values in their historical development may trace the many changes across the several thousand years of Western civilization; but he is bound to note the real progress and also the sudden perils of the quick shift to modern economic processes in many regions of

[4] Compare Edw. Westermarck, *Origin and Development of the Moral Ideas* (London, 1912), 2: 44 ff.; compare also S. A. Cook, *The Laws of Moses and the Law of Hammurabi* (London, 1903), pp. 144 ff.; Fustel de Coulanges, *The Ancient City*, trans. Willard Small, 12th ed. (Boston, 1901), pp. 108 ff.

Asia and Africa. Their recent chronicles impress us as an epitome of Western social history, or as a cartoon of it. We should note the characteristic patterns of the economic development as it discloses in its expanding scope a growing achievement of social values, but also widespread hardships and much confusion.

The economic problem is impressed on our minds today as the issue between capital and labor. In terms of basic social processes it involves mainly agriculture, industry, and trade. Agriculture comes naturally first on our list, for man's first and major property is that of land, real estate, land on which he lives, which he tills and from which he gets his food and subsistence. Society rises above the primitive levels of fishing, hunting, and foraging to to the agricultural stage of settled cultivation of land. Anthropologists have recognized this transition as marking the advance from the food-gathering stage of savagery to the food-producing stage of barbarism. It is also the transition from a largely nomadic to more settled existence, attachment to the tribal land and eventually to one's own home and field.[5] We should keep in mind the historical development from the earliest periods of agricultural life: tribal possession of the soil, with periodic redistribution for individual cultivation, and for the sharing of the produce, the later royal control and exploitation, and then the slow emergence of men's private ownership of their strips of land and the produce of their own work.

If the political curve of progress marks men's rise from slavery to citizenship, the economic road points from serfdom to yeoman freeholding and to farming independence. The earlier stages of this latter road are dismal, and they still darken the lives of hundreds of millions today in many parts of the world. On Egyptian monuments we may see stripped bodies bending under the

[5] Compare V. Gordon Childe, *What Happened in History* (New York, 1954), pp. 23 f.

whips of overseers, ploughing and reaping the crops of king or lord or priest. And are the fellaheen of today much better off, despite the repeated promises they hear of land apportionment? In his travels across the Middle East, Supreme Court Justice William O. Douglas relates a story, indeed a boast, of a Persian absentee landlord, that his estates covered a territory larger than all of Switzerland.[6] Reforms undertaken by the present shah of Iran, however, have been carried out despite the stubborn opposition of the large landowners. Starting with a distribution of extensive crown lands to the tillers of the soil, he has succeeded in initiating legislation which has made more than fourteen million of his peasants owners of the fields which they cultivate. In Mexico the people have been rising steadily from peon serfdom to some considerable degree of farm ownership. Turgenev's *Sportsman's Sketches* portrayed the dismal servitude of the Russian peasants, tied to the soil from which they drew abundance for their masters but the barest pittance for themselves. When Tsar Alexander II emancipated the millions of serfs in the nineteenth century, he began a work of great progressive range. The expectations of those hard-working masses were not fully satisfied, nor have they been realized adequately by the social upheavals which in so many ways have split the world into two warring camps. The success of both the Bolshevik and the Chinese revolutions hinged on the promise of giving to the toiling peasants the lands which they tilled. In both cases, after his initial access to the soil, the plowman found himself restrained and then shackled by a new sort of serfdom under the name of collective farming. In China his home has disappeared along with his farm, and he has been herded in barracks under rigid control of his daily work and food and entire program of life.

In the Western world, we may note the English record

[6] William O. Douglas, *Strange Lands and Friendly People* (New York, ed. of 1952), p. 87.

since Roman and Saxon days; more interesting is the story of the last five or six centuries since Chaucer. In the early English or Anglo-Saxon system, village communities had common unfenced fields from which small strips of an acre or less were allotted to each family. Men had barely enough land to provide their daily bread. With the rise of the feudal system and the growing power of lord, baron, or bishop and abbot, more and more of the land passed into the hands of the mighty, with two important restraints on the common people's freedom. The villager was now a villein, bound to the soil. He could not leave his strip of land to try to better his fortune elsewhere. He had to work certain days on his lord's land as the bailiff ordered him. His corn must be ground at the master's mill, and master's consent was required for any peasant marriage. Great wealth was produced in England, rich harvests and the best wool in Europe for which the weavers in Italy and the Low Countries competed. But the peasant farmers and shepherds led destitute lives which poets like the author of *Piers Plowman* described in bitter verse.

So long as they had abundant labor, lords and abbots could dictate their own terms. In the middle of the fourteenth century, however, the entire social situation was altered by the plague, the Black Death in which more than a third of the population perished. As farmhands became scarce they could secure better bargains, for they were in demand everywhere. Serfs and villeins earned and bought their land and their freedom; the English yeoman class grew in numbers and substance. Parliamentary laws to check increase of wages had some immediate effects, but they also replaced local manorial customs by national legislation; they stirred a nationwide consciousness of common needs and common action. Within a generation after the Black Death came the uprising of 1381, the Wat Tyler rebellion which spilled aristocratic blood all over England and led young King Richard II to grant the rebels' demands. While the pendulum swung back to reaction and Parliament repealed Richard's concessions, the steps forward from villeinage to free land-ownership had been taken. The steps were slow; they mark the advance, very gradual, in the access of English farmhands to land of their own. When the English social historian cites much later statistics to show that farmer-owned land in England had increased by two million acres in a century one is impressed both by the social gain and by its very slow coming.

A generation before Wat Tyler's uprising, the Jacquerie rebellion in France had run its bloody course, with murders of landed gentry at the outset and wholesale massacre of the rebels at the end. The French social gains were scarcely apparent even in promise. Three centuries after the Jacquerie, the French peasants were seemingly as hopeless drudges as ever. La Bruyère's description of them sears the memory: "One sees certain wild animals, male and female, scattered over the country, black, livid, and sunburnt, lashed to the soil which they dig and turn over with unyielding stubbornness. They have something like an articulate voice, and when they stand up they disclose a human face, and in fact they are human. At night they retire to their dens, where they live on black bread, water, and roots. They spare other men the need of sowing, tilling, and harvesting in order to live, and so deserve not to be deprived of the bread which they have sown."[7] Black clouds spread over this landscape, and in the distance one can hear the rumbling thunder of revolution.

As we turn from foreign lands to our own, we start at another stage of land tenure. The American farmer was fortunate in beginning as a freeman. Exceptions can be

[7] La Bruyère, *Oeuvres*, Grands Écrivains ed. (Paris, 1912), 2: 61.

cited: in Virginia, Maryland, and elsewhere transplanted cavaliers held vast tracts by royal grants. New York and New England had their land barons that barred the common farmhands from possession of the soil. There as in old England the economic struggle claimed its victims, for there were resolute Wat Tylers among the Green Mountain Boys of Vermont. But the usual story of the American farm has been quite different. With the opening of new frontiers, the Western Reserve and then the boundless Far West, men moved to new homesteads on virgin soil and peppered the land with farmhouses and barns, which are the characteristic features of the American countryside. From the Ohio to the Pacific this social system of independent farms has set the tone of traditional American life.

From the outset this abundance of available land reflected itself in the large size of individual farms. Father and son reached out for their sections and quarter sections and planned to acquire still more. These expanses of farmland could not be cultivated by the old methods. The ox- or horse-driven plow had to be replaced by machinery, and one of the earliest and most needed applications of industrial engineering has been in modernizing agriculture. On old Scottish hillsides half a dozen men with their oxen might plow through a long day a meager acre or less. On a modern farm in Montana, as we are told, "two men with a 75 h.p. tractor and ten fourteen inch plows can plow an acre, six inches deep, in sixteen minutes."[8] This statement and others like it signify the triumph of American farming, but also some of its difficult problems.

Modern agriculture has been called 90 percent engineering. Not only plowing but also the entire farming process—harvesting, threshing, disposal of crops—has been

[8] Thomas D. Campbell, *Toward Civilization*, ed. Charles A. Beard (London and New York, 1930), p. 166.

mechanized. Labor-saving machinery has made it possible for fewer and fewer men to cultivate more and more land, but by the same token it has been sending millions of farm boys, no longer needed on the farm, to the cities, to industry or trade. Agricultural education and the research of experimental stations have perfected farming processes and increased both the size and the quality of the crops. Industrial chemistry has pointed out ways of using the former waste products of farming, turning cobs and straw into profitable materials. But this sort of agricultural chemistry cannot be undertaken advantageously on a small scale. It involves enormously expensive equipment and operation, and its further development has pointed toward heavily capitalized farming corporations on vast tracts of land. Those who champion this line of progress are reluctant to consider its inevitable consequences, in bypassing or quite stunting the traditional farm homelife that has been regarded as the backbone of our American democracy. Meanwhile the high productivity, overproduction of modern agriculture has left the American farmer at an economic disadvantage. He has to buy his machinery and other needed goods at high prices in an industrial market and must sell his crops on terms that do not yield him a satisfactory living. The government has had to intervene, support prices, and store surpluses. Farm policy has become a controversial political topic.

We may recall again the radical views of Sir Thomas More and other utopians that private property is the root of social injustice and misery. Less sweeping judgment has been applied more specifically to private land-tenure. In an expanding society, so we have been told, private possession of land enables the owner to extort a high rent from those who labor on it or otherwise use it and make it productive. Even when leaving his property uncultivated or unimproved, a proprietor can see it increase greatly in value by the general social improvement of the surrounding land. These two problems, of landlord's rents and the so-called unearned increment, have been treated by radical critics as two varieties of economic injustice. The profits and in some cases the immense fortunes of landed gentry and real estate speculators have penalized the productive worker and have in large measure denied to society its due share in the increased values of land.

A drastic proposal to correct these inequities was Henry George's "single tax." In his *Progress and Poverty* George (1839-1897) urged the abolition of all taxes on productive labor and the replacement of them by a tax on landed estates equal to their rent values. He would not confiscate land or property, but he would tax those who hold it without cultivating or improving it. If the landlord, by extorting high rents, taxes the men who would cultivate or improve his estates, the state should secure these taxes for its needs and thus relieve the productive laboring class of any additional taxes. This single tax system, George declared, would correct the unequal distribution of wealth and power which has destroyed so many civilizations in the past. Instead of endowing idle landlords, it would sustain and encourage productive work and contribute to expanding progress.[9]

Anthropologists have traced the long story of man's pioneering in industry as well as in agriculture. From toilsome dragging of heavy loads men proceeded to log-rolling, as the ancient builders erected the monoliths of Stonehenge and Avebury; then still further speeding their labor, they used end-discs of larger diameter, and then by a stroke of invention, wheels for locomotion. While in these ways the ancient workers were extending the range of their strength, they tamed and harnessed beasts of

---

[9] Compare Henry George, *Progress and Poverty*, 25th ed. (Garden City, N.Y., 1923), pp. 403 f., 525.

burden to do their heavy work. This domestication, and also the discovery and cultivation of new foodstuffs were improving agriculture, while the devising and the ramified use of tools were perfecting industrial skills. The following list has been compiled to indicate the various advances made prior to or about 3000 B.C.—"artificial irrigation using canals and ditches; the plough; the harnessing of animal motive power; the sailing boat; wheeled vehicles; orchard-husbandry; fermentation; the production and use of copper; bricks; the arch; glazing; the seal; . . . a solar calendar, writing, numeral notation, and bronze.[10]

In our civilization, one basic characteristic of the various crafts prior to the industrial revolution resulted in the age of mass production. The earlier industry was largely individual, and it was carried on in homes or in small shops. One more difference: no sharp separation existed between industry and trade. We read the historian's accounts of medieval crafts, and we can see many of them clearly even in this country, at certain Indian villages like San Ildefonso or Chimayo, near Santa Fe. There we can see pottery being shaped and displayed in the front room which serves also as a shop, or rugs woven on looms and hung on the walls in the large room. Or we can drive across the Ozarks and see pots and vases and hooked rugs and rustic furniture spread out for sale on the front porch.

We can readily picture to ourselves the scene of medieval and early modern home industry. Families specialized in certain traditional crafts, or whole villages specialized, like the Taxco silver designer in Mexico. Early trade was likewise an individual or communal barter, a trading of goods among producers. So long as craftsmanship and industry were thus simple and on a small scale, they could preserve their handicraft character. But economic complexity was in prospect. The excellence of some product, which spread the fame of a

[10] V. Gordon Childe, *Man Makes Himself* (London, 1941 ed.), p. 227.

certain master or of his town, the very success in the
disposal of some goods, as it expanded the business,
demanded a more efficient organization of it, of industry
and trade alike. The entire social order of a certain community would be centered on the production and sale
of its choice commodity. Where several industries shared
in the prosperity of a large town or city, a number of
organizations would direct the various enterprises. These
were the guilds of medieval society. Their success might
depend largely upon their exclusive and tightly guarded
use of some special process which sealed the superiority
of their product. "If the absolute monarch could say
L'État, c'est moi, the successful inventor could in effect
say: 'The Guild—that's me.' "[11]

Perhaps even before the craftsmen themselves had thus
organized the industry, they combined for their more
effective trading. These guilds, like our modern professions, had their codes of training and operation—their
apprentices, journeymen, masters—controlling the processes of production and maintaining standards of workmanship. In manufacture and trade alike, this communal
and guild character has been preserved by tradition in
names some of which are of historical interest and others
still identify definite distinguished products: Delft china,
Kerman or Kashan rugs, Damascene or Toledo blades,
Venetian or Bohemian glass, Scottish tweeds.

In the expansion of trade, certain ports rose to prominence, and entire countries vied in navigation. Before
the days of Columbus and Vasco da Gama and Magellan,
the Italian cities, notably Genoa and Venice, led in the
Oriental trade overland. Later Portuguese mariners well-
nigh controlled commerce with India and China, to be
followed by the ship-merchants of Amsterdam and Ant-
werp, and then definitely by the English with their East
India Company and their Indian Empire. By the opposite

[11] Lewis Mumford, *Technics and Civilization* (New York, 1934), p. 132.

route, Salem sent its China clippers across the Pacific, and the whaling trade sealed the fame and the fortunes of American captains.

These names all mark the age of overseas discoveries and also the early spread of the colonial system. We should not overlook the radical change in the industrial and trade relations of Orient and Occident which was produced by the industrial revolution, at the turn from the eighteenth to the nineteenth century. The earlier competition had been for the rare products which Europe wanted from overseas: silk and spices and porcelain, china, or ivory from Africa and gold from Peru. But the later largely colonial trade sought the large Eastern markets for the increasing abundance of European goods produced by the machines of the industrial revolution. An outstanding characteristic of both the economic and the political history of the last two centuries has been the change in the social life of the Western nations, and also in the relations of the Western powers to the nations of the Orient, both due to the replacement of handicraft economy and guild trade by mass production and international trade, both results of the industrial revolution.

All this took place during comparatively recent history. The last third of the eighteenth century had seen the invention of the steam engine. This was followed by the spinning jenny and the power loom and the cotton gin. Before long railroads and steamers ushered in a new era in transportation, and the modern advances in physics and chemistry tapped the boundless resources of nature for industrial use. This progress in the spread of knowledge and in its applications has proceeded with increasing speed, never so amazingly fast as since the onset of the atomic age a short generation ago. Within less than two centuries we can chronicle three stages of industrial history as important as any in preceding time: steam power, electric current, atomic energy.

The advantages of power manufacture can be realized only through an immense volume of output. The initial equipment, installation and operation of the machine plant are so enormous that only very large scale production can make them profitable. Power manufacture required, as it also effected, the elimination of the small craftsman shop. The guild masters had to close their shops and enter the large factory. Competition was now among mass producers, and the industrial enterprises had to expand and even aim at monopoly or risk being swamped in the struggle.

All this is familiar, and the triumphs of the machine age are incontestable. Incontestable likewise has been the human cost of this boasted industrial advance. The plight of laboring men, as well as women and children, in the early years of the industrial revolution was in many ways deplorable, but handcraft production also had not been free from drudgery. The traditional exploitation of drudges has not been limited to modern capitalism.

In turning to the story of modern industrial labor, we should recognize its main successive chapters: harsh driving and destitution at the outset; gradual reform of unsanitary and intolerable conditions of work, due to an aroused social conscience and factory legislation; shorter hours and higher wages exacted by the growing power of trade and labor unions, slowly legalized and exerting their pressure through strikes; and then the contest between labor and capital on more and more nearly equal terms but often at the expense of the consumers. Today the consumer has no lack of opportunity to observe how well organized labor has learned its lesson of hard bargaining, in which only capitalists were supposed to be experts. Greed is not the monopoly of any one social class. But it should temper our judgment to recall the earlier trials of the laboring classes, before the pendulum began to swing the other way.

The large factory which ran the handcraftsman out of business could employ him on its own terms, and those terms were harsh. This harshness was not always due to the employer's callousness. The initial cost of the factory enterprise required cutting costs at every turn; in self-protection the owner seemed compelled to exploit his men. Low wages and long hours were the rule. The first textile plants in England roused almost an insurrection by the handloom weavers, and the owners preferred to locate in new territory to avoid trouble. Schopenhauer wrote bitter words about those early textile factories: "At the age of five years to enter a spinning or other factory, and from that time forth to sit there daily, first ten, then twelve, and ultimately fourteen hours, performing the same mechanical labor, is to purchase dearly the satisfaction of drawing breath."[12] The machine needed coal, and English women drudged in the bowels of the earth sixteen hours daily. Even more shocking was the treatment of native labor in overseas colonies. The scandalous abuse of Congo Negroes by King Leopold's men stirred worldwide indignation. In the gold mines of South Africa from half to three quarters of the workers suffered from lung diseases.[13] Similar though less flagrant conditions in various industries throughout the world have been matters of common knowledge. Upton Sinclair's exposure of the Chicago stockyards, in *The Jungle*, shocked Theodore Roosevelt and led to some congressional reform legislation. The evils of unsanitary conditions were not limited to the working population in the plants themselves or in the adjoining reeking tenements. The chemical industry poisoned the air of whole countrysides; waste products polluted the water courses; both of these conditions have raised one of the most acute problems of our national

[12] Schopenhauer, *The World as Will and Idea,* trans. R. B. Haldane and J. Kemp, 6th ed. (London, 1907), 3: 389.
[13] Compare *Western Races and the World,* ed. F. S. Marvin (London and New York, 1922), p. 216.

economy. In packed slum warrens—they could not be called homes—all comfort, privacy, and plain decency were out of the question. There are two sides to population statistics. We are told that in less than a hundred and fifty years the inhabitants of Lancashire, England, multiplied almost thirtyfold.

Two stubborn evils which still resist reform in many lands are those of women's drudgery and child labor. Even a brief word should suffice to brand the socially disastrous effects of the employment of mothers on the morale and morals of their homes. These miseries are compounded when the neglected children are themselves shoved prematurely into labor which not only deprives them of the opportunities of education and training but also robs them of their youth and stunts them in body and soul. The worst of these evils have been considerably mitigated in our country, but it took long years of seemingly futile struggle for child labor legislation to overcome the opposition of shortsighted or callous employers with their pleas of freedom of contract.

The two sides of the industrial picture can be seen strikingly in some comparative statistics. Despite the tremendous increase in overall production in the industrial countries, there is still great human destitution; but for all that, the general standard of living in the Western countries is steadily rising. The crucial question of social criticism, however, is this: Is the standard of living rising as fast as it should—and as generally? If one could venture a fair answer to this question, it should be one which avoids both despair and complacency. We are told that the per capita wealth of the Western industrial nations varies according to their developed horsepower rate of energy. The impressive increase in the worker's income has been accompanied by steady improvement in the technical and sanitary factory conditions under which he has to do his work. The manifold modernization of plant, equipment, and methods, and the overall expansion of the entire industrial enterprise has greatly enhanced production. Our present annual income is said to match our total national weath of scarcely a generation ago: the statistics get more and more impressive, but they are disturbed by critical analysis of the social distribution of all our vast resources.[14]

A fair judgment of the economic problem cannot be limited to employers and employees, capital and labor. We cannot neglect the large consuming public, and this means that we cannot consider industry alone but industry and trade, the quality and the prices of the industrial products. This aspect of the problem is a main concern of society; it affects labor itself, for the laboring class is a large part of the consuming public, and wages are worth no more than what they can purchase. The Marxists harp on the exploitation of the workers, but the terms of trade may and too often do involve the exploitation of the consuming public, which includes the laborers. A strike may enforce a rise in wages, but as it results also in increase of prices, the eventual outcome may be an added and menacing spiral of inflation. An even worse threat to our social economy is the seeming collusion of management and labor in certain industries to increase both wages and profits at the expense of the consumer. The entire field of repair and service charges in our day provides examples of this fleecing, many of them flagrant.

Our inquiry at this point clearly affects the basic appraisal of trade, the role of the middleman in our social economy—and not only or even primarily the role of the retailing trade but also of the wholesaler and jobber who stand between the producer and the consumer. Everyone who has built a house remembers that for much of his

[14] Compare D. S. Kimball, *Toward Civilization*, ed. Charles A. Beard (London and New York, 1930), p. 141.

equipment he had to visit and make his choice from the display rooms of the various manufacturers, who then delivered the chosen goods on his building site, but only via some wholesale dealers who never even saw the products but just collected their profits on the sale.

The cooperative store movement has been a reform project aiming to protect society from this sort of exploitation. Its beginning was in Lancashire, and the success of these English "Rochdale Pioneers" has been duplicated throughout Great Britain, in Scandinavia, and other European countries. With millions of shareholders, and operations not limited to store distribution of goods but extending into manufacturing fields, into agriculture, textile mills and clothing factories, machinery, automobiles, and even mining, shipping, banking, and insurance, these cooperatives represent an organization of the consuming public to produce and to distribute its needed goods with fair salaries to the operating managers and clerks but without the excessive profits involved in wholesale and retail trade. In the United States the cooperative movement has made no general headway, except in the field of agriculture, where it has attained considerable success.

A related problem confronts industry and trade in the international field, and it is becoming increasingly grave. Three main results of the Second World War were the threatening economic collapse of Western Europe and Japan, the Communist subjugation of the satellites of Soviet Russia and of China, and the crying need of great and small nations all over the world for help in their industrial program and other economic projects. The tremendous American help has led to the rebuilding of the economic structure of Western Europe and Japan, but other non-Communist countries are still the arena of the worldwide struggle between democratic order and dictatorship.

The powers behind the iron curtain operate on the basis of a rigidly controlled industry and trade. The democratic nations have been laboring under the obstacle of trade and tariff barriers. In order to present a united political front to their common peril, they require economic collaboration. Both in Europe and in Latin America nations are combining on the policy of free trade. Outstandingly important are the European Common Market and the European Free Trade Association, engaging together thirteen countries. Despite obstructive complications by still aggressive nationalism, they mark a real advance in civilization. Similar economic collaboration in Latin America indicates the beginning of a wider spread of the basic idea. The major power in industry and international trade, the United States, has not yet entered decisively in this free trade movement. Those who oppose our change of traditional tariff policy urge the need of protecting our American economy and the standard of living of American labor from the deluge of foreign imports produced by cheap labor. Against these advocates of our so-called protective tariff are the champions of a united front by the free nations of the world, which alone can save from Communist incursion the teeming millions of underdeveloped peoples who produce most of the materials which we and the other industrial nations require. These underdeveloped nations can be helped by freer and more liberal trading to rise in the economic scale and gradually to become self-reliant and more reliable fellow members of a worldwide democratic society, capable of resisting the menace of political and social oppression.

We cannot describe accurately the economic trend in American society by any wholesale statement about hours and wages of labor in general, beyond the broad recognition of improved conditions. The increasingly tighter organization of labor unions has perfected their bargaining capacities and has raised the income in certain trades to professional levels. All along the line, hours and wages and conditions of labor are more and more favorable to skilled workmen. But long dismal lines of unemployment and indigence spread even in our land of abundance. A worthy democratic society cannot be reconciled to a placid acceptance of an irreducible minimum of unemployable and destitute masses.

Alongside the high pinnacle of exceptional achievement by the dominant classes in our country, we should rather watch the lower levels: how large and how deeply sunk are our still submerged masses? We must judge and be judged by this, our tolerated minimum. In the words of the elder Lord Asquith, "the test of every civilization is the point below which the weakest and the most unfortunate are allowed to fall."[15] This truth is implied in the agelong wisdom *noblesse oblige*. A society does well to raise its summits of aim and achievement, to honor its geniuses and champions; but all these evidences of superior mastery impose a responsibility to uplift "the least of these our brethren." This humane philanthropic regard is not only good religion but also the essence of sound social intelligence. Ever since classical antiquity democracy has been charged with not caring enough about standards or about waste. In an economy of abundance we are ill advised to be careless about material waste, but we should resist the far more blameworthy carelessness about the human waste of our submerged multitudes.

The genuine solution of this social problem, without which any notion of modern historical progress must be regarded as questionable, cannot be realized by a merely external change of the economic framework. The primary and decisive need is moral. We require a humane regard for men's needs and for their personal dignity that should make it impossible for us to tolerate human degradation.

---

[15] Cited from *Theories of Social Progress*, by A. J. Todd (New York, 1919), p. 125.

Some sociologist ventured the estimate that the invention of the steam engine made available productive power equal to that of a billion men. How immensely must this estimate be increased when we add the productive power of electrical, and vastly more, of atomic energy. This must be reckoned with in considering our so-called labor saving machinery. How can it be made not labor-dumping but really labor-saving, using the forces of nature to improve the conditions and expand the opportunities of men's lives?

This problem is brought into sharp focus in our highly advanced but also greatly mechanized industrial system. The incomparable progress in technological mastery, which is an outstanding characteristic of our age, has stimulated the demand to enable men to get the most uninterrupted productive work out of the available machinery and also to devise machines that would do more and more of the work that has been done by men. These two demands are related but also distinguishable in our two industrial processes of mass production and automation.

The system of mass production has found its fullest operation on the automobile assembly line; no one has outlined its details or urged its merits more effectively than Henry Ford. In his judgment, mass production is "not merely quantity production, . . . nor is it merely machine production. . . . Mass production is the focussing upon a manufacturing process of the principles of power, accuracy, economy, system, continuity, speed and repetition. . . . The normal result is a productive organization that delivers in continuous quantities a useful commodity of standard material, workmanship and design at minimum cost."[16]

This method requires the uninterrupted concentration

[16] Henry Ford, "Mass Production"; compare *Modern Technology and Civilization*, ed. Charles R. Walker, assisted by Adelaide G. Walker (New York, 1962), p. 62.

of each workman upon one specific operation, the production of one specific part of the eventual automobile. Each kind of these parts is then delivered to its appropriate place on the assembly line, where one workman after another puts these various parts into their appropriate places. It is an immensely complicated system of separately simple operations, all working and fitting together like clockwork.

The advocates of mass production methods maintain with abundant evidence that this system, vastly complicated in its most elaborate planning, is simplicity itself in its efficient operation. It secures maximum uninterrupted use of each piece of its multitude of machines and also gets from each operator most efficient performance of his particular work. Mass production carries the principle of division of labor to its logical conclusion, and it makes possible the corresponding mass consumption of its standardized product at a marketable cost. It also makes feasible the increasingly high scale of wages paid in the mass production industry.

But numerous expert investigations at a variety of industrial plants and interviews with men at the assembly lines have reported widespread dissatisfaction. The operatives protest that they are made specific little cogs in the machinery of operation, each one repeating the same little bit hour after hour, every day and month and year, without any sense of design or activity in the work as a whole. How could they endure spending their life in inserting a bolt in a set of leaves of a spring and not even having the time to glance at the next workman down the line who is to put the nut on the bolt and tighten it? The old handcraft system, they say, was far less efficient, more tiring, but not so boring, and humanly more satisfying.

The quandary of this issue concerns more than the workman at the assembly line, for mass production depends upon, but is also a condition of mass consumption. From the point of view of the consumer, the advantages of the new system in reducing production costs, in increasing the quantity and the precision of the products are too obvious to need any discussion. Imagine the likely cost or precision of a handmade paper of pins. Industrial production by the old methods could never have made available the universal distribution in our society of the countless machines and appliances which have transformed our household economy and our daily lives. The workmen at the assembly lines are also consumers. By their tedious repetitive labors they are making possible the modern equipment of their own homes. It is a tangled problem, how to adjust the counterplaying values in the industrial process, where so many provisions for the improved general welfare are procured at so grievous human-personal cost.

Closely related to the problems of mass production, and one way of meeting some, not all, of the workmen's objections to it, are the highly technical industrial methods of automation. It has been described as "the most striking and important creation of the new scientifically based technology," including "streamlined production and assembly lines, integrated control systems for the operation of process plants, tape and other control devices to direct operation of machines, and complex electronic data-processing and retrieval systems known as computers."[17]

The new technology is producing and is to produce still more complicated machines that can be controlled and programmed to operate themselves, to turn out their own products, requiring the minimum of routine workmen's labor but direction of their complex operation by skilled technicians. Its supervision by highly trained operators is the very reverse of routine performance; it

[17] *The New Technology and Human Values*, ed. John G. Burke (Belmont, Calif., 1966), p. 105.

engages all their resources of skill and analysis and execution of a great variety of technical processes. But by its very nature automated machinery would replace the fourteen workmen on Henry Ford's line assembling an automobile spring by perhaps one or two expert technicians. The plain inferences from this fact have been very alarming to the industrial workers, who are disturbed about their future employment. This concern has been shared by some industrial executives who, persistently confident that in the long run technological progress will overcome its labor difficulties, do not fail to acknowledge its likely serious immediate hardships. Social thinkers intent chiefly on the human factor in our industrial system have shared the judgment of Mrs. Eleanor Roosevelt that "we have reached a point today where labor-saving devices are good only if they do not throw the worker out of a job." President Kennedy called the problem of automation "the major domestic challenge of the 1960s."[18] Do the 1970s promise any lessening of this challenge?

A change merely in the economic system, without a moral dynamic in public policies, may only transform social inequities, not remedy and end them. From the Elbe and the Adriatic to the China Sea, the Communist regimes are providing tragic instances of this misdirected social reconstruction. Their basic failure is not merely that they have not given the working masses their promised full share of material resources, or that they have not corrected the great disparity between the incomes of the managing minority and those of the rank and file. The persisting and disastrous evil is that of the ruthless drive of the laboring millions who have only exchanged masters, commissars instead of overseers and bosses. Under the earlier system the workers still had a certain latitude of choice; by organization of labor unions they could hope for better conditions of employ-

[18] Op. cit., pp. 163, 172.

ment, either through the compulsion of strikes or through legislation secured by their political power as voters. But in the Communist system the ruling classes unite economic and political power, industry and trade and government, and the working masses have no recourse. The Communist bureaucratic concentration on educational and technical mastery to provide aggressive and defensive armament equal to any challenge not only presents a mortal threat to the free world but also perpetuates the thralldom of its own masses.

Just as the spreading Communist power is a worldwide menace to free institutions, so the economic problems of democratic societies can no longer be treated in merely regional terms; they demand an international outlook and implementation. The entrance of modern industry into the lives of countless multitudes overseas fired in them economic and social aspirations of nationalism which eventually flamed in anticolonial revolutions, first in India and Southeast Asia and then in the whole of Africa. We who won our own freedom from colonial rule do generally sympathize with the national hopes of remote peoples overseas. On principle the spread of national independence can only be welcomed as progressive. But after the right principle comes the effective practice, and that has been hard and precarious. Leadership is ambitious, sometimes honest, often unscrupulous; the ignorant masses are incapable of meeting the political and economic demands of their new status. We are told that Congo started as an independent nation with scarcely any native university graduates. The new countries need the sympathy and guidance of their former masters whom they have disowned and whom they distrust.

Especially in the reorganization of their social economy, the dark-skinned multitudes lack the skills for effective long-range planning and are handicapped by their still primitive hand-to-mouth improvidence. Aside from their minimal resources, they have neither the resolute thrift nor the equipped ambition needed for industrial success. In the North African campaign during the Second World War the American army required immediate speed in constructing its necessary installations. But native labor was accustomed to its slow drudgery. When the high command tried stimulating a burst of energy by paying much higher wages, the immediate result was that the African workmen, finding their pockets full, took time off to empty them. What confronts those newly formed officially free nations is their inability to meet their heavy responsibilities by initial competent organization. There is a limit to the ability of the Western nations to help them, and in their desperate need those native rulers are quite ready to listen to the Communist powers. Their very rise to the level of an independent national economy, as it presents to them some immediate opportunities and much greater though distant prospects of a more abundant life, likewise embroils them in instability and confusion and threatened collapse. Their new freedom is like our atomic energy: a marvelous promise but also a dire hazard.

CHAPTER ELEVEN

Social Order and Personal Freedom

ARISTOTLE DESCRIBED MAN not only as a rational animal but also as a political animal, a social being, the perfection of whose capacities is realized in the life of the state. In both of these essential qualities of man's character, the rational and the political, there is a duality involving a contest, but also a harmony through and beyond the contest. Reason, the intelligent direction of thought and activity, is a stern discipline, a control and curb of resistant wayward mind, but it is also the way of the mind's reliable self-expression, realization of truth. So in the political range: social order is attainable only in a system of established laws which are intended to restrain insubordinate wills; yet only within the range of secure law is it possible for the individual to pursue and to attain true freedom, a personal career of social fruition. In this chapter we should undertake to trace the direction and degree of freedom which history records in this interplay of law and liberty.

In the progress of Western self-government a gradual emphasis on four constructive principles has been noted: rationality, justice, compassion, and freedom.[1] The realization of each of these four has been impeded by deep-rooted recalcitrant passions which even our boasted modern democracies have not outgrown. As we trace the historical rise from primitive to civilized social order and institutions, we are repeatedly shocked to recognize traits and impulses characteristic of savage mentality, which are still stirring in us, perhaps submerged and disowned, but persisting to embroil our higher purposes. Against this confession, however, we may also find that some of our better social values are deeply ingrained in human experience, with early dim promise in very primitive societies. Go back as far as we may, the darkness is never altogether black; reach upward to whatever height, the light is never perfect. Social progress would then be marked not by a finality of attainment but by a more steadily assured upward direction.

The state is a system of social order; its fruition is to provide the right and reliable conditions for men's productive activities in a social medium of mutual limitation and cooperation. The vitality of social order needs the dynamic of individual initiative and "the ambition of power."[2] The state cannot suppress these spurs to activity, but they must be directed and disciplined so as to safeguard the common peace and to allow fair initiative to one's fellowmen.

Man's gradual rise to reasonable citizenship and to a social order of justice and political freedom may be studied in the historical evolution of systems of laws. Primitive societies had no distinctively personal responsibility for an individual's actions, nor yet a personal recognition of a socially authoritative system of rights and wrongs. The savage was not free as an individual: without acknowledgment or even awareness of formulated laws, he was entirely controlled, but also protected, by tribal custom. Not yet a fully conscious person, he was first and last a tribesman. Tribal traditions and mores governed his

---

[1] Compare John Bowle, *Politics and Opinion in the Nineteenth Century* (London, ed. of 1954), p. 9.

[2] R. M. McIver, *The Modern State* (Oxford, 1928), p. 46.

entire conduct, his relations to his fellow-clansmen and also to aliens. A bloody quarrel with a stranger embroiled forthwith two tribes. The victim, alive or dead, required tribal vengeance or compensation, with which other tribes of the larger society were not directly concerned. Individual retaliation or tribal feud did not involve a recognized respect for general basic rights or for the conditions of common peace.

A tribesman's actions, however, might hurt more than one alien, might stir more than a feud between two tribes. The felon's own tribe, even while custom-bound to defend him, might find him unmanageable, and other tribes might feel umbrage or sound an alarm. Beyond the immediate tribal embroilment, a sense was developing of the needed preservation of the larger social order. A flagrant outrage might bring other clans to support the victim's tribal demand for punishment. Not only a felon but any other dangerous disturber of the social order, a rebel or even a reformer, might thus arouse a general resistance. When Mohammed, in the name of Allah, denounced the customs of the Arab tribes in ways which threatened the traditional worship centered around Mecca, his own tribe, the Koreish, whose prosperity depended upon its direction of the Meccan fairs and festivals, abhorred him personally and yet was tribally bound to defend him. Thereupon, it is reported, a plan was devised that an alliance of men from many tribes should assail Mohammed. His Koreish fellow-tribesmen could then, without disgrace, evade the customary duty of defending him. So Mohammed felt well advised to seek safety in flight, his *hegira*.

On very primitive levels, where tribes lived largely within their own borders and the alien was a rare intruder, the tribal outlook would prevail over any real recognition either of individual personality or of the larger intertribal social order. But in the course of his-

torical development, with increasing mobility and ramified contact of various tribes, the actions of each individual
became the object of more and more general concern.
The expansion of centralized political power, in the transition from primitive to barbarian societies, served to super-
impose the ideas of law and legal punishment over those
of tribal injury and restitution by vengeance or compensation. The murderer had struck and mutilated his victim's
tribe, but beyond this, he had outraged the chief's and
the king's peace. Just as the royal power prevailed more
and more over tribal control, exacting tribute and enforc-
ing submission, so the royal authority came to assume the
final decision, alike in satisfying individual and tribal
claims and in imposing the larger social verdict.

The ascendancy of royal power in the evolution of
laws was bound to include much arbitrary enforcement,
but the king's will was not altogether capricious. The
authoritativeness of laws was bound to depend upon their
recognized traditional sanction. Be it in India or Israel
or Greece or Rome, as people had laws, they believed
them to express immemorial social custom, even religious
authority. The code of Manu in India, however dubious
its ancient authenticity, was commonly revered as dictated
by God, and so were the Decalogue and the priestly
Mosaic code in Israel. Themis, whose scales of justice
top the domes of our courthouses, was a Greek goddess,
and not only Themis but likewise Zeus and Apollo were
worshiped as the primal lawgivers. In Rome also law,
the legal sanction, was religious in its origins.[3]

Thus in two ways tribal feuds were subordinated to the
larger social power. The king's will imposed its verdicts
in the punishment of crimes, and royal judicature sustained its force and authority by its appeal to revered
customary and religious sanctions. The increasing ex-

[3] Compare Sir Henry Maine, *Ancient Law* (New York, 1888), chapt. 7;
Fustel de Coulanges, *The Ancient City* (Boston, 1874), Bk. 3, chapt. 11.

pansion of the scope of operative law, spanning over tribal boundaries, did not directly surmount the primitive dismissal of the alien as having no valid rights against the tribesman. In many ways the alien was still an outlaw, literally, without recognized claims in court.

The slow advance beyond these primitive survivals may be traced in the judicial codes and practices of various countries. Roman jurisprudence provides probably the most notable instance of this legislative expansion. The earlier Roman law was explicitly law for Romans, for the patrician citizens of the Roman realm: civil law, *jus civile*. Its aegis and also its control must have sufficed for the original state of Rome and during the early stages of the spreading Roman power. But as the republic and then the imperium reached over land and sea to encircle the entire ancient world in its dominion, the regulating of trade between Roman citizens and foreign merchants and the administration of order among alien multitudes in Rome and in the far-flung provinces of the empire required, alongside of the old patrician code of civil law, legislation of more expansive and ramified scope. The gradual institution of the so-called *jus gentium,* law of nations, had far-reaching implications. As the city of Rome became the Eternal City, and its banners proclaimed the universal empire, so Roman law and Roman peace, *Pax Romana,* came to signalize universal principles of order and law, justice natural and fundamental. The meaning of the *jus gentium,* law of nations, was expanded to signify natural right, *jus naturale.* In the thought of the Roman jurists, some of them Stoic sages, this idea led to the conviction of the basic rights of all men whatever, a principle of all-human justice and equality before the law. So Ulpian declared in the third century of our era: "All men, according to natural right, are born free and equal."

This instance of the developing ideas in Roman jurisprudence expresses significantly some characteristic trends in the progressive conception of social order. In the early system of Roman civil law legal protection was limited to the Roman patrician citizens. The law of nations indicated a change of practical expediency in dealing with the growing multitudes of aliens in Rome and the provinces rather than an abandonment of the traditional principle of the superior and exclusive character of the Roman patricians. But in the expansion of the law of nations to signify natural right, Roman jurisprudence was moving toward a deeper recognition of the basic rights of all men, beyond actually operative legislation. Large classes of men might not be able to gain effective recognition of these rights, but the rights themselves, they felt, were essentially theirs; by inherent principle they ought to prevail. They did not prevail in Rome, nor have they prevailed fully anywhere at any time. The persistent declaration of them may be derided by cynics as hypocritical lip service. More truly, or at any rate at its best, exalted professions of this sort express insistence of the maturing social conscience on high imperatives toward which the historical processes are ascending, although too slowly.

The system of laws that protects the peaceful neighbor and citizen also restrains and stands ready to punish the delinquent. Social progress is marked alike by the more assured safeguarding of the acknowledged rights of law-abiding people and also by the less ruthless and more reasonable treatment of the lawless. The history of crime and punishment provides significant expression of this twofold advance. If we inquire into the ground of punishment, what motivates and what justifies it, the alternative answers find formulated statement in the principal penological theories. Why should the criminal be punished? Because he is guilty, and his crime demands *retribution*.

Because society must be protected and the criminal and others must be *deterred* from further crimes. Because the criminal must be disciplined, *reformed,* and reclaimed for law-abiding life. The emphasized terms distinguish the three main directions of thought in penology. In broad outline we may say that men's judgment has proceeded from a confusion of retributive and deterrent motives toward some view of reclamation and reform.

Deeply rooted passions of resentment or primitive impulses of retaliation, prior to any acknowledgment of law, seek rational justification in the doctrines of retribution, and subtle legalism may give them solemn philosophical formulation. If the retributive demand expressed only vindictiveness, it would fail of moral justification. Hegel reasoned that retribution was the revindication of the system of law which the criminal had defied and violated. Retributive punishment restores and reconstitutes the sovereignty of law. Judge and jury dare not fail to impose their verdict; the criminal's lawlessness must be solemnly refuted. Thus, as it might be said, the murderer has still a right—the right to be hanged.

Unlike retribution which in plain or in abstruse terms would "even the score," the doctrine of deterrence takes a practical forward-looking approach. Society must be protected, the lawbreaker must be punished to prevent him from further offenses and to check criminal impulses in others.

In actual operation the inflicting of punishment through the ages has expressed both retribution and deterrence. If deterrence and prevention were the explicit aims, penalties might be more severe for offenses of common frequency and very light for the rarest crimes. The shoplifter in our society might then fare worse than the murderer. But it is argued, the law metes its severity of punishment according to the gravity of the criminal violation which the social order suffers and which it is resolved to deter and prevent. There seems to be a retributive strain in this mainly deterrent reasoning. And neither of these doctrines nor both together would quite suffice to explain, let alone justify, the penal barbarities of tradition.

Lest we mistakenly comfort ourselves by thinking that only primitive and barbarian races were ruthless in punishment, we should recall that as late as modern times not only burglary and horse-stealing but theft of some shillings were capital crimes under English law. Counterfeiters were burned after being garroted. "In the Bishop of Ely's prison the gaoler prevented escapes by chaining his prisoners on their backs on the floor, and fastening a spiked iron collar about their necks."[4]

Against the black record of legal inhumanity, the modern history of prison reform manifests a slow but growing sense of reasonableness in the treatment of criminals. The increasing use of the term *reformatories* indicates the trend toward social reclamation in prison methods. The felon is still recognized as an enemy of the social order, but society that judges and punishes him is now also endeavoring to understand him. What conditions of individuality, upbringing, and milieu warped his social outlook, turned impulses and will into a criminal career? How should prison life be ordered for him, to reform him if at all possible, to reclaim him for law-abiding citizenship? These are hard questions, and no responsible prison warden would claim to know the specific answers in all individual cases. Personality eludes routine classification, and even in wholesale statistical terms we are still short of meeting adequately many glaring problems and avoiding misdirection. First offenders and young delinquents are still liable to be lumped with hardened felons where they become not reformed but

---

[4] L. T. Hobhouse, *Morals in Evolution,* 3d ed. (New York, 1915), p. 124.

more likely stiffened in criminal mentality. Against this persistent evil may be cited encouraging reports of multitudes of reclaimed criminals for whom prison discipline and training have resulted in a return to decent life. Here again are hard obstacles in the ingrained attitudes of society. The reformed criminal may leave his prison cell, ready to return to honest work, but will society accept him? Even the most sincere advocates of prison reform may be reluctant to welcome him to responsible tasks. The brand of Cain is never quite effaced; society urges itself to forgive, but it is not able to forget. Is this due to understandable insecurity and caution, or is it a case of deep-lying rancor, a righteous indignation which no actual change in the criminal's character can quite extinguish?

The fair-minded reader may be trusted to share the general tenor of the preceding discussion, insofar as it deals with the criminal individual. But he would be critical of our system of law enforcement which, in its justified respect for the accused citizen's constitutional rights, actually allows criminals and their lawyers to take advantage of the numerous loopholes in court procedure and either escape conviction altogether or postpone its actual consequences by going free on bail pending long-protracted appeals. And more emphatically our law-abiding public has been shocked by the failure of our law enforcement agencies to deal effectively with organized crime. Most notorious in its field as the giant criminal corporation in America is the Mafia, which has quite outgrown its Sicilian parentage and is operating in this country under the name of La Cosa Nostra, "Our Thing."

From its main headquarters in the New York area the Cosa Nostra reaches out with its thousands of members and their henchmen into many cities throughout the land. It is either doing its share or actually controlling a wide variety of shady and criminal activities: gambling, narcotics traffic, loan sharking and other forms of swin-

dling and extortion, burglary, larceny, murder, bribing of
public and business and labor union officials—with nefar-
ious versatility and baffling skill in evading the firm hand
of the law. The revenues of this far-flung criminal empire
run reportedly into astronomical figures.

Senator John McClellan, chairman of the Criminal
Laws and Prosecution Subcommittee, has cited in a recently published article a list of cases in which a "dis-
heartening failure" of justice is "due in significant part
to shocking judicial leniency in sentencing convicted
mafiosi." He quotes President Nixon's words to Congress
summing up the distressing facts: "We have not substantially impeded the growth and power of organized
criminal syndicates. Not a single one of the 24 Cosa
Nostra families has been destroyed. They are more firmly
entrenched than ever before."[5]

The highly complex organizational mastery which
characterizes our legitimate corporations in business, industry, and finance has found its parallel in the field of
organized crime in which the Cosa Nostra is the chief
but not the only expert. This heinous threat to our national security demands more determined and effective
resistance by our law enforcement agencies. The promise
of more stringent legislation is a hopeful sign.

The problems of crime and punishment and prison
reform lead us directly into the related one of prisoners
by capture, in war or in primitive manhunts, and so to
slavery. Anthropologists and social historians may point
out a paradox here. Our initial judgment of slavery would
be analogous to our view of Muhammadan polygamy.
Morally degrading as it has proved to be in its persistence
through later and higher stages of family morals, polygamy
was actually, in its first institution by Mohammed, a
reform of the previous general looseness in Arabian re-

---

[5] Compare Senator John McClellan's article "Weak Link in Our War
on the Mafia," in *Reader's Digest* (March 1970), pp. 56 ff.

lations of the sexes. Slavery likewise became common and institutionalized during the transition from primitive to barbarian societies. The savage on the warpath did not take or keep prisoners. He killed those whom he defeated in war, often killed and cooked them, and between battles he went on cannibal hunts. It was mainly after he moved from fishing and hunting to tilling the soil and to relatively stable labor that, needing more hands to toil and bring him profit, he changed from massacre to enslavement.

The victors wanted to have free but also reliable service. Captive women's toil involved less hazards than that of men who might take vengeance despite every precaution of master or overseer. Children trained for a life of servitude promised least risk. Some American Indians made the children of their slain war prisoners drink the blood and eat the brains of their parents, believing that this would stifle filial affection and attach them to their new life with their masters. Whether they were children or adults, male or female, slaves were valuable property requiring care and prudent treatment. There is perhaps unwitting irony in observing that slaves were often treated as members of the family: sons and slaves were both servitors profitable to their lord. Enslaved children might be adopted and reared with the born boys and girls. A skillful or very reliable slave, as he earned the respect and trust of his master, enjoyed also his hospitality. He could even sit at a chief's table or take a puff at his pipe or give advice in the management of the estate.

At this level of social morality there were no ideas of personal dignity or individual rights. The master's exploitation of the slaves' labor and also his care for their well-being were both directed by a sense of good management. The toil of slaves gave their lord leisure and the comforts of it. Servant girls and women tended to the needs and whims of their mistresses. A society of slave-owners, freed from the need of drudgery, came to regard all manual labor as beneath the dignity of freemen and turned to more genteel manners and to culture. In their own ways, slaves also had some prospects. As beasts of burden were domesticated, thralls were released from yoke and halter; with the perfection of tools and utensils, and later of rudimentary machinery, slaves' labor could be turned to more profitable uses. But always the basic motivation prevailed: feeling no guilt of oppression or exploitation, the slaveowners sought ease for themselves by the toil of others in their power.[6]

In the advance from barbarian toward civilized societies, the slave, bondman, serf, or plebeian manifest in the evolution of their social status the progressive reorganization of states, both political and economic. Even in barbarian countries a favorite slave might be freed by his master or might earn and purchase his freedom. In Babylonia marriage of a slave with a free woman was admissible, and while a slave was still regarded as so much property, he could look forward to owning himself eventually. So the master's brand on a slave's body could not be impressed indelibly; it could be altered; it could be erased altogether.[7]

Throughout antiquity the primitive origin of slavery in the thralldom of war prisoners may be traced. The war captives were the foreigners, or they were the subjugated natives held in bondage by the invading and established victors. Tradition and even religious cult and authority may reinforce the exploiting motive, to keep the master race and class dominant. The old social system of India not only distinguished the several castes but excluded millions as untouchables. A Parsee high priest of Karachi denounced this system with its hopeless outcasts as far worse than the usual slavery.[8]

[6] Compare W. G. Sumner, *Folkways* (Boston, 1907), p. 261, citing Sir Henry Maine, *Ancient Law*.

[7] Compare S. A. Cook, *The Laws of Moses and the Code of Hammurabi* (London, 1903), pp. 159 ff.

[8] Compare Maneckji Musservanji Dhalla, *Our Perfecting World* (New York, 1930), p. 211.

The Egyptians had organized enslaving expeditions; they swooped upon neighboring peoples and dragged them captive to toil in the fields or in the building of temples and pyramids. The slaves had no personal rights whatever in Egypt, but their very number allowed them some prospects. As even uncounted thousands of captive thralls did not suffice for the stupendous public works of the Pharaohs, native laborers were impressed to meet the demand. So foreign slaves worked alongside of Egyptian peasants; intermarriage in the course of time mixed them all as a lower populace of serfs. They are the ancestors of the modern fellaheen. Like their fellow drudges across the Red Sea or countless multitudes of natives in the vast black continent to the west and south of the Nile, they are developing a keen desire for decent subsistence and independence. But as they gain some self-rule, agelong ignorance and inexperience often plunge their new social order into chaos. Only years of hard trial, with some success and much failure, and much understanding help by the civilized world, can prepare them for a productive and reliable life of free, responsible citizenship.

Slavery in the Western world has had two phases. The first concerns classical Greece and more extensively Rome. The second, in Christian Europe, led to the modern slave traffic overseas, European and American, a dark blot on our civilization.

In ancient Greece as in other lands, slavery had early origins in the enforced servitude of war captives, in the subjugation of native races by the invading Hellenes, and in the contempt of classical Greeks for all alien barbarians. The spread of slavery and serfdom was a phase of the expanding social economy which exploited the toil of landless men without rights. Cruelty to war prisoners was immemorial custom. Harshness and insult recognized no differences of rank or dignity in conquered aliens. In the *Iliad* Andromache bewails her dreaded capture, should her lord Hector be defeated and Troy be ravaged by the Greeks. After the combat Achilles drags Hector's corpse tied to his chariot. In Sparta the conquering Achaian race, the Spartiates, held the native tribes whom they had subjugated in state-controlled servitude. These so-called helots were farmed out to Spartan citizens to work the land. Helots had no rights of citizenship; any resistance on their part was suppressed ruthlessly.

If any justification for slavery and serfdom was needed, Hellenic reflection supplied it by its sharp distinction between Greek citizens and barbarians. The alien had no inherent human rights against a Hellene. Plato and Aristotle took this low view of slaves. While recognizing some criticisms of slavery, Aristotle called slaves animated tools and distinguished them from other animals.[9] Yet the actual ability and intelligence of many slaves earned them individual recognition despite their formal degrading status. The practice was sometimes better than the theory. The youth of many a proud Greek house were educated by their slave pedagogues, and in Plato's dialogue *Meno* Socrates elicits the inborn mathematical intelligence of a slave boy. The lofty theory rested largely on prevailing power. Although on principle no Greek citizen could be enslaved, wars between Greek states led to cruel treatment of captives, of which Athens herself was guilty. Contrariwise, Greeks, Athenians, ran risks of enslavement when voyaging overseas. Plato himself was captured by pirates and was saved from enslavement only by ransom.

The history of slavery and serfdom in ancient Rome is a representative feature of the several stages of Roman history. The introduction of slave labor into the Roman economy on an increasingly large scale was made possible by the spreading Roman conquests, first of their adjacent Italian territories and then of land after land until the

---

[9] Compare Aristotle *Politics* 1253ᵇ, 1254ᵇ.

Romans became the masters of the ancient world. In earlier days before the Empire few citizens had slaves, and even a high patrician's estate might include scarcely a dozen. During the imperial period both Rome and the provinces became crowded with slaves. The influence of abundant slave labor on Roman life and morals was various. Slaves of exceptional ability and high personal character gained the esteem of their masters; as freedmen some even rose to acknowledged high dignity. Epictetus was the outstanding example. Some of the captives who were marched after the chariots in triumphal processions brought to Rome their cults and rituals, gained Roman converts to their faiths, and eventually turned the capital into a museum of religions. But many more found it profitable to pander to the indolence and lusts of their masters and became factors of moral corruption and degeneration.

In the Roman treatment of slaves may be noted prudent exploitation rather than humane regard, also shocking cruelty, some of which persisted during the later period of gradual admission of slaves and plebeians to the protection and rights of Roman law. Of atrocities there was a horrible surfeit which discourages citation. We read that Roman ladies at their primping used their slave-maids' backs as pincushions. The fish in Vedius Pollio's ponds were fed on slave-meat. Caesar Augustus sentenced a slave to crucifixion for having killed and eaten one of his favorite quails.[10] On the opposite side of the record is a growing condemnation not only of inhuman excesses but in the imperial period also of the whole institution of slavery. Legislative reform in this field was motivated both by realistic statesmanship and by the higher moral outlook of Roman philosophers and jurists, notably Stoics. The safety of Rome demanded an integration of slaves

[10] Compare W. E. H. Lecky, *History of European Morals from Augustus to Charlemagne* (London, ed. of 1913), 1: 303.

and plebeians into the body politic of the Imperium. Legal philosophers also reasoned that the emancipation was morally imperative. Even while slavery still persisted it was condemned as against the law of nature.

The chronicles of slavery in Hebrew, Islamic, and early Christian societies do not allow of unambiguous appraisal. They record pity for the victims of slavery rather than condemnation of the institution; or they express high precepts in contrast to harsh and even heartless practices; or they indicate slow measures of mitigating evil conditions. Mohammed found slavery deeply entrenched in Arab social economy and sought to correct its more flagrant abuses, but he did not or could not abolish it. Freeing a slave was a merit in Islam, but keeping slaves was not denounced; only excesses of cruelty were condemned and were regarded as a just ground for freeing the victims. No Muslim could be enslaved, and a slave's conversion to Islam by right earned his freedom. Moral abuse of a bondwoman by her master was stigmatized. In general, Islam's treatment of slavery combined good professions and partial reforms with much evasion and ruthless practices.

Hebrew customs, in strict application, limited slavery only to Canaanites and other Gentiles; by right no Israelite could hold a fellow countryman in servitude. Actually there were many Hebrew slaves, and the law was concerned to lessen their misery. A debtor could not be enslaved permanently; he was bound in servitude only for a stipulated period; slaves were to be freed in the seventh year of service. The record appears disturbingly twofold. An Israelite father could sell his own sons into bondage, and likewise his daughters into concubinage. But a slave could not be slain by his master and had certain implicit rights, might even acquire property of his own and purchase his freedom. Some of the earlier abuses were reformed by the Deuteronomic code, and the later prophetic and priestly thinking pointed toward radical improvement though it scarcely achieved it. The unevenness of the Old Testament view of slavery may be judged by the readiness with which modern defenders of the institution have assembled biblical texts in support of their position.

While the New Testament could not be regarded as decidedly abolitionist, the basic emphasis on Christian love and the universal outlook of the gospel pointed toward humanitarianism of all-Christian fellowship. As the apostle Paul wrote, "by one Spirit we were all baptized into one body—Jews or Greeks, slaves or free" (1 Cor. 12:13). Actually there was no initial unqualified rejection of bondage. Paul appealed to Philemon to treat his runaway slave Onesimus as a beloved brother, but he still sent the slave back to his master, even though he declared that he thus sent his very heart. The patristic chronicles of slavery pointed toward reform. Like the Roman philosophers, especially the Stoics, the fathers of the church deplored the practice, even disowned the institution on principle, but scarcely undertook a resolute emancipation. The actual progress of plebeians and slaves in status and rights during the later imperial period affected large Christian multitudes, and peculiar Christian conditions contributed to this social advance. A slave could gain honor for his class by suffering martyrdom for his faith. The church of Saint Vitale in Ravenna, today a monument of marvelous mosaics, was dedicated by Justinian to a slave's memory.[11] Tradition records several Christian bishops who had been slaves, ecclesiastical parallels of Epictetus. In the early medieval period slavery in Western Europe tended to become serfdom, villeinage, attachment to the land rather than personal thralldom. Then by slow steps of enfranchisement the tillers of the soil won their economic freedom.

[11] Compare Lecky, op. cit., 2: 69.

The advance was nowise uniform, and historical record has some surprising features. The Domesday Book, of eleventh-century England, records some 25,000 slaves held by clergy and laity. One should have expected the church to take a lead in the resistance to slavery, and we do read of bishops selling church treasures to purchase the freedom of slaves. Yet social historians also tell us that the monasteries were among the most reluctant to free their slaves. In the fifteenth century Pope Nicholas V accorded to Portugal the subjugation of Western Africa into perpetual servitude. When the Jesuits were expelled from Tsarist Russia in 1820, they were charged with holding 22,000 serfs in Poland. Throughout Russia peasant serfdom was a tradition on the vast landed properties. The serfs were legally a part of their master's estate. As Gogol's novel *Dead Souls* indicates, the landowner paid taxes on them; they were bought and sold as property even as the soil which they tilled.

The spread of slavery in Western countries is a fact humiliating to the believer in social progress. The evidence that, after centuries of attaining gradually more humane social conditions, Europeans and Americans were still capable of such brutalities toward their black fellowmen must shock any easy confidence in the reliability of social advance. The barbarian layers are still thick under the civilized crust. The hard struggle for racial justice and civil rights in our own day is a challenge to any complacent optimism. Negro slavery in Negro lands has been an immemorial iniquity which primitive tribes have not outgrown. The dismal reflection is not that savage ways of life have not advanced further toward humane civilization, but that the most civilized peoples can show so much surviving barbarism.

The Negro slave traffic seems to have been spurred by the opening of the African Gold Coast to Western exploitation. Trading cotton and gin for ivory was profitable, but more lucrative still was the traffic for black toilers needed especially in the Caribbean colonies and on the American cotton plantations. More horrible than the treatment of the Negroes by ship captains and traders was the official legal dismissal of them as so much property. In the British colonies Negroes and cattle were listed in the same bills of sale; in the southern United States the slaves were defined as "chattels personal in the hands of their owners . . . to all intents and purposes whatsoever."[12] But it should be noted that, while the French *Code noir* described the slaves as *meubles*, household goods, French and also Spanish and Portuguese colonial slavery approximated the condition of serfdom; it bound the Negroes to the soil; they could not be sold at large.

In the modern antislavery movement English Quakers were pioneers; William Wilberforce was a notable champion. British slave trading was abolished in 1807. Slavery in the French colonies had been prohibited in 1794, but Napoleon restored it, and final French abolition had to wait until 1848. The abolition movement in the United States contains the names of John Brown, W. L. Garrison, and Harriet Beecher Stowe; it became a national issue and led to the crisis of the Civil War and President Lincoln's Emancipation Proclamation. But the official abolition of slavery did not extirpate entirely the deeply rooted evils of racial injustice. In varying hostile opposition and in shifting advance or retrogression, the correction of flagrant abuses in our country and in other lands does not end the social conflict. With new hope the deprived masses demand more extensive freedoms, but these demands spur renewed resistance by certain conservative classes, "the white backlash." The stiff *Apartheid* policy of South Africa and the firm insistence

---

[12] Compare Edw. Westermarck, *The Origin and Development of the Moral Ideas* (London, 1906), 1: 705 f.

on white supremacy in Rhodesia are instances of unyielding racialism.

Our own American experience manifests in different ways the bitter convulsiveness of the racial problem. Despite our proclaimed program of civil rights legislation, its application has been condemned as too slow and inadequate. The deliberate speed urged by the courts presumably expressed a recognition of the truth that a radical reform in racial relations would involve the necessarily gradual change in social attitudes. But "deliberateness" has also been used to justify persistent delaying tactics by entrenched advocates of white supremacy who would hold the old line as long as possible and would yield the very least that they must. This sort of recalcitrancy has aggravated the resentment of the Negroes and increased their demands. The civil rights and other reforms which were not granted adequately in the 1950s were no longer viewed as sufficient and acceptable in the 1960s. While the large majority of the Negro people are still marked by patience, growing multitudes of them, especially of their youths, have been stirred to riots of criminal violence, thievery and arson and bombing in towns and cities and in the nation's capital. This violence has not shown judgment or discrimination. It has struck at colleges and universities which had opened their doors to blacks needing the higher education that would lift them to a better life and career. Even worse than the actual riots and resulting destruction has been the spreading loss of sympathy for the needed reforms by multitudes of whites who have been shocked by the criminal excesses of the black rebels. This vicious circle is aggravating the tangled problem of racial justice in our society.

Despite the extensive civilizing work by the great colonial powers in sanitation, education, agriculture, and industry, the long exploitation of native masses has left searing wounds of hatred which are hard to heal. The record varies: the Philippines provide an eloquent contrast to the Congo. Great Britain's efforts to prepare colonies for self-government, not always successful, have provided some good basis for stability in the newly established independent states. But how reliable is this expected stability? Nigeria, which had been hailed as the model of successful transition from colonial to self-governing status, has shocked the world by the unspeakable barbarism of its civil war. Throughout the world in various ways former colonial states are mismanaging their present proclaimed independence and are aggravating crises in international relations. Their problems are not all political; they complicate regional economic and social stability and are a threat to international peace.

Modern technological advance has expanded the problems of this chapter, of social order and personal freedom, to a worldwide scale. The social range in which we have to live has become increasingly global. Accordingly the systems of laws and institutions of security and peace essential to personal welfare can no longer be framed or administered in local or even in merely national terms. For good or for ill we find ourselves in worldwide involvement which rules out any isolationism as unrealistic. We live in an age when not only our personal well-being but our very existence hinges upon the outcome of some crisis far away which may threaten a nuclear war. Are we to regard with disdain or with pity the cramped outlook of some of our neighbors for whom even national exclusiveness would not suffice, who demand strictly local or regional self-determination? Too stubborn "states' rights" demands seem like distressing tribal atavism.

These reflections on contemporary actualities and ways of thought may help us in any fair survey of the agelong problem of war and peace in the historical course of international relations. Even a first glance at the facts which we are to review should rule out any bland optimism, but the irony to which we are repeatedly driven must not yield to skepticism or dour negation. We shall have to steer between the horrible and the hopeful.

War is by general consent a deadly cancer in the international organism, but it also appertains to a certain developed degree of an international order of life. The lowest order of tribal savagery does not involve the conditions of waging war in the stricter sense of that term. "War has been defined as the legal condition which equally permits two or more hostile groups to carry on a conflict by armed force."[13] While it is the greatest obstacle to the full realization of a truly civilized law-abiding life, war may be seen as itself the result of emerging civilization and legality. It is a destructive upsurge of defiant force, but defiant to a system of law. Parasitic in its spread, it draws its resources of violence from the increased advances of technology and can become most horrible in the most advanced civilizations. By the irony of inverted progress, it has become such an unthinkable nightmare in our atomic age that in our "hope of despair" we dare to deem it no longer a possibility.

In the earliest stages of savage life, when feud and vengeance govern the hostile relations of tribesmen and tribal groups, the various procedures of bloody retaliation and compounding payment yield in the course of time to a law-enforcing control by a superior authority of judge, chief, or king. Then the conflict of forces swells the feud into a war. Even after the general submission of men to the sway of law, they would reserve for themselves a recourse to strictly personal settlement of issues judged to affect their honor. The historical persistence of dueling has been agelong. Civilized states have condemned the individual duelist's spurn of law-abiding trial, but in the

---

13 Quincy Wright, *A Study of War* (Chicago, 1942), 2: 718.

relations of states to each other the old reliance on the verdict of superior force continues.

Beyond head-hunting and cannibal raids, the border clashes, dynastic jealousies, and conflicting claims to fertile lands embroiled barbarian rulers in bloody wars. The cruelties of ancient battles are on record in monumental inscriptions, in historical chronicles Egyptian or Assyrian, and more familiarly to us in the Old Testament. What is most distressing is the flagrant or unwittingly proud candor with which victorious kings recited and engraved the record of their bloody mutilations of their defeated enemies. As a relieving contrast we have occasional advocates of mercy with visions of peace. The prophet Isaiah sang a promise of the day when the nations shall beat their swords into plowshares, and even in bloodthirsty Assyria the king Tiglath-pileser III set some of his captives free in the sanctuary of Shamash, the god of righteousness and mercy.[14]

On the topic of torture and other cruelties in war the historical record is undecided. Some writers believe that they can trace a fairly long chronicle of lessened ferocity. But they advise not to attribute this gradual abatement of horror to any spread of benevolence. Rather has it been due to the actual increasing elimination of the bloodier lords of battle in every country. History agrees with epic poetry in illustrating the Gospel verse that "all who take the sword shall perish by the sword." Be it in the *Mahabharatta* or the *Nibelungenlied,* the epic bards chant the battles, the victories, and sooner or later the death of one proud warrior after another. So it goes from the first page of the *Iliad:*

> Achilles' wrath, to Greece the direful spring
> Of woes unnumber'd, heav'nly Goddess, sing!
> That wrath which hurl'd to Pluto's gloomy reign

[14] Compare L. T. Hobhouse, *Morals in Evolution,* 3d ed. (New York, 1915), p. 249.

> The souls of mighty chiefs untimely slain;
> Whose limbs unbury'd on the naked shore
> Devouring dogs and hungry vultures tore.[15]

History repeats the same agelong story in prose.

Historical evidence can provide proof for a plausible thesis that warfare through the ages has abated in its ferocity; but how repeatedly the record is upset by counterinstances, our own day has shown with tragic emphasis. We read a striking recital of the diminishing savagery of English warfare, from the wars of Stephen and Matilda in the twelfth century to the wars of the Roses in the fifteenth and those of Roundhead and Cavalier in the seventeenth. We are reminded of Montesquieu's words in eighteenth-century France, that "slaughters of prisoners made by soldiers after the heat of the action are now condemned by every civilized nation."[16] But how often the evidence runs the other way. Medieval bishops and popes may have banned on pain of excommunication any fighting on Sundays or during Lent; by the "truce of God" they were to limit battles to the first three days of the week. But the Thirty Years War of the seventeenth century recorded atrocities which reduced Germany to a desert of devastation and in which Protestants and Catholics vied in violence. And we who read the historical chronicles of the past are shocked by our own more recent memories of Rotterdam and Warsaw, Dachau and Buchenwald. They are another story humiliating to the optimistic historian.

Significant and enlightening is the gradual change, unmistakable though not thoroughgoing, in the popular attitude toward war. Traditionally the heroic souls have been celebrated in victory and mourned in death. This temper of evaluation is deeply ingrained; it serves to

---

[15] *Iliad* (Pope's translation) first page.

[16] Montesquieu, *Esprit des lois,* 15. 2; compare Alex. Sutherland, *Origin and Growth of the Moral Instinct* (London, 1898), 1: 454 ff.

maintain the strong appeal of the old epics, and we may note its expression in our less poetic estimates of the great warmakers of history. The name of Richard the Lion Hearted still sounds sweet in English ears, and tourists along with Frenchmen are thrilled by emotions different from horror and dismay on approaching Napoleon's tomb under the dome of the Hôtel des Invalides. The warlike tone is nowise extinct, but there is a change from pride in ferocity to apology for severities as unavoidable, or to lying denials of the historical record. Germans and Russians accuse each other of the frightful slaughter in Warsaw. These self-exculpations, so different from the ancient boasts of primacy in horror, are not without significance. In their false apologies they strive to appeal to a recognized popular sentiment which condemns atrocities. As Rochefoucauld told us, "Hypocrisy is the tribute which vice pays to virtue." The Kafir or Hottentot is quite candid in making his own distinction between good and evil: "Good is when I carry away someone else's wives and cows, and evil is when mine are carried away from me."[17]

Against the historical and psychological background suggested by the previous comments, we may consider more closely the causes or incentives to war, and more particularly the problem which war or the threat of it presents to our age of worldwide crisis. The incitements to war in our modern life are many, and some of them are ancient. There is the angry wound of outraged national pride or bitter rancor or envy burning for revenge. There is the pressure of seething populations which cannot be contained within existing national boundaries and which would dignify aggression as a public necessity. There is the surging protest of races still outside the pale of civilization, whose souls have been aroused enough

---

[17] Vladimir Soloviev, *War, Progress, and End of History* (London, 1915), p. 16.

to claim justice and to dream of equality, who have emerged from colonial servitude to acknowledged formal independence but who are not yet really capable of self-government and are still largely pawns in the global conflicts of great powers. The tangle of international trade and tariff barriers condemns some nations to virtual serfdom and others to futile labor. And the radical problem of some form of coexistence by powers of conflicting ideologies requires a settlement without which no merely political peace can prove enduring.[18]

In one of the most extensive works on warfare published in our time, Quincy Wright's *Study of War,* four conditions of modern life are cited as deep involvements in the problem of international hostilities: 1) the shrinking of our world resulting from modern technology; 2) the acceleration of history; 3) the progress of military invention; 4) the rise of democracy.[19] Science and technology, with perfected communication and transportation, have expanded worldwide travel and exchange of goods and ideas, have made all nations interdependent in every way. With their manifold closer contacts, cooperation but also conflicts have become more common. "Acceleration of history" has also been the result of the modern technology and its extensive wider communication of ideas and the implementation of them. Social change all over the world has become increasingly rapid. Primitive conditions of life are becoming more and more exceptional. Social statisticians tell us that, while in the days of Columbus one out of every four persons on earth was a savage, today less than 5 percent can be reckoned as primitive, and the next half-century would probably alter most of them.

In the special field of military operations, technical invention of wholly new horrendous armaments has revolutionized the entire procedure of war, strategy and tactics

---

[18] Compare R. A. Tsanoff, *Ethics,* 2d ed. (New York, 1955), p. 361.
[19] Compare Quincy Wright, *A Study of War* (Chicago, 1942), 1: 3 ff.

alike. Just as it has replaced the traditional soldier class by universal military service, it has changed the old warfare between armies by a new frightful total war among entire nations, without any noncombatants. The fourth condition of modern life, the rise of democracy, indicates a spreading national consciousness in the various countries, the importance of public opinion in determining the foreign policies of governments which is swaying the balance of decision in times of crisis. We may recognize that this popular dynamic has often been the tinder of flaming war, but as it has become more enlightened and effectively vocal it may also prove to be a growing power in international peace.

We should face our contemporary war record forthrightly in all its frightfulness, which no optimistic apologies can gainsay. How is one to judge Hegel's reported comments, made immediately after the Napoleonic campaigns, that "modern wars are carried on humanely. One person is not set in hate over against another."[20] Contemporary sociologists and historians have charged that in our twentieth century man has been more barbarous, more brutal and bloody, more inhumane to his fellowman than any men of the past. The bare statistics here are more gruesome than any grim condemnations. According to the sociologist Pitirim Sorokin, mankind has suffered during our two world wars more destruction of life and the resources of civilization than have been recorded during the preceding eight centuries.[21] Very evidently the historical record shows that man has not lessened his greed and aggressive lust of conquest. What ground do we have for hoping that men will ever change their nature and beat their swords into plowshares? Twice in our century democratic freedom has been salvaged, but only salvaged, in a precarious truce. It is now facing its third and hardest

---

[20] Hegel's *Philosophy of Right,* trans. S. W. Dyde (London, 1896), p. 340.

[21] Compare Wright, op. cit., 1: 237, citing P. Sorokin.

trial. The atomic bomb did bring the Second World War to an abrupt end in the Pacific; but the incredible expansion of atomic armament since Hiroshima has magnified beyond calculation the horrors of any future war. In terrible irony, just because of the unthinkable universal ruin which menaces us all, we are unwilling to resign ourselves to its imminence.

Before the outbreak of the First World War Norman Angell tried to check the brewing storm with his book *The Great Illusion*. It was translated into many languages and read all over the world, and while it failed to avert war it helped to spread the conviction of the "complete economic futility of conquest," the vanity of seeking "a place in the sun" by fighting for it, the radically and finally destructive effects of war all-around. More recently Arnold Toynbee has brought his all-historical outlook upon this dismal issue of war and civilization. In his book of that title he puts in terse statement his conclusion that war is "the proximate cause of the breakdown of every civilization . . . man's principal engine of social and spiritual self-defeat."[22] He traces repeatedly the eventual undoing of the warlike. This is "the burden of Nineveh," and it is exposed throughout the world in the ultimate futility of every bellicose aberration of despotic or national rapacity. Militarism is suicidal. In view of the tragic historical record, it is distressing to read the periodic glorification of war, as, for instance, the following by the Prussian commander Hellmuth von Moltke: "Perpetual peace is a dream—and not even a beautiful dream—and War is an integral part of God's ordering of the Universe. In war, man's noblest impulses come into play: courage and renunciation, fidelity to duty and a readiness to sacrifice that does not stop short of offering up life itself."[23]

[22] Arnold Toynbee, *War and Civilization* (New York, 1950), pp. vii, viii.
[23] Compare Toynbee, op. cit., p. 16.

Mankind has not yet learned its tragic lesson, not even during the past frightful half-century. The urge of aggression spurns every effort to settle conflicting demands by negotiation; it forces peace-seeking statesmen to defend justice and freedom by armed resistance. But the darkness of dismay in which the present crisis plunges us should not blind our minds to the recognition of the upward strain in men's thinking and in their striving for a better day. In the stormy days of civil war in Holland and in the flame and desolation of the spreading Thirty Years War in Germany, Hugo Grotius saw clearly and formulated the principles of international law in war and in peace. Condorcet likewise wrote his historical outline of the progress of the human mind during the bloodiest days of the French Revolution and the Terror. Today also men throughout the world are pursuing in thought and in active policy the principles of a world-order of peace and justice and freedom. But, again throughout the world, aggressive forces, and they are not all Communist, are exploiting every occasion to stir conflict and expand their spheres of control by all the tactics of rebellion and war, cold or hot. Our American dominance as a world power has led us to believe that we have the task of policing the world and defending freedom wherever menaced. But this terrestrial assignment is overtaxing our resources and capacities; it strains our best judgment and divides our people in harsh conflicts of policies and principles, as most emphatically shown in our tangled military involvement and undeclared war in Vietnam. We seem to be in a dual quandary. Our humane devotion to justice and freedom, we declare, compels us to challenge violent aggression with armed resistance; but it also forbids us to fight our enemies with our total destructive power. So we seek some justifiable and hopefully effective strategy between those of Mahatma Gandhi and Genghis-Khan.

The pursuit of the principle of a world order of justice

and peace has found expression in the formulation of a law of nations. A clear statement of the reason for it has been given by one of the greatest English jurists, Lord Mansfield: "The law of nations is founded on justice, charity, convenience, and *the reason of the thing,* and confirmed by long usage."[24] This basic justice and this reasonableness in the interrelations of peoples and states have been the agelong aims of enlightened men, but they have been obstructed by avid nationalism: both impulses evident in the meetings of the United Nations. This world-wide international forum of available negotiations is also an available vast platform for aggressive propaganda. The humanitarian appeals to international understanding are deafened by violent diatribe. But in their basic principles these conferences represent the steady endeavor of enlightened statesmanship to achieve a platform of recognized international standards of right, by reliance on which all nations, great and small, can secure their rights through fair negotiations. The global expansion of international relations, which is one mark of contemporary civilization, does incite unprincipled despots to exploit the new global tactics and armament for a more fateful enslavement of humanity. But it also inspires the world's best social conscience to reach toward unprecedented human welfare. "That mankind shares a common heritage is a creeping concept that may yet overshadow the claims of national sovereignty."[25]

[24] Quoted by J. L. Brierly, *The Law of Nations,* 4th ed. (Oxford, 1949), p. 69.
[25] Elizabeth Mann Borgese, "The World Communities," in *The Center Magazine* (Santa Barbara, Calif., Sept.-Oct., 1971), p. 11.

CHAPTER TWELVE

Intellectual and Aesthetic Values

A NOTED contemporary anthropologist has stated: "Of all our present creeds, none is more firmly or widely embraced than . . . belief in the attainment of knowledge as an unconditional good in prospect."[1] Aristotle's description of man as a rational animal and of the pursuit of knowledge as the characteristically human activity—"All men by nature desire to know"—is sustained in the history of thought by men's positive or negative appraisals of life. There has been a persistent correlation between skepticism and pessimism; contrariwise, intellectual reassurance, rational or experimental, has tended to give our basic attitude toward life a positive if not altogether optimistic tone. The belief in social progress is thus vitally concerned with the question whether intellectual values are attainable and reliable. So we are told: "The great aim of nature is intellectual development."[2] No other satisfaction in life would quite suffice, if men's characteristic pursuit of knowledge were to be exposed as futile.

Our problem here has two aspects. Is reliable and expansive knowledge attainable? And if it is attainable, how is it related to the realization of the other values of life? The interplay of these questions, which is one of exploration and criticism of men's intellectual capacities, is ever disturbed, both in individual experience and in social judgment. Scripture and poetry alike may move us to ponder in dismay that what we come to know may prove lamentable in the learning. So reflects Ecclesiastes: "In much wisdom is much grief: and he that increaseth knowledge increaseth sorrow" (1:18). This sort of comment expresses the tragic dilemma of our present age. It is well to keep it in mind from the outset.

Our inquiry into the progress of knowledge brings to our attention the dependence of technical advance on scientific progress. The two terms might just as well have been cited in the opposite order. The intellectual course has not always been from craft to insight, nor yet from pure to applied science. Men built pumps before they understood their operation; they forecast eclipses before they had any scientific grasp of astronomy. The sight of Stonehenge stirs us to marvel: how can we explain those amazing feats of structural execution, achieved without the technical machinery made possible by modern scientific mastery of mechanics? The moving of heavy blocks on tree rollers led to the discovery and use of the wheel, with its incalculable improvement in transportation. Much later, in explaining the operation of pumps through understanding the conditions and laws of air pressure, modern minds expanded, in theory and practice alike, the whole field of meteorology.

It would be superfluous to argue the main case of the actual growth of knowledge, certainly in details and to a great extent in fundamentals. What is more informing and to the point is to consider some of the characteristic features of man's maturing intellectual mastery, but then also to acknowledge its more important limitations, very apparent and maybe real and basic.

One great mark of the attainment of knowledge is recognized better if we note its dual aspect. Fruitful scientific exploration in any field requires specialized methods which may involve a high degree of abstraction. Investi-

1 R. R. Marett, *Faith, Hope, and Charity in Primitive Religion* (Oxford, 1932), p. 132.

2 J. W. Draper, *A History of the Intellectual Development of Europe* (New York and London, ed. of 1905), 2: 394.

gation must isolate its specific problem, fasten upon it and pin it down for explicit and definite solution. But as the problem is thus mastered and solved, it spreads and is ramified in implications; the special conclusion shows its bearing on other topics and issues; the one answer opens up a new variety of questions. In the very fencing off of our property for precise survey, we find the extent of its contacts with some neighboring estates and its actual but previously unsuspected adjacency to others. The scientific explanation of pumps leads to advances in various fields, to barometers and altimeters and thermometers. The discovery and understanding of X-rays, important in nuclear physics, bear fruit in transforming modern surgical procedure. The agricultural, industrial, and medical involvements of modern chemistry provide numerous examples; in one field after another, the understanding of nature seems to require acute concentration of specific inquiry, but then it yields its fruitage in widely ramified directions.

Another feature in the advance of knowledge, closely related to the one which we have just been considering, is its cumulative operation, involving periodically some startling, accelerated tempo. Some historians of civilization, recording the decline and fall of so many social projects and institutions, have also noted the more reliable vitality of intellectual activities. George Sarton, writing in the disastrous years of the Second World War, observed that "scientific activities are the only ones which are cumulative and progressive."[3] This aspect of scientific progress seems to be natural to the higher life of man. A scarcely noticeable but deeply pulsing tendency of thought that propels it in a certain direction seems suddenly to sweep forward victoriously. Even so one may scarcely observe in the apparently calm flow of the waters

[3] George Sarton, *The Life of Science* (New York, ed. of 1948), p. 24; quoted here from R. B. Perry, *Realms of Value* (Cambridge, Mass., 1954), p. 306.

of Yellowstone or Iguassú the seething surge that will presently hurl them thundering toward and then over the brink of the waterfalls. Note the creative impetus and acceleration of knowledge in the whole field of chemistry stimulated by the work of Lavoisier, or the rushing flood of invention in every branch of industry which marked the second half of the nineteenth century.

The seemingly steady and undeviating course of thought may bring it to a crossroad where it swerves radically toward wholly new ground. So we have seen rivers that have flowed smoothly across endless plains reach the barrier of some mountain height, and instead of skirting it and flowing on their level course, suddenly veer and plunge into its rocky bounds. The whole history of thought records such radical deviations. The shift of mental interest from mythology to investigation of nature which began in the sixth century B.C. marks the beginnings of Western science and philosophy. It took a dramatic turn to greatness in classical Athenian thought stirred by the Socratic concentration on self-understanding. Across some twenty centuries, at the crossroad of civilization in the Renaissance, the one city of Florence manifested the teeming fertility of creative genius with its dynamic vision of a new world to explore and exploit and recreate.

Future historians will record the even more amazing advance of science and technology in our atomic age which we are not yet able to comprehend adequately. It seems to illustrate both the increasing tempo and the radical veerings and shifts of intellectual momentum. Professional experts dramatize their statements of the marvelous progress of physical science and technology in our generation, beyond all previous ages, by telling us that the majority of physicists and engineers who have ever lived throughout history are still alive. It is not quite a hundred years since Jules Verne baffled his age with his fantasy *Around the World in Eighty Days.* Eighty days—

and they are now minutes for our astronauts. And as to radical turns of knowledge into new directions, what is more dynamic than the change of course from classical to nuclear physics?

The history of civilization records striking instances of what may be called migrations of intellectual centers of activity, and in many important centers an ascendancy and a decline. Consider classical antiquity: Athens, inconspicuous in early Greek philosophy and science, rose to outstanding dominance which it maintained for some two centuries, but then it declined without promise of resurgence at home, though with unparalleled influence on all later thought. It was followed by Alexandria, which became a world mart of ideas and doctrines, with its museum containing not only the greatest library of antiquity in all languages but also an ancient institute of advanced studies, which included, among others, Euclid and Hipparchus.

The migration of intellectual leadership takes often unpredictable and very strange turns. The descendants of the Arab camel drivers who, if tradition is right, burned the Alexandrian library were soon to become the medieval world's most zealous bibliophiles, leaders in philosophy and science, transmitters of classical wisdom, especially the Aristotelian, to the Western world. For long centuries European medical schools taught from the treatises of Arabian Avicenna; and Dante sang in his *Divine Comedy* of Averroës of Cordova "who made the great commentary."

The historians and chroniclers of knowledge usually write of its advance and transmission from culture to culture, but also of its eclipse and loss. Its inheritance is unreliable even under normal conditions of social stability; political or military crises may quite efface it. The broad curve of history may point from crude simplicity to social complexity and culture; but in many cases the direction has been reversed. Herodotus wrote of the developed and highly specialized medical practice in ancient Egypt, quite in contrast to present-day conditions in that country. A visitor to the lost Inca citadel of Machu Picchu cannot comprehend the masterly skill of its builders, working without machinery. On an old wall in Cuzco is a heavy dressed slab of stone with twelve angles in each of which, as in a jigsaw puzzle, other heavy stones fit perfectly without any mortar. And in the anthropological museum of Lima one can see not only the most delicate textile and spider web embroidery, done presumably with fish bone needles, but also mummy skulls showing marks of cranial surgery. The crushing of all this ancient knowledge and skill by the conquistadores, as they ground down the Indians to menial labor, snuffed out that ancient mastery.

In social practice knowledge is not always an abiding possession; it is not in itself assured of permanence. No idea remains unalterably valid. Of course, this may only show the self-reconstitutive character of intellectual activity. But the more searching question would still confront the mind of its own fundamental reliability. Repeatedly in history the expanding domains of thought have been menaced by skeptical incursions.

Although this skepticism has not always concluded on a note of utter negation, ever since antiquity it has challenged the confidence of productive reflection. Note the Sophistic distrust and dismissal of any alleged knowledge in the beginnings of Western science and philosophy, or even the more disturbing skepticism of Pyrrho and his successors, the more disturbing because it challenged the greater and more mature intellectual mastery of classical Athenian philosophy and invaded even the Platonic citadel of reason. Again and again in the history of thought, periods of intellectual achievement have been unsettled by some upsurge of doubt and disillusion. After the greatest achievement of Scholastic reason, in Saint Thomas Aquinas's *Summa Theologica*, Duns Scotus, "the

Subtle Doctor," himself a preeminent master of Scholastic logic, distrusted the professed rational foundations of his Christian faith and relied rather on the fiat of his pious will. Five hundred years later Hegel was declaring that the secret nature of the universe could offer no permanent resistance to the courage of science. Like a blast against this rational assurance, Schopenhauer concluded that "the more intelligent a man is, the more keenly aware is he of the darkness that surrounds him."[4] Byron, in an ironical couplet in his *Manfred,* despaired of science as "But an exchange of ignorance for that/Which is another kind of ignorance."[5] The eminent physicist Sir James Jeans writes: "Many would hold that, from the broad philosophical standpoint, the outstanding achievement of twentieth-century physics is not the theory of relativity with its welding of space and time, or the theory of quanta with its apparent negation of the laws of causation, or the dissection of the atom with its resultant discovery that things are not what they seem; it is the general recognition that we are not yet in contact with ultimate reality."[6]

Neither knowledge nor ignorance can be certified and guaranteed by an array of impressive quotations. Despite common opinion to the contrary, the basic implications of skepticism are not invariably fatal to intellectual reliance. The recognition of error, fallibility, and incertitude need not be a declaration of intellectual bankruptcy. It may well serve as evidence of a more searching and exacting intelligence. The conviction which many minds have shared with Spinoza, that truth is to be sought through the exposure of error, is significant at more than one level. Not only is truth outlined and defined by the clearance of errors, but in the very disclosure of error a perfected capacity for recognition of truth is revealed.

[4] Schopenhauer, *Sämtliche Werke,* Paul Deussen Edition (München, 1913), 10: 584.

[5] Byron, *Manfred,* 2: iv.

[6] Jeans, *The Mysterious Universe* (Cambridge, Eng., 1934 ed.), p. 111.

Furthermore, error may well serve to determine the area of available insight.

Scientific research and philosophical reflection lead us to recognize that nature has neither top nor bottom. But this would be mistakenly regarded as a skeptical conclusion. Rather it should signify to us the boundless range of available inquiry in every direction. The searching mind is always intent on comprehending, on grasping the reality which it investigates, and it aims at the utmost available simplicity of statement, at some abstract rational principle. Nature, however, seems both to gratify and to admonish our persistent reflection; at times it sagely disillusions us. In realizing the ultimate inadequacy of some sort of knowledge, we gain in wisdom, we learn that we must pursue our probing at some deeper level. So Alfred North Whitehead teaches us basic understanding: "Nature appears as a complex system whose factors are dimly discerned by us. But is not this the very truth? . . . The aim of science is to seek the simplest explanation of complex facts. We are apt to fall into the error of thinking that the facts are simple because simplicity is the goal of our quest. The guiding motto in the life of every natural philosopher should be, Seek simplicity and distrust it."[7]

The problem of man's progress or of his stagnation and frustration in attaining intellectual values is not settled by a critical reply to the general challenge of skepticism. Beyond even an encouraging reply to the question whether reliable knowledge and understanding are available at all, we have to consider the problem of what kind of knowledge is within our reach. The student of progress is disturbed here not so much by the questioned reliability of the intellect generally, but by its patently serious limitations of scope. We may call this the Pascalian

---

[7] Whitehead, *The Concept of Nature*, p. 163; quoted here from H. O. Taylor, *Freedom of the Mind in History* (London, 1924), p. 208 n.

quandary. Pascal was a master of both analytic and experimental methods. Had he not even as a youth reasoned out in his own unaided way Euclid's theorems; had he not proved and perfected the laws of air-pressure? He was clear in his conviction that the geometrical method was the best method of the mind: it defined its terms and it proved its propositions. But while he thus reaffirmed Plato's requirement of rational analysis as a condition of philosophical reflection, Pascal regarded a man who was merely a rational geometer as a skillful artisan. The science in which he worked and excelled could attain valid conclusions in its special fields, but it did not yield understanding and was not even, as science, cognizant of the problems which are of the deepest human concern: the problem of belief in God, of man's duty and moral values, man's ultimate role and destiny. For all man's knowledge of details, "the end of things and their first principles are hidden from him in impenetrable mystery."[8]

Thus we recognize here our two inquiries. We are considering our mind's capacity or incapacity to attain what may be called intelligence in valuation, reliable insight into our spiritual principles and prospects which affect us most profoundly. And we are also asking what bearing, if any, scientific knowledge and perfected technology have on these deeper human interests and values. These two inquiries are distinguishable but also related. Here we are raising the problem of the limitations of strictly intellectual inquiry to its physical-scientific factual scope. If we are to gain assurance of our available valid knowledge of nature, do we not require a conception of knowledge and of the conditions and testing of the knowing process which are inapplicable to men's so-called spiritual experiences?

Students of the history of philosophy will recognize

[8] Pascal, *Oeuvres*, Grands Écrivains ed. (Paris, 1904), 12: 78; 10: 4 f.; 12: 13.

at once the terms of the Kantian vindication of scientific knowledge, in *The Critique of Pure Reason*. Kant (1724-1804) concluded that scientific, universally valid knowledge of the world is possible so long as nature is considered as a necessarily connected system of events in space and time. To Kant himself this conclusion did not warrant unqualified negation or skepticism in morals, art, or religion. While he disavowed any theoretical metaphysics that would justify intellectual conviction of those ultimate issues, he did recognize available grounds of moral-dutiful conduct, aesthetic judgment, religious belief and devotion.

Kant's idealistic successors sought to achieve a metaphysics which would integrate nature and spirit. The outstanding philosophical system guided by this strategy was Hegel's dialectical idealism. But to many minds Kant's critical limitation of knowledge to its physical-scientific scope pointed toward a more unyielding naturalism. Matters of moral conviction or aesthetic taste or religious devotion should not be regarded mistakenly as understandable. This sort of conclusion has led many thinkers toward outright and unqualified materialism; not merely agnostic disavowal of any knowledge of God but a decisive atheistic negation of religion and of all alleged spiritual realities. Other minds of naturalistic commitment have acknowledged with some vague tolerance a certain range of conviction and taste and faith, but have definitely restricted intelligent statements to the factual scientific domain.

In our day we may note a spreading tendency, both in philosophical reflection and in more popular common reaction, to regard ethical and aesthetic judgments as merely emotive reactions, not subject to validation and unavailable for proof or disproof. As if by way of crushing rejoinder, in the field of religious discussion, some devout existentialists not merely disavow but disdain any intellectual basis or proof of religious faith as necessary ground. Their devotion seeks direct encounter with the Divine and requires not valid conclusions but life-consuming consecration. At this point our thought is embroiled in greater quandary by the fact that, while the existentialism of Kierkegaard and Barth would dismiss reliance on intellectualism in order to emphasize unwavering theistic commitment, Sartre's existentialism is initially and finally atheistic. These issues indicate some of the perplexities which confront the study of progress in men's quest for certainty, in that desire which Aristotle described as the natural activity of man, the rational animal.

Our quandaries increase when we turn to the second of the two questions mentioned above: What bearing do the attainment of scientific knowledge and its applications in perfected technology have on the other values of personal and social welfare? Our fair answer will depend upon the values which we are considering and even more upon the values which we emphasize and exalt. If, without prejudging the course and outcome of our inquiry, we may anticipate some of its evident aspects, it will be seen that the historical evidence does not warrant an answer of exclusively positive nor an exclusively negative valuation. Here, even more strikingly than in the survey of some other fields of human experience, the advance of theoretical and practical mastery is seen to manifest an expanding range of perfection and its satisfactions, but also an ever graver hazard of misdirection and frustration. The option and liable outcome of one or the other of these alternatives depends mainly upon our choice among contending values: upon that all-important humane insight without which we lack wisdom but of which it is debatable that we have any reliable knowledge.

Growing intellectual mastery in scientific knowledge and its various technical applications can be shown to increase greatly our ability to produce or to prevent certain conditions and results of our natural environment: to do or to omit as we choose. We can and we do achieve greater and more various and more effective implementation of what we choose to do. But our eventual well-being or breakdown or disaster, while it involves this scientific-technical competence, depends basically upon our intelligence in choice, depends on how we choose. The engine which we operate may propel us to a desirable destination, but it may also sweep us to destruction. Our very first thought about our state of affairs in this atomic age drives this point home.

The advance in man's understanding of the laws of nature and in his technical exploitation of its resources has been spectacular. Amazingly perfected communication in telegraph, telephone, radio, television, and incredibly accelerated travel and transportation have made it possible for men and nations to be in immediate contact, closer to each other on the opposite ends of the earth than they could be to their fellow-townsmen a bare century ago. But though they may thus be factually close together, they may yet be worlds apart in their purposes, hostile and the more destructive mutually because of their deadlier capacity to attack each other.

The spread of univeral education not only at elementary levels but also in college and university studies has greatly multiplied throughout the world, especially in our Western lands, the theoretical and technical competence which in unusually creative minds achieves important inventions. This range of productive intelligence has been expanded beyond belief by the recent perfected administrative operation of scientific teamwork which in one short generation has swept us definitely into the atomic and space age. Telstar and weather forecasting satellites, nuclear-powered ships and peaceful exploitation of atomic energy may already be signaling a new and more blessed civilization. Three centuries ago John Dryden looked forward to our marvelous day:

. . . We upon our globe's last verge shall go,
And view the ocean leaning on the sky;
From thence our rolling neighbours we shall know,
And on the lunar world securely pry.[9]

But these boons so amazing are also so dire a hazard that our daily lives seem to us a fearful gamble. In Goethe's *Faust* we read the dismal reflection, though it is attributed to the devil, that man's use of his intelligence has been to perfect his competence in corruption: "He calls it reason, 'tis his power increased/To be far beastlier than any beast."[10]

This problem of the relation of growing scientific and technical mastery to social welfare does not concern only the bearing of intellectual progress to other social values. We also ask: How does the growing intellectual mastery affect the present course and future prospects of intellectual activity itself? Two of the institutions of higher learning in the state of Texas proclaim on their main edifices the exalted worth and the liberating power of the pursuit of truth. On the main building of the state university are engraved the words of the apostle: "Ye shall know the truth, and the truth shall make you free." On the cornerstone of Rice University one may read the judgment of Democritus, that he would rather discover the cause of one fact than become king of the Persians. These are noble expressions of the high worth of intellectual values and of the life devoted to the pursuit of knowledge and truth. But what happens when the intellectual energies of men are claimed more and more by research of immediate technical application, industrial or military? Increased knowledge and technical mastery can surely perfect the external conditions of daily life and multiply greatly the available natural resources for our effective use. This progress has furthermore enabled

---

[9] Dryden, *Annus Mirabilis* (Oxford, ed. of 1915), p. clxiv.
[10] Goethe, *Faust*, Pt. 1, Prologue in Heaven, Bayard Taylor's translation.

America to defend freedom against tyrannical incursions. But beyond the still unallayed fear of a third world war is another hazard, perhaps less terrifying but very fundamental, the threat to men's intellectual activity itself.

In medieval Scholastic culture a dogmatic authoritarianism concentrated men's thought and purposes on religion and theology. The beginnings of modern thought in the Renaissance were marked by an upsurge of unbound intelligence pressing forward in every direction for the rights of free investigation and free expression. The modern mind did not ignore practical application, but it resisted dictation or constriction. The lures of industrial profit or the exactions of war emergency in our time have to a considerable degree regimented the former "republic of minds," the world society of scientists and scholars. In medieval scholasticism science was regarded as the servant of theology, but today it tends to become the cook of industry and the recruit of armament. The freedom of spirit, essential to intellectual culture, seems to be in a precarious state. Aside from the industrial and military canalizing of research, we may note overt or implied depreciation of humanistic studies: as though the humanities were only second choice for one's intellectual career, for minds that are not quite up to the principal goals of intelligence, in science and technology.

The confidence of the believers in social progress is being tested these days by the violent disturbances in our institutions of higher education. The traditional reliance on trained intelligence as a guardian of the higher values of life was emphasized especially by the liberalism of the Enlightenment. Despite the frightful Terror of the French Revolution, Condorcet persisted in his assurance that the spread and perfecting of modern education would pilot mankind to ever greater progress. But throughout the world today the universities, which have been trusted to nurture the maturing intelligence of the future guardians of a progressive social order, have been swept by the insurgence of riotous and destructive excesses.

These outbursts of violence in various countries have been incited by different factors, but they also manifest some common sources of propaganda. In many of them a well-organized hard core of rebellious leaders are evidently doing their part in the worldwide Communist program of stirring trouble. But the spread of disaffection is due to a variety of causes in different countries. In Latin America, as we have been told, university riots have long been endemic, indigenous to a society in which an educated young intelligentsia sees slight prospect of acceptable careers. In Japan the Communist infiltration has been fanned by resentful nationalism and by frustrating social and economic conditions. In Paris, as is well remembered, student rebellion against administrative and social grievances was a factor in terminating Charles de Gaulle's government. So variously in other countries.

The problem of violent unrest in American universities is particularly distressing because our nation has been the chief testing ground of Enlightenment liberalism. More than in other lands our universities have respected the principles of academic freedom, have offered higher education to the large body of young men and women preparing for the greatest variety of careers, have sought to make satisfactory residential and other provisions for their students' welfare. In fact university students in the United States have been traditionally so peaceful that certain critics have commented on their apparent indifference to public affairs. The recent radical change in this respect has been ascribed to different causes: primarily and still chiefly to the war in Vietnam. The whole problem has been aggravated by the disabilities of poverty in a highly affluent society, by the gravely menacing conditions of pollution, and by grievances against administrative and governmental policies. The Negro insurgence has added flame to the fires of revolt. Any forthright consideration of the student spirit of unrest in our colleges and universities is bound to recognize the justification for a strong protest against conditions and policies which require reform. What is sorely disturbing is not the protesting spirit itself but the violent and destructive expressions of it on the part of the mostly highly gifted and best-educated young minds in our society. The great majority of our university students do not participate in the active protests and nowise in the violent riots. But the problem still remains that a great number of students do rebel, riotously and destructively. Is the most widely available higher education so unreliable a guarantee of a progressive and intelligent, responsible way of life?

Thus we are led to recognize that our modern age has shown dramatically both promise and threat in its intellectual advance. Science and its applications can raise our whole civilization to unprecedented heights, but they also confront us with the hazard of irretrievable ruin. The fateful alternative hangs upon our choice of values, upon a wise humane insight which science and technology cannot formulate but which is a fundamental need in this age of world crisis.

We turn now to the problem of social progress in the fields of aesthetic values. The creative imagination is perhaps the most characteristically individual expression of personality, and unique genius is in many ways unavailable for historical appraisal. But the general direction which creative activity is likely to follow, the sort of art which is apt to flourish is to a considerable degree determined by its social-cultural medium. This latter aspect, clearly, is more apparent in the popular reaction to artistic activity, the creative response or the vulgarity or the stolidity of the public.

The recognition of the social expressiveness of art may be overemphasized in some sort of sociological aesthetics. Without going to such lengths we should acknowledge the social interrelations of the various aspects of civilization. What we divide conveniently in our academic departments is really organic and interwoven. The arts are creative ways of expressing the various outlooks on life in the history of civilization, from early antiquity to the modern age. The spirit of a historical epoch or a culture may be viewed in a variety of artistic media, and that spirit or prevailing tone may be disclosed in the ascendancy of some art or the decline of others. Its expression in pictorial or plastic forms may share in spirit with its poetry or drama or music. The characteristic classical genius is recognizable in Sophocles as truly as in Pheidias. Dante's *Divine Comedy* is the poetic version of the Christian view of human life and nature, which found embodiment also in the medieval cathedrals. The upsurge of dynamic creative power in the Renaissance, so evident in Leonardo Da Vinci and Michelangelo, is revealed also by Erasmus and Shakespeare. The spirit and outlook on life in our present world find both portrayal and exposure on some walls of our art museums and in our dramas; they can be read in our poems and novels.

Our approach to the arts in their close relation to the native character and direction of a cultural epoch is fully justified by the historical evidence. Our specialization in cultural activities is modern fashion and practice. The earlier origins and structure of our civilization were marked by a more integral pattern. Taboo and mana and magic were not only germinal ideas in primitive religion but also gropings toward scientific knowledge and practical mastery. The dance and the drama had definite religious beginnings. The Greek word *techné* which we translate as "art" appears in our modern languages in the forms of technique and technology. In fact, classical an-

tiquity did not have a specialized concept of "art," or
"*objets d'art*," or art museums.

The arts in the antiquity of our Western civilization
were expressions of the creative imagination motivated
by religious zeal and social-patriotic devotion. The ancient
sages had their inspiration in the folktales and legends
of immemorial cults. The *Iliad* and the *Odyssey* were not
only the first and still the greatest epics of our Western
world; they were also a Greek Bible. When the Ark of
the Covenant was brought to its shrine in Zion, King
David leaped and danced before the triumphant parade.
Even so young Sophocles danced before the marching
Greek warriors after the victory at Salamis. The Parthe-
non of Athens was not only a masterpiece of architecture
and sculpture but also a temple to Athena Parthenos, the
tutelary goddess of the Athenian people and the imaginative embodiment of the power and glory of the Athenian
state. Pheidias who designed and largely executed the
sculptures and carvings of this religious and patriotic
shrine was not an exclusively artistic genius. His art was
also a dedication to his city-state and to its immortal
goddess.

The close integral relation of the arts to the religious
cults and the social-political pattern and order of a people's
life was bound to determine artistic development and also
delimit some of its manifestations and forms. This direction and restriction may be noted especially in several
ancient civilizations which were controlled by a firmly
established priesthood and religious tradition; for example, the Egyptian preoccupation with men's destiny
after death determined what may be called the funerary
strain in their art. And Egyptian sculpture cannot be
understood without a clear recognition of the zoomorphic
strain of animal worship in their religious tradition. Many
of their gods and goddesses had animal heads, as we see
them displayed on the monuments. If the head was that

of a sheep, the deity was Mut; if a crocodile, then it was Sebek; if a bull, Apis; or an ibis with a long beak, then it was Thoth; if a jackal, Anubis. The statues of the pharaohs or the deities with human heads must have provided a welcome change to the artists.

Religious beliefs and practices may thus direct artistic design and execution. Religious doctrine and social tradition may also restrict or entirely rule out certain forms of art. We have been speaking of sculptures; but a radical shift of attitude occurs as soon as we use the word *idols*. When the religious and cultural development of a people reached the stage of monotheism, the rejection of all idolatry would terminate the major part of the sculptor's art. So the prophetic reformation of the religion of Israel rejected all graven and molten images of God as abominations. The other great religion of Semitic origin, Islam, followed Judaism in proscribing idols, and in its orthodoxy it went further: it denounced any depiction of living forms. A departure from this rigor, by the Shiah sect of Iran, made possible the distinctive expressions of Persian art. Orthodox Muhammadan genius found its outlets of perfection in incredibly versatile arabesques, in mosaics or rug-weaving or in architecture, from the Taj Mahal of Mogul India to the Alhambra of Moorish Spain.

The attitude of Christianity toward this use of graven and molten images was varied in its historical development. The Roman Catholic tradition, as it in so many ways overcame but also inherited various forms of classical culture, replaced the paintings and sculptures of Greek and Roman paganism by Christian images. The Eastern orthodox churches, while using icons and mosaics, opposed any statuary in the churches as idolatrous. This sharp disagreement was in fact one of the factors in the separation of Eastern orthodoxy from the Roman papal hierarchy. While Byzantine and Russian art produced masterpieces of iconography, it had no sculpture. In later years we may note the rigor of Puritan reformers in this respect, the resolute clearing of the new houses of Christian worship of any images whatever.

A similar survey of other aspects of the creative imagination would disclose the same cultural interplay, the active social interrelation of the arts and general culture, especially on the religious side. The medieval Gothic cathedrals impress us as humble prayers in stone. Turn from them to the Cathedral of Florence, in which the spirit of the Renaissance seems to contend with Christian contrite piety. Alberti beheld it in an emphatically Renaissance mood: "Who will hesitate to call this temple the abode of delight? Wherever you look you see everything designed for joy and good cheer."[11] Imagine such a comment about the Cathedral of Chartres!

The transition from medieval to modern culture is manifested very significantly in the ascendancy of secular literature not only in the revival of the *literae humaniores,* the more humane letters of classical culture, but also in the rise of the vernacular literatures of the modern European nations. The examination of aesthetic progress in our society can be pursued on more objective lines just because our modern society has become so decidedly secular; it can be pursued also because of its growing specialization which has allowed us a more specific artistic expression.

The individual aspect of great artistic production, as in each case the creation of unique genius, would seem to set art apart from any appraisal in terms of historical progress. In most other fields of human experience progress has been held to signify an advance in value from earlier to later historical stages. This chronological upward curve of perfectibility is obviously not illustrated in the arts. Homer or the Homeric bards began epic poetry

---

[11] Compare O. Dittrich, *Geschichte der Ethik* (Stuttgart and Berlin, 1906), 3: 347.

and seemingly forever sealed its unapproachable perfection. There is no better instance of this aspect of supreme creative mind, the timelessness of its consummation which defies analysis in historical terms. This does not mean that the *Iliad* and the *Odyssey* are entirely beyond explanation, but that there is bound to remain a final element of artistic perfection which is not the result of anything social or historical but is simply its creative self, the utterance of genius.

With all this due acknowledgment of the unique individual element in great art, we still must recognize other aspects of the career and achievements of creative mind which bring us back to its social milieu in the historical process. For all his creative individuality, an artist —be he a painter, sculptor, poet, dramatist, or composer— is partly and in many cases decisively affected by the time and place and culture of his life and activity. What would Michelangelo have become if he had been born in Israel during the prophetic reform; or Sophocles or Shakespeare as contemporaries of Anselm; or Dante in the age of Voltaire; or Beethoven in Mohammed's Arabia? The old Latin proverb, *poeta nascitur*, the poet is born, needs revision. Poets and other artists are born and also "made"; that is, their native genius requires the right environment for its full realization. The Gospel parable of the sower and his seeds teaches us here its aesthetic truth. Of the same seed, some may fall by the wayside and some among the thorns, but some of it on good ground to yield a good harvest. Who knows what multitudes of creative minds, like "mute inglorious Miltons," never had the right social ground which could fructify their genius?

In considering aesthetic values we are naturally apt to emphasize in our thought the creative artist and his work; but we should not ignore the importance of the artist's public. Art is creative but it is also, basically, communication. As the Roman poet Martial put it, "he does not write whose poems no one reads." An artist who regards himself unjustly neglected may defy the apathy of his age, but still he must be reckoning on some future more responsive generation. Like Charles Lamb, he may protest: "Hang it all, I shall write for antiquity!"— but it should be an antiquity yet to come. The historical appraisal of artistic progress involves a judgment of the public's taste and the corresponding aesthetic experience of society in various epochs.

The relation of the artist and the public is mutual; it is an interplay. The artist who needs a public and to a large degree depends upon it for the full fruition of his powers, also influences his public, redirects it to new artistic expressions and satisfactions, and may in some cases be capable of creating a new public by the stimulating power of his radical genius. The artist or poet or composer may be wooing and winning a congenial public, or they may be laying siege to reluctant or quite unresponsive reception. Their success or their failure may both be relatively immediate or at long range, lasting and steady or with some remarkable rise and fall, lapse and revival of vitality, flashing fame and then oblivion. Wagner opened a new door, and Beethoven before him, to a whole new world of musical expression. Their vital appeal has remained strong, and in Beethoven's case supreme. The public response to Brahms, now one of spreading and deepening favor, was initially partial and precarious. As to Bach, or rather the Bachs, a generally favorable reception to several composers of that name was followed by the emergence of Johann Sebastian to uncontested dominance.

The pictorial and plastic arts provide similar instances of the rise and steady or wavering eminence. Michelangelo stormed his citadel and has remained in full possession; but Raphael, whose name seemed destined to become the synonym for supreme painting, has lapsed somewhat from his once preeminent sway.

Literature, and especially poetry, affords us instances of even more immediate interplay of artists and the larger public. In the case of painting and sculpture, unless we have access to art galleries, our response to the artist's appeal must rest on our study of copies. And the appreciation of music requires for most of us its execution by virtuosos or orchestras or radios or phonographs. Only the trained musician can enjoy Mozart or Beethoven directly by reading their scores. The poet's work, however, is directly in our hands, to read and repeat and cherish. Here there is no question of good or imperfect copies, of fine or deficient performance: we have the original, and the quality of its appeal and of our response to it, the entire aesthetic experience, test directly the poet's genius and our capacity of appreciation. There need be no third party between us. In dramatic poetry, to be sure, this is not quite true, as far as the complete artistic appeal or response is concerned.

As evidence of the enduring vitality of artistic genius and of the reliable public possession and progress of aesthetic values, literature, poetry, can be most revealing. Here also we are impressed by instances of the abiding but also of the unstable character of artistic fame and what it connotes. Dante, supreme in his day and in the Renaissance, seemed thereafter to lose ground for more than two centuries before returning to acknowledged eminence. The splendor of Victor Hugo and Lord Tennyson, crowned masters for our fathers, has dimmed in our time, and who can foretell the likely power of their appeal to our children? In judging literary fame, the evaluation of critical judges and the general public reaction must both be considered, and these two may often disagree. Even if we were to say, the intelligent public, and justify our qualification, still we shall find frequent disagreement. There are acknowledged and unquestioned masters that are no longer read widely: Milton is an outstanding example. There are writers who have lost much of their early acclaim by leading critics but still command the firm loyalty of the public. In his day Ivan Turgenev, even in French translations, was hailed as the finest artist since Sophocles. More recent professional criticism, Russian and foreign, have depreciated Turgenev considerably, but they have not weakened his popularity. Even in the Soviet regime, despite his opposition to communism from its early inception, Turgenev is being read in Russia at the rate of a million copies annually.[12]

We have been inquiring in various ways into the historical stability and progress of aesthetic values, and the general impression seems to be varied, justifying neither optimistic assurance nor pessimistic negation. Our own day provides ready instances of both attitudes; considered judgment remains undecided. The impressive widespread revival of the study of the best books in individual reading and in organized groups has revived the old classics and made them the cherished choice of millions. Even on a much broader scale, the literal flood of paperbacks is supplying to multitudes of new readers the best literature of the world. One is amazed in looking over the shelves not only in bookshops but also in drugstores and on newsstands the seemingly inexhaustible variety of fine reading matter offered at popular prices. Splendid it would be, we might surely call it progress, were it the whole story; but along with the masters are the literary hacks and quacks and panders: trash and perfumed garbage cheek by jowl with the gold treasure of the ages. What judgment of the public's evaluation are we to draw from this conglomerate heap?

The arts are factors influencing the character and moral values of society. Even more characteristically they are strong imaginative expressions of the conditions and experiences of men and women. The literature of the

---

[12] Compare the Soviet *Bolshaya Encyclopedia*, Article on Turgenev (Moscow, 1962), vol. 43.

Renaissance is a prime source for the student of Renaissance mores and morals and life and character generally. Future historians will read of the state and direction of our minds and lives in the literature and other arts of the present day. Are we confused and dismayed by the impression of disorder and dissolution of values in so many of our writers and painters and composers? They are only echoing the chaotic din of our age.

We may protest and ask: Are our lives only a chaotic din and dissolution of values? An artist's portrayal reveals the manner and condition of the life which he depicts, but it also discloses and exposes the clarity or the distortion of his reflection. Goethe and Hegel both remarked that no one is a hero to his valet, not because there are no heroes but because he is a valet. And long before them Plotinus declared that a great contemplation makes a great object of contemplation. Dostoyevsky in his *House of the Dead* portrayed in searing words the moral squalor and horror and ignominy of the Siberian convicts with whom he, a political prisoner, had been caged, but he also caught and reflected the occasional ray of light and possible redemption in the midnight gloom of their accursed lives. Our own age needs more master artists that will reveal to us and preserve for posterity our contemporary life and character along its entire gamut, in full integrity and balanced insight.

CHAPTER THIRTEEN

Moral and Religious Development

No COMMENT on our contemporary culture is more common than that of the woeful contrast between our technical mastery and our moral confusion and decay. This ethical dismay is neither exclusively recent nor exceptional. Intelligent men through centuries have noted that people have attained more knowledge and skill than they can be trusted morally to use. In prose or in verse we hear Tennyson's refrain, "Knowledge comes, but wisdom lingers." We should appraise critically this judgment and understand its significance.

Our problem demands a recognition of the kind of solution we can reasonably expect. It may be that the intellectual realm is a boundless territory of unending exploration and discovery, whence the advance of knowledge and technology follows naturally. Morality, on the other hand, while its forms of personal and social expression may vary with the changing cultural and institutional milieu, may involve basically certain principles of human character and conduct which abide throughout. Henry Th. Buckle (1821-1862), comparing moral and intellectual laws, concluded that the dynamic of advance in history is along the intellectual, not the moral line. A really progressive civilization should include a twofold growth, in virtue as well as in understanding and skill. Yet while realizing the needed interplay of these two, Buckle maintained that the advance of knowledge has not been stimulated by distinctively moral motives, nor has growing intelligence led to more virtuous character. The curve of progress is in the intellectual field. "To do good to others, to sacrifice for their benefit your own wishes; to love your neighbor as yourself; to forgive your enemies; to restrain your passions; to honor your parents; to respect those who are set over you; these, and a few others, are the sole essentials of morals; but they have been known for thousands of years, and not one jot or tittle has been added to them by all the sermons, homilies, and text-books which moralists and theologians have been able to produce."[1]

This view of morality, ostensibly pessimistic, also has overtones of positive evaluation. It regards moral insight as a fundamental and abiding human possession. There can scarcely be progressive gain in man's moral enlightenment and conviction because there has been an initial moral mastery. Men here are like the reputed Bostonian who felt no need to travel because he was already there. This alleged moral competence has been asserted even by thinkers skeptical of our intellectual reliability or growth in understanding. Voltaire, quite dubious of the availability of real knowledge, upheld the universality of basic moral principles: "Dervish, fakir, bonze and talapoin, all declare everywhere; 'Be just and beneficent.' "[2]

Historical evidence, however, points to much radical development in moral ideas and practices: in men's selection and graduation of their cardinal virtues and of their vices, also in their changing views of both, in their distinction between moral performance and inner spirit and motivation; in their outlook on the scope of moral relations and duties. The detailed systematic study of these differences has been the work of descriptive ethics. The moral philosopher is confronted by the variety of

---

[1] H. Th. Buckle, *History of Civilization in England* (London, ed. of 1885), 1: 175, 180.

[2] Voltaire, *Oeuvres*, ed. Moland (Paris, 1878), 13: 181.

proposed theories among which he has to make his choice, all of them claiming to rest on tested moral experience. Wary of the likely dogmatism of any rationalistic doctrine of the Highest Good, Francis Bacon urged as a required preliminary the direct empirical study of men's actual and varied conduct and men's operative judgments of approval and condemnation. Progress in this fruitful line of inquiry was greatly stimulated by the studies of Darwin and by his successors whose treatises on the evolution of morals have expanded greatly our knowledge not only of the origin and development of moral ideas and practices but even of their earlier antecedents, of the possible gradual approaches to them in animal behavior. We have already noted the leading works in this field, and here we shall concentrate our attention on the later history of civilization, with its critical reflection of ethical theory and its growing complexity of moral problems.

Consider first the scope of recognized moral territory: men's views of the range of moral values and their grada-tion of them, the cardinal virtues of tradition, of tradition varying with culture and epoch. Any review of ethical reflection in Western civilization naturally begins with the Socratic-Platonic view of the good life. It expressed the classical ideal of harmonious self-realization through self-understanding. The principal teaching of Socrates, that the unexamined life is not worth human living, that virtue is knowledge, emphasized the central importance of critical intelligence to control men's desires and direct their will-energies. Plato's systematic perfection of these basic principles is expressed in his table of the cardinal virtues. The good life manifests control of men's appetites by reason (temperance), rational direction of their ag-gression or resistance or defense (courage), intelligent outlook and insight (wisdom), harmonious due distribu-tion of emphasis on all human interests and capacities, the virtue par excellence, justice.

Aristotle's classical ethics of the rational or Golden

Mean, while it shifts somewhat the Platonic ideal of harmony to one of balance between the extremes of excess and deficiency, maintains the classical ideal of rational control and direction as the essence of morals. Aristotle's naturalistic procedure is manifest in his expanded or rather more detailed table of virtues to express the life of rational balance in the various fields of conduct: thus recognizing, for instance, the virtues of liberality, intelligent self-esteem, right ambition, friendly civility, and others. Of importance here is his consideration of honor and pleasure. He values honor but observes that the attainment of it depends upon those by whom it is accorded to a person, and that therefore it cannot be regarded as the highest moral excellence. The consideration of honor raises the issue of honorable conduct and in particular the virtue of veracity. The pursuit of truth, of valid knowledge, was outstanding in classical evaluation, but truthfulness is not inscribed explicitly on the Greek lists of highest moral attainments. The earlier Greek Homeric tradition here seems to have been one of ambivalent judgment. Wily Odysseus was admired for his resourceful cunning, but we also read Achilles' forthright outburst in the *Iliad*, directed precisely at the "son of Laertes, Odysseus of many wiles": "Hateful to me as the gates of Hell is he that hideth one thing in his heart and uttereth another." As a dramatic comment on this moral issue, we may recall the dialogue in the *Philoctetes* of Sophocles, in which Odysseus endeavors to win over Neoptolemus in a plot of trickery:

Neoptolemus: Thou deem'st it, then, no shame to tell a lie?
Odysseus: Not if success depends upon a lie.[3]

Regarding the pursuit of pleasure, both Plato and Aristotle mediated between indulgence and abstinence. Unlike the uncritical hedonism of Aristippus, for whom the

[3] Sophocles *Philoctetes* 108 f., trans. F. Storr, Loeb Classical Library.

wise man is a connoisseur of pleasure, like a bee that
knows how to suck nectar from the bitterest flower, Plato
advocates a rational curb on passionate pleasure-seeking,
and Aristotle, while admitting pleasure among the positive
values of life, would not regard it as the Highest Good.
After Aristotle the ethics of pleasure became a central
issue between the Epicureans and the Stoics. Epicurus
regarded the attainment of pleasure as the chief value of
living, toward which all control and right direction of
life should aim. In opposition to this ethical program,
the Stoic sages urged rigorous conformity to reason, without any concession to the desires and passions, rational
serenity in all vicissitudes, *apathy.*

The history of Greek and Roman ethics reflects the
characteristic classical outlook on life. The progress which
its historical development manifests is not a rise from
lower to higher—from Plato and Aristotle to Cicero and
Epictetus—but rather a cultural expansion of outlook, from
an Athenian to a Hellenistic perspective. The spreading
culture and the intermingling of races in the expanding
Roman empire, the ancient melting pot of civilizations
which made Alexandria a world forum of ideas and ideals
and Rome a veritable museum of religions, was fertile
ground for new prophets and sages and saviors. Within
this diversity of doctrines and turmoil of cults Christianity
took root and in its development gave moral redirection
to the Western world.

The turn from classical to Christian morals was a turn
from secularism or humanism to contrite otherworldliness.
This radical transition is revealed clearly by a comparison
of Aristotle's table of virtues with the beatitudes in the
Sermon on the Mount: Blessed are the poor in spirit;—
they that mourn;—the meek;—they that hunger and thirst
after righteousness;—the merciful;—the pure in heart;—the
peacemakers;—they that have been persecuted for righteousness' sake. These are not the virtues of self-reliant

energetic living, but we are not to misinterpret Christian morality as life-denying. It subordinated all human desires and ambitions to the earnest doing of God's will. The true fulfillment of man was not to be found in external mastery or advantage but in the deepening of the inner life and in godly devotion: "For what is a man profited, if he should gain the whole world and lose or forfeit his own self?"

Christian reflection did not reject the principles and values of classical ethics, at least not altogether, but it subordinated them to its religious emphasis. Even in their secular perspectives, while the cardinal virtues of Plato were good, they were not the essential and final good, not "the better part." So Saint Ambrose called them, in a phrase that is not so perverse as it sounds, "splended vices," and he reinterpreted them all four in the spirit of Christian loyalty. Saint Thomas Aquinas likewise exalted the higher theological virtues of Saint Paul's triad: faith, hope, and Christian love, *caritas.*

The upsurge of aggressive humanism during the Renaissance is distinguished strikingly by the revival of secular self-reliance. The return to Epicurean hedonism, as by Lorenzo Valla, was only one expression of the invading worldliness. The new spirit found expression on different levels of individualism. On the one hand, we may find Giordano Bruno's emphasis on unwavering integrity in the pursuit of truth, without any supine conformity to dogmatic authoritarianism. Under the championship of capitalized Truth a new table of virtues for the life of free productive inquiry was outlined, including among others Law, Judgment, Culture, Philanthropy. On the other hand, this very release of men from authoritarian restrictions led multitudes to willful abandonment of moral standards and principles. This dissolute worldliness may be noted in the meaning which the word *virtù* came to have in Renaissance usage. It did not signify virtue in the traditional moral sense; it meant rather astute effectiveness and finesse in whatever a person might undertake, be it even thieving or revenge or profligacy or murder: whatever suited one's desires, carried out with the skill of a master.

From our side of the Atlantic, we find this varied ethical outlook illustrated in Benjamin Franklin's *Autobiography,* in his list of thirteen virtues by which he proposed to guide his daily conduct: "Temperance, Silence, Order, Resolution, Frugality, Industry, Sincerity, Justice, Moderation, Cleanliness, Tranquility, Chastity, Humility: Imitate Jesus and Socrates."[4]

The last phrase in Franklin's statement expresses the modern spirit at its best, correlating the Christian values with those of classical antiquity. In morality as in other human activities, the history of our civilization has been a process of expanding range and complexity. Progress in this field would depend upon the right direction and choice between contending values, in an increasingly vaster scope, with ever more important alternatives. Instances of such progress are notable, but also grievous misdirections. We may recognize especially the disparity of performance and motivation: despite our appeals, we may be condemned by one or the other. As we noted before, hypocrisy is called the tribute vice pays to virtue. The tribute is also an acknowledgment of commonly recognized standards of conduct. A hypocrite does not really conform to the standard in his actual conduct, but he does not defy it in his profession, however insincere. Men's actual performance rarely follows their avowed principles, but acknowledgment of principles and standards is a normal preliminary to moral progress in conduct.

So we may read and understand the self-glorification of conquering despots graven on cuneiform tablets or

---

[4] *Benjamin Franklin's Autobiographical Writings,* ed. Carl Van Doren (New York, 1945), p. 626.

monuments of victory in Nineveh or Babylon, boasting of the thousands of defeated victims, slain or tortured or mutilated. In our day Hitler and Stalin actually multiplied this black record beyond belief, but in the denial of their atrocities lies a recognition of the higher moral consciousness of contemporary civilization. What great modern artist would boast of his murderous exploits as Benvenuto Cellini, that he had stabbed his enemy with *virtù*, right in the public square among his cronies. The Communist, now rattling his atomic weapons, now chanting professions of peace in controversy, indicates the dual drift in our moral climate.

As it is with atrocities ancient or modern, so it is with international aid. The least suggestion of it in antiquity would have been suspected as some sort of a Trojan horse. This kind of suspicion is nowise extinct in our day. Throughout the world needy nations great and small have acknowledged our American readiness to spend and tax ourselves in projects that might lift them to a more decent level of existence, yet many of the peoples we have helped have joined our critics in declaring that all those loans and grants and services have been motivated only by selfish reckoning of our own interests. We may acknowledge the high motives of philanthropy, but we are apt to distrust any alleged or proposed conformity to it in project or in action.

One important mark of moral progress or rather one test of it may be recognized in the expanding range of acknowledged moral relations and obligations. The curve of development seems to point from clannishness to broad humanitarianism, from tribal or national limitations, to or toward some degree of international morality. Whittier's stanza comes to mind as a hopeful prospect. We should remember his noble struggle against slavery:

> Yet sometimes glimpses on my sight,
> Through present wrong, the eternal right;

And, step by step, since time began,
I see the steady gain of man.[5]

Even at the present time, we can scarcely regard international morality as more than a goal, in many respects still dim and distant. Nevertheless, it is today a recognized goal. Moral tribalism persists in barbarian lands, and even the most advanced societies are not free of national exclusiveness. But the best social conscience of our day does look beyond traditional boundaries, even though our actual conduct still belies our lofty professions. Advance in acknowledgment of all-human moral outlook has been due to the evidently ruinous results of the flagrant disregard of it, but repeatedly a moral atavism has driven modern statesmanship to dismal retrogression. While diplomacy formulated its elaborate procedure of negotiations and formalities in the declaration and conduct of war, armistices and peace treaties, the record of our age is distressing with its return to undeclared war and disregard of international law: Japan's attack on Pearl Harbor, Hitler's invasion of Russia and the Low countries, Communist incursions in Asia, and the present worldwide dread of abrupt eruption of atomic war. And what about U.S. incursions in S.E. Asia?

Public morals, especially in international relations, provide striking evidence of historical progress but also of backsliding or collapse. The record is not very different in some other fields of activity involving moral values. In the economic area, the progressive advance from slave labor, serfdom, and villeinage to the emancipation of workingmen in the modern free enterprise system is an outstanding instance of moral progress. But the historian of our time must record also the check to further advance and the moral breakdown represented by the Communist economy with its compulsion of the workers by overmastering state control. On the other hand, the enormous

[5] Whittier, "The Chapel of the Hermit."

power gained by organized labor has been profitable but also restrictive to the individual worker and has embroiled our modern system in conflicts and strikes with disregard for the common welfare.

Another field may be mentioned, in the more personal relations of family life, in which the history of civilization is a record of the emancipation of women and in the gradual spread of monogamy. Even in Muhammadan lands polygamy has become increasingly exceptional. Marriage by capture and by purchase survive only in the very primitive areas. Even the formally respectable *mariage de convenance* is becoming an anachronism. But the spreading instability of modern family life, precisely in the more advanced countries, is depressing, especially the callous attitude with which it is regarded. The scrambling and unscrambling of countless families is leading in effect to a modern revival of promiscuity, demoralizing to the children and responsible for many of the shocking evils of juvenile delinquency. This is the seamy underside of the generally enviable record of progressive freedom of modern men and women in genuinely monogamous lives.

Modern development in history thus relates to problems in various fields of individual and social activity. They all in one way or another have a moral aspect and involvement. The thought of our age is confronted with the conviction of crisis, but a crisis which on a closer study is disclosed in a dual perspective: either as a brink or as a threshold.

This chapter deals with two very debatable topics in the study of social-historical progress: of these two, religion has been even more controversial than morals. Throughout history it has signified the highest ideal of man's devotion, but it has also been the animus of grim oppression and the most bitter strife. In its own speech it has been exalted as the source and sanction of man's best attainments: "The fear of the Lord is the beginning of wisdom." Even a secular mind like Goethe observed that no religiously stolid age or people have produced poetry of the highest worth. Yet from outside the temples godless men have flouted religion with taunts of scorn and defiance. Lucretius, who might be cited as a classic rejoinder to Goethe's tribute, praised his master Epicurus in great hexameters for his emancipation of men from superstitions: *Tantum religio potuit suadere malorum.* "Such is the power of religion, evils in life to engender." In our day Communist propaganda has branded religion as "opiate for the people." Deeper insight into this issue may be gained from the old Roman epigram *Corruptio optimi pessima*—"The corruption of the best yields the worst." This insight could also be revealed in our study of other high values of our experience: love, patriotism.

On principle we should expect that religion, professedly man's highest spiritual expression, should signify also his progressive spiritual ascent. It is of interest to note this kinship of religion and progress: the quasi-religious element of faith in progress often persists in minds to which traditional forms of religion have lost their appeal. So we are told by a penetrating student of the historical march of ideas, Antoine A. Cournot (1801-1877): "No idea . . . is closer to the family of religious ideas than the idea of progress. . . . Like religious faith, it has the virtue of uplifting souls and characters."[6] In considering the religious aspect of the problem of social progress, two related inquiries should be distinguished. Does history disclose a progress in religion? And what has been the effect of religious beliefs and practices upon social well-being: has religion been an upbuilding or a retarding factor or even a hostile influence, resistant to human progress?

---

[6] Antoine A. Cournot, *Considérations sur la marche des idées* (Paris, 1872), 2: 425; cited here from Lord Acton's *Lectures on Modern History* (London, 1912), p. 324.

The multiplicity of proposed definitions of religion indicates its variety of manifestations in historical development. Ancient languages have different words to describe the religious experience of their respective cultures, but for the general and basic character of them all we have to share the Latin term *religio*. If we ask, what is the fundamental meaning of religion—as including but not reducible to that which the Hindu Brahmin called knowledge or devotion or faith, which was law to the Buddhist, the doctrine to the Confucian, the way to the Taoist, obedience and submission to the Arab, faith to the Christian—the answers would also be many, expressing many traditions and ways of approach. They should be considered as aspects of a more comprehensive view.

The traditional definition of religion as belief in God is partial and historically limited. Its inclusion of tribal monolatry and polytheism and pantheism and monotheism and deism may be criticized as ambiguous; it may also be regarded as a merit of historical comprehensiveness. This definition precludes a religion like Confucianism, which is not concerned with any form of theism, and Buddhism, which in its original expression was explicitly atheistic. Should we expand the concept of God to signify spiritual Reality, or the Ultimate, or the Infinite, it may be objected that these would be alternatives of, or alternatives to, theology—a variety of beliefs and doctrines. It has been held, however, that religion is not fundamentally a belief, a creed, not basically an intellectual experience, but rather and essentially a form of practice—and not merely outward obedient conformity to sacrifices and ritual but devout practice, charged with emotional intensity—as Matthew Arnold called it, "morality touched with emotion." Preeminent expressions of this element of feeling by saintly mystics have always evoked the deepest religious veneration. So Friedrich Schleiermacher (1768-1834), without quite dismissing either theology or godly works, exalted religion as "a sense and a taste of the Infinite."

These various views of religion would describe the experience itself and also its object. Our term *worship*, a word of wide and deep connotation, has the merit of expressing both of these aspects of religion. It includes the idea of that which is worshiped, a worshipful attitude toward it, and the translation of belief and feeling into a devout life. All the way through we may note the central importance of value-connotation in the religious outlook. The object of religious worship, call it God, or the Divine, or the Holy, or the Infinite, as the supreme in value and the heart of religion in its various stages and aspects has been its concern with the conservation of values and of the highest values. A stanza by Goethe comes to mind here:

> The best that each one has and knows
> He names it God, his God, bestows
> Upon him, heaven and earth above,
> His fear, and where he can, his love.

We have used the word *concern;* in our day religion has been defined as man's ultimate concern or as man's deepest solicitude.[7] These are very significant insights insofar as they connote utmost devotion. But concern and solicitude may also suggest insecurity and may not come up to conviction. We may propose a view of religion as men's conviction of the supreme reality of the highest values, or more broadly if also more vaguely, as men's deepest and utmost response to the Highest.

In turning now to the question whether there has been a progress in religion, I should obviously disavow any intention of adequate survey. Only some significant high-points in the history of religion may be recognized. We

---

[7] Compare Paul Tillich, *Systematic Theology* (Chicago, 1951), 1: 12; R. B. Perry, *Realms of Value* (Cambridge, Mass., 1954), p. 463.

might study religion, the definition and the historical development of it, in an altogether neutral or even in a negative spirit, even as we may consider the definition and the history of magic. Or we may examine religion as we examine art in its different aspects and historical development, as a fundamentally significant experience and expression of reality. The present discussion proceeds from the latter standpoint.

Whatever our basic view and evaluation of religion may be, the study of its development does lead us to recognize certain progress in rising and more maturing cultures. We may consider only one instance: the Judeo-Christian religion. The biblical writings, as they have been reinterpreted by competent modern scholars, provide us with an impressive record of religious advance, both in men's view of God and of their relation to God, the religious experience. The early religion of the Hebrews was tribal monolatry emphasizing ritual and external observance. Yahveh was the God of the tribes of Israel and of the Israelitish soil, even as other gods with other names were the tribal deities of other peoples and other lands. When the Hebrew chieftain Jephthah fought a successful battle, he rejected the pleas of his enemies: "Wilt thou not possess that which Chemosh thy god giveth thee to possess? So whomsoever Yahveh our God shall drive from before us, them will we possess" (Judg. 11:24). When Naaman the Syrian general was healed of his leprosy by the prophet Elisha, he vowed that in his own home he would offer sacrifices only to Yahveh. So he asked Elisha for "two mules' burden of earth," so that he could stand on Israelitish soil in order to worship Israel's God.

From this tribal ceremonial ritual, the prophets of Israel, starting with the eighth-century prophets, led the people toward a higher religion, to the worship of a universal God exacting personal devotion in righteousness

and justice and mercy and love. The attainment or rather
the advocacy of this ethical monotheism and personal
religion marked one of the summits of spiritual advance
in history. Its inspired utterances, by Micah and after him
by Jeremiah and "Second Isaiah," are in dramatic contrast to the speech of the earlier tribal cult of Yahveh:
"He hath showed thee, O man, what is good, and what
doth the Lord require of thee, but to do justly, and to
love mercy, and to walk humbly with thy God" (Mic. 6:8)?
"Am I a God at hand, saith the Lord, and not a God afar
off (Jer. 23:23)? "Who hath measured the waters in the
hollow of his hand, and meted out the heavens with a
span, and comprehended the dust of the earth in a measure, and weighed the mountains in scales, and the hills
in a balance (Isa. 40:12)? "Whither shall I go from thy
Spirit, and whither shall I flee from thy presence (Ps.
139:7)?

It can scarcely be held that this ethical monotheism
was fully grasped by the people or adopted by the priests
of Israel. The challenge of John the Baptist indicates
the extent to which the old religious ceremonial tribalism
persisted, long centuries after the prophetic call to reform:
"Bring forth . . . fruits meet for repentance; and think
not to say within yourselves, We have Abraham to our
father; for I say unto you that God is able of these stones
to raise up children unto Abraham" (Matt. 3:8-9).

Jesus of Nazareth spiritualized thoroughly the idea of
God, of the Kingdom of God, of men's personal experience
and worship of the divine. He told the woman of Samaria
that God is not enclosed or enshrined anywhere, on the
Samaritan mountain or in Zion's temple: "God is spirit,
and they that worship him must worship in spirit and in
truth" (John 4:20). The Kingdom of God is not "Lo here!
or lo there! for behold, the Kingdom of God is within
you" (Luke 17:21). And the Sermon on the Mount records
the deep spiritual reinterpretation of the religious life,

from external observance to most intimate personal devotion and fulfillment.

The skeptical appraiser of religious progress would interpose here: Has Christendom through its long centuries come up to the Sermon on the Mount, to the religious vision of the Gospels, any more truly than the Jewish people and the Jewish priests came up to the spiritual challenge of the prophets? The sublime ascents of religious geniuses have scarcely been matched by a corresponding rise in spiritual level of popular insight and aspiration. In this respect religion is like art and unlike science. While we cannot maintain that the historical course of intellectual attainment since classical antiquity has been marked by an uninterrupted advance, we do recognize that by and large the later science is the better. No such chronological curve of steadily maturing perfection is notable in art or in religion. In these two fields of human activity creative genius has repeatedly reached summits of perfection and sublimity which were not merely contemporaneous expressions of their age but ideal heights which later generations might approach but scarcely surmount. In this respect Buddha and Jeremiah are like Sophocles and Pheidias. Even more truly than the great masters of art, the religious geniuses have given supreme and abiding utterance of some spiritual values, have sanctified a new religious tradition. But we should acknowledge that these sublime utterances and visions have also lifted men's eyes from high to still higher ideals. Thus we may perceive the rise from the prophetic reformation in Israel to the deeper and more universal spiritualizing of religious values in the Christian gospel. Historically the older gospel and its revision or radical reform have developed side by side. Occasionally, as in the heroic faith of Zoroastrianism, a profoundly significant religious appeal has lost its power and become only a noble episode rather than a vital, ongoing religious alternative.

To the devout member of each religious confession nothing is higher than its own ideal. Even the thoroughly objective student of the history of religions cannot rank in a spiritual hierarchy all the great prophets and saviors. But he would be sure that, whatever the hierarchical order, it does not necessarily follow historical sequence. Mohammed is not more sublime than Jesus because he comes later. Historical progress in religion may well be traced on a very broad scale, from primitive monolatry and fetishism to polytheism to monotheism or pantheism, from crude ritualism to godly righteousness. But when spiritual growth has reached its fuller maturity, its ascents to sublimity are various and we cannot grade them confidently in every respect. What the course of history may reveal here is progress in the truer and more intelligent devotion of men to their avowed savior's ideals. Here again religious progress parallels the artistic in the growing enlightenment and appreciation attained by the public.

This approach to the problem of religious progress appears reasonable, but we are directly embroiled in a perplexity. In the course of history savage and barbarian rituals have proved less difficult to practice and perfect than the worship and piety of the higher religions. The loftier the ascent, the more arduous it is. The spreading and deepening problems seem ever to outstrip the solutions; the farther the saint reaches, the less within his grasp is the holiness to which he aspires. Here is the religious parallel to the moral truth which we have been told, that the blessings of a satisfied conscience are least enjoyed where they are most nearly deserved. In the realm of spiritual values progress is not in their complete possession and enjoyment, but in the fuller recognition of them as ideals still before and above us. And in the saint's aspiration toward holiness is his consciousness that the ideal toward which he strives must include his own

endeavors to pursue it. Josiah Royce (1865-1916) expressed this truth clearly: The best world for a moral
agent is "one that needs him to make it still better."[8]
Only, unlike intellectual or moral commitment, the commitment of religious piety is not wholly self-reliant but
worshipful: worshipful humility before the ideal, worshipful devotion to pursue it.

In considering the relation of religious beliefs and
practices and institutions to general social welfare, the
positive appraisals of devout praise are readily forthcoming. In order to approach a reasonable balance of
evaluation, we should attend to the skeptics and de-
tractors. Even without a hostile animus, competent social
historians have traced the record of organized religion as
an obstacle to progress, especially in the intellectual field.
Distinguished works like *The Conflict of Religion and
Science* by J. W. Draper (1811-1882) and *History of the
Warfare of Science and Theology* by A. D. White (1832-
1918) indicate in their titles the substance of their arguments. Dismal records of organized religion expose its
suppression of critical thought and reform in the persecution of branded heresy. We are told that the fires of the
Spanish Inquisition in Toledo did not die down for over
a century. The clerical trials and tortures of alleged
witches fill some of the blackest chapters of Western
history. The martyrdom of Giordano Bruno, the imprison-
ment of Galileo and before him of Roger Bacon are
tragic instances of the hostility of the surpliced power
to scientific advance. Bitter intolerance and bigotry have
repeatedly locked religious opponents in bloody conflicts.
The one foul memory of Saint Bartholomew's Eve should
suffice. The Thirty Years War between Protestants and
Catholics in the seventeenth century reduced Germany

[8] Josiah Royce, *The World and the Individual* (New York, 1900),
2: 340.

to a desert. The bloody hostilities of Hindus and Muhammadans in India and of Protestants and Roman Catholics in Ireland are contemporary parallels.

This dreary record cannot be dismissed, but it is only one side of the ledger of critical reckoning. Intense conviction that so often turns into violent bigotry is also a condition of heroic and creative pursuit and attainment of high values. A historical survey and appraisal of patriotism would be confronted by a grim array of aberrations and atrocities, not unlike those of religious fanaticism. Neither patriotism nor religion would stand utterly defamed by such a judgment. The other side of the picture, the rest of the story, is not less striking, and it is more enlightening.

Against the dark aspects of ecclesiastical dominance in the persecution of witches and heretics stands the eminent record of the medieval church in its gradual civilizing of northern Europe during the long "Dark Ages." The Order of Cluny, established at the beginning of the tenth century and founding hundreds of monasteries throughout Europe, became a living power of social reform, giving chivalry a moral tone, emphasizing duties and responsibilities, the conviction of personal dignity in the system of feudalism.[9] Organized religion which resisted the advance of secular thought was itself the medium of enlightenment and learning through long years of general ignorance

We should not fail to recognize, across the long span of various cults and religions throughout history, a basic concern for fairness and charity and goodwill. The Golden Rule of our biblical-Christian tradition has been paralleled in various forms in other religions: not only to do to others as we would that men should do to us, but to avoid retaliation and return good for evil. So Taoism taught men

---

[9] Compare Maurice de Wulf, *Philosophy and Civilization in the Middle Ages* (New York, 1922), p. 27.

to requite hatred with goodness; and the Buddhist *Dhammapada:* "Let a man overcome anger by love, . . . the greedy by liberality, . . . the liar by truth." Not only in the higher reaches of religious development but also at its lower levels religion has stirred and nourished the socially binding power of goodwill. A distinguished modern anthropologist maintains that "real progress is progress in charity" and observes that "the true function of religion is to enlarge charity." The spread of charity on a universal scale may be impeded by the irreconcilable plurality of religious faiths, yet it needs a religious dynamic as its motivating power.[10]

We seem to be confronted by a paradoxical contention of values in which good and evil are productive of each other. Religion has been the cohesive power in men's higher life, welding common spirit and solidarity and devotion. It has been in all ages the expression of men's groping and reach after the ideal. Religion has also been the animus of dissension and controversy and strife; it has stirred and stubbornly preserved superstitions and bigoted ignorance. And yet, as Robert Burns wrote, "The light that led astray/Was light from heaven."[11] Where good and evil, high and low values seem to be thus intertwined and interacting, how are we to judge not only of progress but also of the right hierarchy of values? Milton wrote in his *Areopagitica:* "Good and evil we know in the field of this world grow up together almost inseparably; and the knowledge of good is so involved and interwoven with the knowledge of evil and in so many cunning resemblances hardly to be discerned." This passage was cited by the author of *The Golden Bough* as a motto for his book *The Devil's Disciple: A Plea for Superstition.*

[10] Compare R. R. Marett, *Head, Heart, and Hands in Human Evolution* (New York, 1935), p. 40; compare also Marett, *Faith, Hope, and Charity in Primitive Religion* (Oxford, 1932), pp. 164-78.

[11] Compare T. R. Glover, *Progress in Religion to the Christian Era* (London, 1922), p. 339.

What J. G. Frazer (1854-1941) had in mind was to show that in social history many solid institutions rest on rotten foundations: "The odd thing is that in spite, or perhaps by virtue of his absurdities man moves steadily upward."[12] Even in the murk of savage superstition we may see gleams of spiritual vision; but again, the full noonday of religious enlightenment has been repeatedly clouded by dark bigotry.

Few instances disclose this duality more strikingly than those provided by the evolution of prayer, itself a most revealing aspect of religious experience. Three broad stages of this development have been pointed out.[13] At the lowest one, prayers are typically incantation spells, magical rites, by the expert performance of which benighted tribesmen believe that they can impose their wills on the occult powers in nature and accomplish their purposes, of bringing rain or checking a blight or bane or destroying an enemy. As sooner or later these incantation spells expose their futility—as Chantecler oversleeps and wakes to see the sun rise despite his failure to crow—men turn in their prayers from motives of magical compulsion to cajolery, to pleas and petitions. At this second stage of prayer, what men entreat their gods to give them discloses their views alike of deity and of the order of nature. Maturing insight gradually affects men's sense both of the seeming efficacy and, more important, of the religious appropriateness of their petitions.

It is at the second stage that we may note, amidst the usual benighted pleas, surprising occasional evidence of a higher spiritual attitude and also strange lapses from much higher ground. The tribesman may beg and wheedle and even resort to threats: "Why art thou so stingy? If thou dost not amend, we shall also forget thee, and then

---

[12] J. G. Frazer, *The Devil's Advocate: A Plea for Superstition* (London, 1927), pp. vii, 4.

[13] Compare L. R. Farnell, *The Evolution of Religion* (London, 1905).

thou canst go and eat grasshoppers." This from a Zulu; but then amazingly and, of course, not at all characteristically, this outburst from Martin Luther: "If we should finally become angry towards Thee, and no longer bring honor and tribute to Thee, how wouldst Thou continue?"

But common worshiper and seer, prophet and theologian are alike humbled and exalted by a deeper sense of the divine. Prayers become the expressions of a communion with God, consecration and submission of the pious will. Instead of seeking by spells and holy magic or by wheedling and entreaties to engage the occult Power to accomplish their own will, men's prayers in various ways tend to approximate to the prayer in the Garden of Gethsemane: "Thy will be done." Even though, as the worshiper kneels, he may be intensely engrossed by his special need and plight, he may be brought by his prayer itself to a deeper sense of his real need, to commit himself and his will to God and be blessed in godliness. This higher attitude in prayer may be noted in all the great religions. So the Psalmist prayed: "Create in me a clean heart, O God." And Socrates: "Grant me to become noble of heart." And later, in Rome, Epictetus: "Do with me what thou wilt." Yet strange and inspiring instances of it may be cited from the most primitive stages of religious evolution: "Thou knowest what is good for us: give it to us."

Along the entire course of growing spiritual maturity, higher and lower values contend for dominance. The saint may cry out: *"De profundis!*—I call forth from the depths!" Despairing contrition alternates with unyielding hope. Medieval demonology feared the versatility of Satan's wiles; he might enter the blessed service itself and assume the Blessed Host in the eucharist. The saint who had overcome and rejected the deadly sins of carnal living and was reaching the consummation of his monastic austerities was warned not to be lost and betrayed at his very goal by the sin of *athymia,* hermit despondency.

Most strikingly did John Bunyan (1628-1688) drive home a similar conviction when he concluded his *Pilgrim's Progress* with the words: "I saw that there was a way to Hell, even from the Gates of Heaven, as well as from the City of Destruction."

A study of the belief in social progress could scarcely end with a formal concluding chapter. The general outlook on the historical process toward which our various inquiries have inclined us is the view of ongoing civilization as an expanding range of men's activities, affording greater opportunities for high achievement but also graver hazards of downfall. The evidence from various fields of human experience reported in the second part of this book was intended to test the soundness of our general view.

The conception of belief in progress as the belief that the historical course of events records growing improvement does not connote any growing reassurance or complacency. This has been patent throughout our study. It does not connote clear and decisive finality in our judgment as to what the higher and better values really are in any specific situation. We recognize the importance of moral and other value development both in active pursuit and realization of acknowledged high and better values and also in more intelligent and critical understanding of what is better. Genuine historical progress must be progress in truer understanding of the ideal goals as well as progress in the realizing of them.

If we were to aim at terseness, we might say that a progressive civilization is one which increases man's value potential. It is advance in the scope of available improvement and rise in values. By the term *available* here it is not meant that the attainment of the higher values is assured, nor even that it can reasonably be expected. It may be very problematical or precarious. We mean that it is a really acknowledged alternative: we have arrived at the stage where it is clearly presented as a goal or a challenge, recognized as a duty and a worthy purpose. Persons as well as societies and nations come to such rendezvous with high destiny.

We can thus perceive that a progressive civilization involves, along with its prospects of greater rise in values, not only the hazards of a graver downfall but also the evil of failure to perceive the available higher ascent. We have in this recognition a meaning analogous to the Christian idea of the sin of omission. Man's first step in the performance of his duty is to gain a clearer acknowledgment of it. We are brought from our twofold reflection to the Socratic first principle of moral philosophy in our Western civilization, that virtue is knowledge. So progress is increase in insight and outlook as basic to intelligent realization.

The continual rearray of the course of progress is also a rearray of the line of battle. This is the dramatic or heroic note in personal careers and in the historical process. Walt Whitman wrote brave words with which this study may fittingly close: "It is provided in the essence of things that from any fruition of success, no matter what, shall come forth something to make a greater struggle necessary."[14]

[14] Compare Lewis Mumford, *The Condition of Man* (New York, 1944), p. 337.

The Promethean Fire-Bringers: Pioneers in Social Progress

FOLKLORE IS THE TREASURY of the traditional mind. Primitive society was retrospective in its outlook; it relied on beliefs and practices of immemorial antiquity, tested and tried, preserved in myths and tribal customs, imparted to growing youths with solemn authority and allowing of no deviation. But the spirit of rigid conformity to tradition was embroiled in a paradox; for while it rejected and punished any hint of radical change in its own midst, it honored its great ancestors who had led it to new heights by their inventive power and who had devised the customary practices and framework of living which their successors were resolved to maintain without any change. This has always been the conscious or unwitting perplexity of the reactionary: he resists any nonconformity and cleaves stubbornly to traditional forms, but these forms in their early days must have been advocated by original and radical minds, of whom on principle he should disapprove.

In some fields of activity the basic conditions of human life have set a premium on fruitful invention, and this is nowhere more evident than in the application of knowledge to technical mastery. Here even the most conservative mind is on the lookout for productive improvement. Though suspicious of any religious or social or political programs of reform, he is ever ready to hear about technical improvement or reconstruction. Primitive tradition has preserved in folklore its eulogy of the great inventive pioneers of mankind. Ancient bards, epic and dramatic poets have sung the glory but also the trials of their careers. This strain in folklore and poetry reveals a basic insight and a social philosophy of life, expressed not in systematic doctrine but in praise of the leaders in social pioneering. One of the first and greatest epoch-making forward steps in human progress was the discovery of the production and the uses of fire.

Men's discovery of the production of fire is not to be confused with their experience of fire or their knowledge of some of its sources. Throughout time fires of various origins have been more or less common, whether in volcanic regions or in coal or peat combustible deposits or far more frequently wherever flashing bolts of lightning split the storm clouds and set trees ablaze in the forest. Primitive man was all too familiar with these terrors of unsubdued fires in nature; he fled from them or bowed down before them in abject worship. But was he ever fireless in the sense that he did not have the art of the production, the steady possession and use of fire? Even in this more restricted sense of the term *fireless,* modern anthropologists have doubted that any known tribes were ever really devoid of fire, although some instances have been cited, in Australia or among some hill tribes of India. What matters is the degree of mastery in the use of fire. Folklore abounds in myths of the great heroes who with their wisdom or bravery or guile gained the possession of fire and taught men how to use it. Until their mastery of this art men could have only the sporadic and unreliable sources of fire in nature.

Numerous ways of fire-making have been recognized by anthropologists, but the principal varieties are few in number: the stick-and-groove or fire-saw or fire-plow, where a strip of bamboo or other readily inflammable wood is rubbed briskly across another; the fire-drill, where a sharpened rod is held in a hole or socket and revolved rapidly until it inflames some dry leaves or whittlings in the hole; the striking of a spark by the use of flints or iron; the use of crystal lenses for focusing sun-heat on some rapidly combustible tinder; and sundry variations of these methods. This briefest recital does not begin to report the endless accounts given by anthropologists of primitive fire-making throughout the world.[1] Outstanding are the myths of the great fire-bringers that have been animated by the creative powers of religious adoration or poetic genius.

The Vedas of ancient India worshiped fire as their chief god on earth. It was called Agni, a name which in other Indo-European languages has given us simply the word for fire: in Latin, *ignis,* and in Slavic languages *ugni* or *ogn.* In some of the very ancient hymns to Agni, in the *Rig-Veda,* we have almost a list of the various ways of fire-making. In citing a part of this hymn some explanations are interpolated, which are probably obvious. "Thou, O Agni, art born to shine forth; thou art born from the skies [in the sun], thou from the waters [in bolts of lightning in rain storms], thou from the stone [in flints], thou from the wood and herbs [in the rubbing of sticks and leaves], thou king of men, thou bright one!"[2] The devout poet, in worshipful adoration, exalted the god to universal supremacy:

> To Agni I present a newer mightier hymn, I bring my
> words and song unto the Son of Strength,
> Who, Offspring of the Waters, bearing precious things,
> sits on the earth. . . .

[1] J. G. Frazer, with the ample documentation familiar to readers of his *Golden Bough,* collected a great number of these tales in a volume entitled *Myths of the Origin of Fire.*

[2] *Rig-Veda* 2. 1. 1; compare F. Max Müller, *Physical Religion* (London, ed. of 1898), p. 145 ff.

When he was kindled, through the power and majesty his
    fiery spendor made the heavens and earth to shine.
His flames that wax not old, beams fair to look upon of him
    whose face is lovely, shine with beauteous sheen.
The rays of Agni, him whose active force is light, through
    the night glimmer sleepless, ageless, like the floods.

. . . .

What Matarisvan piercing, forced by frictions, Herald of
    all the gods, in varied figure
Is he whom they have set mid human houses, gay-hued as
    light and shining forth for beauty.[3]

In ancient Iran there is an episode from the great
Persian epic of Firdousi, the *Shah-Namah* or the *Epic of
Kings,* in which Hushang, the slayer of dragons, hurls a
stone at a serpent, misses his aim, but cleaves a rock, from
which fire spurts in flames for the use of man:

That there was fire in stones he also found
And then light kindled in the world around. . . .
The slight stone struck upon a heavy rock,
And thereon fell in pieces with the shock.
Out of both stones there sprang a flame of light,
And the rock's heart itself was rendered bright. . . .[4]

Moving westward toward Europe, we have the great
fire masters, Vainamoinen and Ilmarinen, in the national
epic of Finland, the *Kalevala.* Here is plain folklore
exalted to poetic heights. The toothless witch Louhi
wickedly stole the sun and the moon and also fire. Ukko
the creator then struck new sparks of fire from his sword
and hid them in the clouds; but the precious flame rolled
out and fell to the bottom of the sea. There it was gulped
by a small powan fish, which was swallowed by a gray

[3] Compare Hymns of the *Rig-Veda,* trans. R. T. H. Griffith (Benares,
1896).
[4] *The Shah-Namah of Firdousi,* trans. Alex. Rogers (London, 1907),
p. 11.

trout, and it in turn by a large pike. After long epical angling, Vainamoinen caught the great fire-fish and, ripping its entrails, released the fire-flame and ordered it to serve men's needs:

> Better go thou to my village,
> To the hearth-stones of my people;
> Hide thyself within my chimneys,
> In my ashes sleep and linger. . . .[5]

The other hero of the *Kalevala*, Ilmarinen, the Finnish Hephaestus or Vulcan, trained the fire to serve men's industrial needs by coaxing iron to let itself be melted and hammered into weapons and tools and utensils:

> Now the master, Ilmarinen,
> The renowned and skilful blacksmith
> From the fire removes the iron,
> Places it upon the anvil,
> Hammers well until it softens,
> Hammers many fine utensils,
> Hammers spears, and swords, and axes,
> Hammers knives, and forks, and hatchets,
> Hammers tools of all descriptions. . . .[6]

The worship of fire as a deity, Agni, was not exceptional. Fire naturally inspired men to adoration. Universally it had a major role in religious ritual in all forms of sacrifice. The altar fires were sacred, and a major function of the priestly class was to preserve the purity of the holy flames. This was the duty of the vestal virgins in ancient Rome, whose chief, the Pontifex Maximus, was dominant in Roman religious ritual. Fire was of such importance in the Zoroastrian religion of ancient Iran that it has been called fire worship.

[5] *Kalevala*, Runo 9, trans. J. M. Crawford (New York and London, 1889), 2: 698.
[6] *Kalevala*, Runo 9, op. cit., 1: 111 f.

The chief fire-bringer of the world's mythology, Prometheus, the Greek hero of progress, stands out in his moral and spiritual significance, a dramatic embodiment of a creative philosophy of life. The Promethean legend is first given to us in Hesiod's *Works and Days* and his *Theogony*. Prometheus, the son of the Titan Iapetus, took pity on the hardships of men who were living like beasts and wore themselves out to earn a bare and crude existence. He judged that men's first need was the possession of fire to protect them from the rigors of winter, to cook their food, and to melt metals to be molded into tools and utensils. But fire was hidden by Zeus who, as Hesiod says, planned sorrow and mischief against men. So Prometheus stole the fire of Zeus from heaven, hid it in a hollow stalk of fennel, and brought it to men. For this gift which enabled men to rise from beastly savagery to civilization, against the will of the high god, Prometheus suffered a dire doom. Zeus nailed him in chains against a rock in the Caucasus; daily the eagle of Zeus pecked at his liver, and at night the liver grew back, so that the torture of the hero could be inflicted over again. Thus the champion of human culture suffered for more than twenty thousand years, until finally Heracles slew the vulture and delivered Prometheus.

This is the legend of the Greek fire-bringer in its main outlines. Folklorists have pointed out significant features which it shares with fire myths in other cultures. The hollow fennel stalk in which Prometheus brought down the fire from heaven is the Greek version of a common way in which fire was transported by nomadic tribes. The very name of Prometheus betrays his character as the fire-bringer. This name has been derived from the Sanskrit word *pramantha* which in ancient Indian signified the upper parts of the fire drill.

It is in the great tragedy of Aeschylus, *Prometheus Bound,* that we have the most famous version of the myth. The master dramatist could not openly glorify the fire-bringer Prometheus and condemn the high god Zeus for torturing the culture hero, champion and benefactor of mankind. But by giving Prometheus full dramatic and sublime utterance, Aeschylus portrayed the tragic nobility of his character. He also revealed the great pioneer as conscious of his fate, noble but tragic; in a mighty speech, right in the middle of the drama:

> . . . Think not I am silent thus
> Through pride or scorn. I only gnaw my heart
> With meditation, seeing myself so wronged. . . .
> List rather to the deeds
> I did for mortals; how, being fools before,
> I made them wise and true in aim of soul.
> And let me tell you—not as taunting men,
> But teaching you the intention of my gifts,
> How, first beholding, they beheld in vain,
> And, hearing, heard not, but, like shapes in dreams,
> Mixed all things wildly down the tedious time,
> Nor knew to build a house against the sun
> With wickered sides, nor any woodcraft knew,
> But lived, like silly ants, beneath the ground
> In hollow caves unsunned. . . .
> For lack of drugs
> Men pined and wasted, till I showed them all
> Those mixtures of emollient remedies
> Whereby they might be rescued from disease. . . .
> Enough said now of this.
> For the other helps of man hid underground
> The iron and the brass, silver and gold,
> Can any dare affirm he found them out
> Before me? none, I know! unless he choose
> To lie in his vaunt. In one word learn the whole—
> That all arts came to mortals from Prometheus.[7]

The great drama has deep spiritual significance. At a decisive crossroad and crisis in Greek religious reflec-

[7] *Prometheus Bound,* trans. E. B. Browning, ll. 505 ff.

tion, Aeschylus seemed to express a conviction of a radical quandary in the faith of men. Deity is presumably perfect: but why should Zeus act so unjustly in blocking to men their path to the higher life of civilization? Perhaps the gods themselves rise from guile and ruthlessness to justice and mercy:

> I know that Zeus is stern;
> I know he metes his justice by his will;
> And yet, his soul shall learn
> More softness, when once broken by this ill:
> And curbing his unconquerable vaunt
> He shall rush on in fear to meet with me
> Who rush to meet with him in agony,
> To issues of harmonious covenant.[8]

So we may contrast the Zeus portrayed in *Prometheus Bound* with that expressed in the first great Chorus of the *Agamemnon:*

> Zeus—by what name soe'r
> He glories being addressed,
> Even by that holiest name
> I name the Highest and Best.
>
> On Him I cast my troublous care,
> My only refuge from despair:
> Weighing all else, in Him alone I find
> Relief from this vain burden of the mind.[9]

Yet in that first Orestean trilogy the abysmal problem of evil still baffles religious conviction.

The Promethean theme expresses the nobility but also the tragic lot of the creative pioneer in the onward march of civilization. The Promethean motive in human life is the motive in the upward and forward will, the spirit of the prophet, the radical reformer, even the utopian

---

[8] Op. cit., ll. 226 ff.
[9] Aeschylus *Agamemnon*, trans. Lewis Campbell (London, 1890), ll. 162 ff.

visionary, ever ready to spend himself in following the gleam of the higher and better social order yet to be. The mythological portrayal of the social pioneer and radical reformer as the fire-bringer has profound significance. For fire, a beneficent power for human use and betterment, is also a dire element of destruction. The hymns to the fire gods in various religions are hymns of praise to the benign deity but also terrified hymns of his angry devastation. Even so the bright hopes of men for a reformed social order have clashed with their stiff conformity and their fears of any radical change.

Do we not have here, in immemorial antiquity, the twofold social conviction which split early societies into contending classes, conservatives and liberals or more emphatically reactionaries and radicals? The social order has even been involved in this issue between established tradition and urgent reform. The traditionalists in any society have been those who honor and guard the old established customs and beliefs. They preserve the continued stability of the common life. This is their merit, but it has its serious defects. For if their conservatism were never challenged, and they were left in sole dominion, social life would stagnate in stiff and often antiquated customs. On the opposite side, there are the radical reformers who are ever critical of the old order and strive to change and improve it according to their own preferred designs. They are the leaders of progress in human life. But were they to have their way without any resistance from the traditionalists, they might plunge society into disorder and anarchy. Conservatism and change, stability and spurring advance are both needed, for their active interplay and counterplay make possible the expansive vitality of social institutions.

Civilization cannot spare its reformers, but it dare not be gentle with them, for they propose radical changes that may bring blessings to men but might also threaten disaster. This is the tragic note in the career of the social pioneer and prophet. We ourselves may see how this tragic element in radical change, promising great gains but also menacing dire doom for mankind, is illustrated in our new age of atomic energy. We are amazed by the promise of incredible new mastery and use of hitherto untapped boundless energies of nature, but we are also aghast at their destructive power.

The poet Shelley, himself a radical spirit of reform, expressed the hope that ultimately the higher values would prevail. In his own drama *Prometheus Unbound* he portrayed his hero in his "courage, and majesty, and firm and patient opposition to omnipotent force" and also as "exempt from the taints of ambition, envy, revenge, and desire for personal aggrandisement." Shelley looked forward to an ideal consummation, the thought of which sustained his hero in his dire tortures: "To love and bear; to hope till Hope creates/From its own wreck the thing it contemplates."[10]

It is not only fire, and more broadly technology, that baffles men's reflections on social progress. In a larger perspective, the Promethean theme has expressed men's perplexingly dual attitude toward other radical changes in their thought and activity. Men reach forward, but they also draw back. There is the promise of progress, but there is also the dread of possible misadventure. This double tension has found expression in religion and poetry. In the Babylonian epic *Gilgamesh,* the hero of that name, smitten by the terror of imminent death, seeks out his ancestor Utnapishtin (the Babylonian Noah) and secures through his advice a branch of the tree of eternal life. But while he is taking a swim in deep waters, a serpent snatches the branch from his reach and a voice from above declares that immortality is for the gods, not for men. Two tales in the book of Genesis are of similar

[10] Shelley, *Prometheus Unbound,* end of Act 4.

purport. Adam and Eve are banished from the Garden of Eden for having eaten from the forbidden tree of the knowledge of good and evil. And when men start building the tall Tower of Shinar, to reach unto heaven, God frustrates their hopes by confusing their language so that they cannot understand each other's speech: an ancient theory of comparative philology! Boundless desire for knowledge was suspected by the populace as impious presumption. The medieval commonalty suspected the seemingly omniscient Gerbert as having trafficked with the devil, to whose devices he probably owed his elevation to the papacy as Sylvester II. The revival of learning and also of worldly sensuality in the Renaissance gave rise to the popular tales of Faust and Don Juan; and in the seventeenth century, Pascal, himself a distinglished scientist, denounced the "triple abyss" of pride, curiosity, and lust.[11] Throughout folklore and mythological epos and ironic reflection men have expressed their deep sense of the contending good and evil involved in any radical change in the social process: as a likely step of progress, but maybe precarious and fraught with possible dire hazards.

[11] Pascal, *Oeuvres,* Grands Écrivains ed. (Paris, 1904), 13: 440.

Index

abortion, 227

Adventism, 52

Aeschylus, 30, 363-65

aesthetic progress: problems of, 324-33; its social-cultural involvements, 325, 329; dependence on religious beliefs and practices, 326-28

aged, killing of, 227

Agni, fire-god and fire-bringer in Vedic India, 360-61

agriculture, modern, technical advance in, 259-60

Alberti, 328

Alcott, Bronson, 204

Alexander, Samuel, theory of emergent evolution, 154-55

Alexander II, tsar, 257

Alexander VI, pope, 87, 89, 91, 94, 191, 223

altruism and egoism, 149

Ambrose, St., 47, 339

"Ancients and Moderns, quarrel of," 74-77

Angell, Norman, 306

Anselm, St., 329

Aquinas, St. Thomas, 48, 51, 314, 339

Arabian medieval thought, 109

Archimedes, 108

Aristippus, 337-38

Aristotle: and the doctrine of eternal recurrence, 24; his views of historical progress, 28; modern resistance to, 71, 73, 74; mentioned, 5, 76, 77, 109-10, 123, 180, 279, 319, 337-38

Arnold, Matthew, 345

art. See aesthetic progress

Asquith, H. H., Lord, 272

atheism, 173-74

Augustine, St.: philosophy of history, 44-45; ideas of the kingdom of God, 44, 47; recognition of secular progress, 45, 46; condemnation of Pelagianism, 47; mentioned, 34, 36, 37, 53, 54, 78

automation in modern industry, 275-76

Averroës, 313

Aviceanna, 313

Bach, Johann Sebastian, 330

Bacon, Francis: his New Atlantis, 196-200; his influence on the establishment of modern academies of sciences, 200; mentioned, 71-72, 77, 110, 205, 336

Bacon, Roger, 49, 351

Baillie, John, his view of the idea of progress, 180-81

Barth, Karl: providential version of existentialism, 172-73; mentioned, 319

Baxter, Richard, 58

Bayle, Pierre, skepticism of, 83-84

Beethoven, Ludwig von, 329, 330, 331

Bellamy, Edward, Looking Backward, 2000-1887, utopian plan, 207-9

Berdyaev, Nicholas: existentialism of, 170-72; mentioned, 181

Bergson, Henri: his doctrine of creative evolution, 155-58; mentioned, 153

Bible, the. See Old Testament; New Testament

birth control, problem of, 228

Boccaccio, Giovanni, 225

bodily well-being and household economy, 237-48

Bodin, Jean, 69-71

Bolingbroke, Henry St. John, 91

Bossuet, Bishop, 78-79, 101

rationalism, Platonic, 183-89; Descartes's, 73; Leibniz's, 84-85; Hegel's, 121-24
reform, social, problem of conservatism and liberalism, 366-68
religious progress: problems of, 343-57; controversial views of, 343-44; varieties of proposed definitions of religion, 345-46; in the Judeo-Christian tradition, 347-52; conflicts with intellectual advance, 351-52; in the evolution of prayer, 354-55
Renaissance thought, the idea of secular progress in, 61-64, 68-73; skeptical strains in, 62-65
Revelation, Book of, apocalyptic ideas in, 39-41
Ripley, George, 204
Rochefoucauld. See La Rochefoucauld, François de
Ronsard, Pierre, 74
Roosevelt, Mrs. Eleanor, 276
Roosevelt, Theodore, 267
Rousseau, Jean Jacques: condemnation of civilization as a corruption, 92-94; mentioned, 5, 90, 124, 127
Royal Society of London, 77, 88, 200
Royce, Josiah, 351

Saint-Simon, Claude Henri de, social evangelist of progress, 133-34
sanitation, 239-41
Sarton, George, 311
Sartre, Jean-Paul: atheistic existentialism of, 173-75; mentioned, 319
Savonarola, Girolamo, 190
Scaliger, J. C., 74, 76
Schelling, F. W. J., 119, 124
Schiller, Friedrich, 122
Schleiermacher, Friedrich, 345-46
scholasticism, 48, 62
Schopenhauer, Arthur; pessimistic denial of historical progress, 149; mentioned, 27, 150, 151, 267, 315
Schweitzer, Albert, 38, 39
science. See intellectual progress

Scotus, Duns. See Duns Scotus
Seneca, 28, 29-30, 226
serfdom and its abolition, 257-60
seventeenth century, secular progress during, 64-82
Shaftesbury, Third Earl of: optimism of, 85-86; mentioned, 83, 84, 86, 88, 91
Shah Namah, 361
Shakespeare, William, 325, 329
Shelley, Percy Bysshe, 125, 367
Sinclair, Upton, 267
"single tax," 262
skepticism, invasions of, 314-15; in early modern thought, 62-65; Bayle's, 83-84; Voltaire's, 89-90; Hume's, 95-96; Pyrrho's, 314; Pascal's, 316-17
slavery, 288-97
Smith, Adam, economic optimism, 113-14
socialism. See communism
social order and personal freedom, 279-308
Socrates, 75, 76, 222, 336, 355
Sophocles, 30-31, 242, 325, 326, 329, 337, 349
Sorokin, Pitirim, 216, 305
Southey, Robert, 125, 126-27
Spencer, Herbert: evolutionary theory of, 138-39; theory of universal progress, 143-45; mentioned, 127, 153
Spengler, Oswald, 86, 161-65
Spinoza, B., 165, 315
Sprat, Bishop, 88
Stalin, Joseph, 341
Stevenson, Robert Louis, 94
Stoics: doctrine of eternal recurrence, 25; advocates of historical progress, 28-30; mentioned, 109, 338
Stowe, Harriet Beecher, 297
Swift, Jonathan, 94, 124
Sylvester II, pope, 368

Taoism, 352-53
technology, economic values, and human progress, 249-78; in modern agriculture, 259-60. See also intellectual progress
Telesio, Bernardino, 195

DATE DUE

APR 3 0 2008	